Invasion Scare

Also by Michael Glover

Wellington's Peninsular Victories
Batsford, 1963

Wellington as Military Commander
Batsford, 1968

Britannia Sickens
Leo Cooper, 1970

Legacy of Glory
Charles Scribner & Leo Cooper, 1972

1815: The Armies at Waterloo
Leo Cooper, 1973

An Assemblage of Indian Army
Soldiers and Uniforms
Perpetua Press, 1973

The Peninsular War: A Concise History
David & Charles, 1974

Rorke's Drift
Leo Cooper, 1975

General Burgoyne in Canada and America
Gordon & Cremonesi, 1976

Wellington's Army
David & Charles, 1977

A Very Slippery Fellow
O.U.P., 1978

The Napoleonic Wars
Batsford, 1979

A Gentleman Volunteer
Heinemann, 1979

Warfare from Waterloo to Mons
B.C.A., 1980

Warfare in the Age of Bonaparte
B.C.A., 1980

The Velvet Glove
Hodder & Stoughton, 1982

The Fight for the Channel Ports
Leo Cooper, 1985

An Improvised War
Leo Cooper, 1987

That Astonishing Infantry
Leo Cooper, 1989

INVASION SCARE
1940

Michael Glover

We must expect . . . to be attacked here
on the Dutch model before very long and
we hope to give a good account of ourselves.

> Winston Churchill
> to President Roosevelt, 18 May, 1940

On the first day of the invasion parachutists
dropped out of the sky like a vast flock of
vultures. Most of them were disguised in
Allied or Dutch uniforms, others came down in
the uniform of Dutch policemen and began to
direct the population in the streets.

> *Daily Express*, 13 May, 1940
> (of the German invasion of Holland)

LEO COOPER
LONDON

First published in 1990

Leo Cooper is an independent imprint of
the Octopus Publishing Group, Michelin House
81 Fulham Road, London sw3 6rb
LONDON   MELBOURNE   AUCKLAND

A CIP catalogue record for this book
is available from the British Library

ISBN 0 85052 2625

Typeset in 11/13pt Linotron Baskerville by
Hewer Text Composition Services, Edinburgh
Printed in Great Britain by Redwood Press Ltd, Melksham
and bound by Hunter & Foulis, Edinburgh

For Leo
with thanks

Contents

Illustrations

Acknowledgements

Many people have helped with this book but I am particularly
grateful to David Curnow, Adrian Digby and Charles Longley.
As always John Andrews and Judith Blacklaw of the Ministry
of Defence Library have been strikingly helpful.
I am also very much indebted to my brother Buster
but all the inspiration and a lot of the work
came from Daphne who, for the twenty-first time,
kept the whole show on the road.

Maps

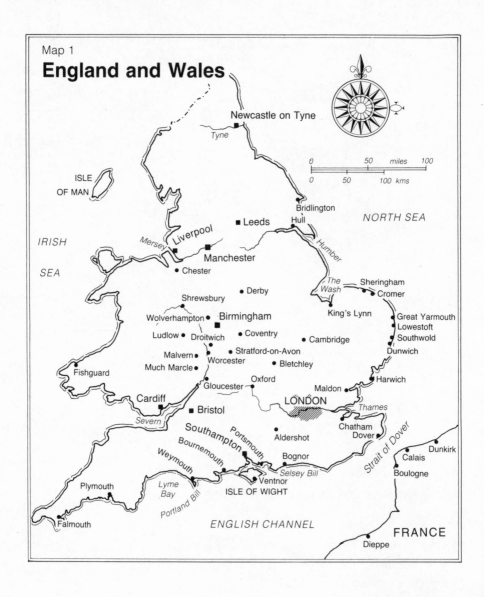

Map 1

England and Wales

Newcastle on Tyne

Tyne

ISLE OF MAN

IRISH SEA

SEA

0   50   miles   100
0   50   100 kms

Bridlington
Hull
NORTH SEA

Leeds
Mersey Liverpool
Manchester
Humber
Chester

The Wash Sheringham
Cromer
Derby
Shrewsbury
King's Lynn
Great Yarmouth
Lowestoft
Wolverhampton Birmingham
Ludlow Droitwich Coventry Cambridge Southwold
Dunwich
Malvern Stratford-on-Avon
Much Marcle Worcester Bletchley
Fishguard
Oxford Harwich
Gloucester Maldon
Cardiff LONDON
Bristol *Thames*
Severn Chatham
Southampton Dover
Portsmouth Aldershot
Bournemouth Dunkirk
Weymouth Bognor Calais
Selsey Bill Boulogne
Plymouth *Lyme Bay* Ventnor
ISLE OF WIGHT
Portland Bill
Falmouth ENGLISH CHANNEL
FRANCE
Dieppe

Strait of Dover

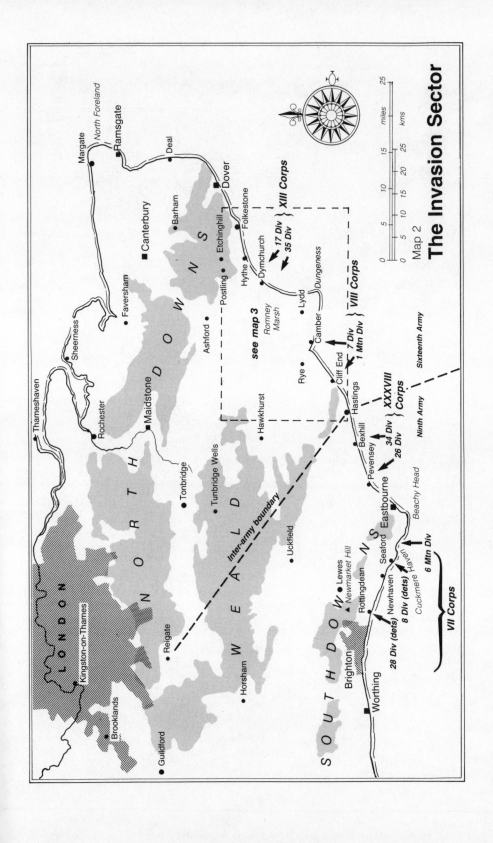

Map 2 The Invasion Sector

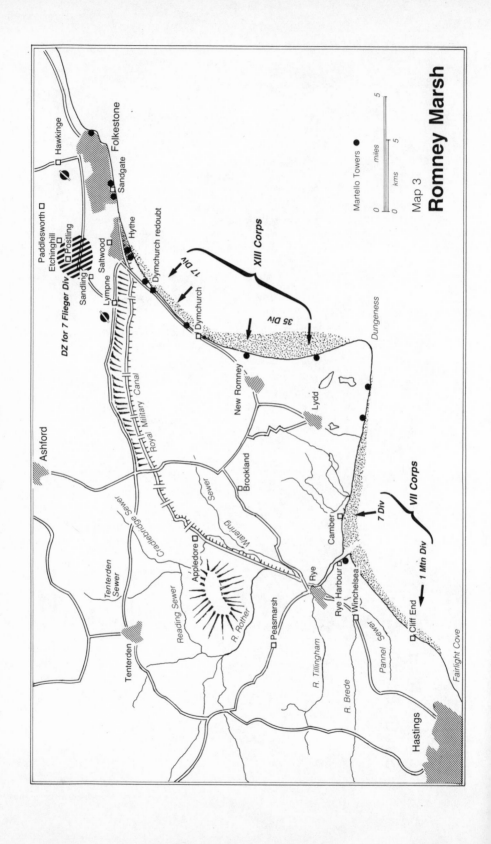

Map 3 **Romney Marsh**

Martello Towers ●

miles
kms

Hawkinge
Folkestone
Sandgate
Paddlesworth
Etchinghill
Postling
Hythe
Saltwood
Sandling
Dymchurch redoubt
Lympne
DZ for 7 Flieger Div
17 Div
Dymchurch
XIII Corps
Ashford
Royal Military Canal
35 Div
Dungeness
New Romney
Lydd
Cradlebridge Sewer
Brookland
Sewer
Tenterden Sewer
Watering
Reading Sewer
Appledore
Camber
VII Corps
7 Div
R. Rother
Rye
Rye Harbour
Peasmarsh
Winchelsea
Tenterden
R. Tillingham
1 Mtn Div
Cliff End
R. Brede
Pannel Sewer
Hastings
Fairlight Cove

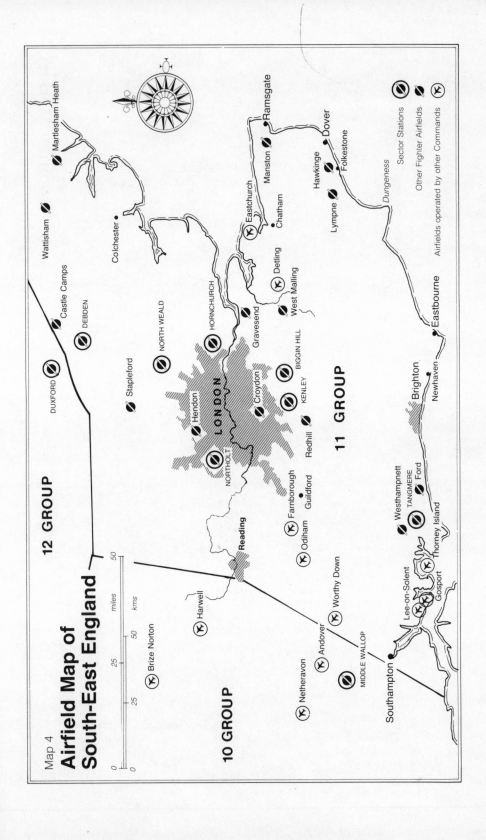

Map 4

Airfield Map of South-East England

12 GROUP

10 GROUP

11 GROUP

LONDON

miles

kms

0   25   50

0   25   50

Sector Stations

Other Fighter Airfields

Airfields operated by other Commands

Martlesham Heath

Wattisham

Colchester

Castle Camps

DEBDEN

DUXFORD

Stapleford

NORTH WEALD

HORNCHURCH

Hendon

NORTHOLT

Reading

Brize Norton

Harwell

Netheravon

Andover

Worthy Down

Odiham

Guildford

Farnborough

Redhill

Croydon

Gravesend

West Malling

Detling

BIGGIN HILL

KENLEY

Ramsgate

Manston

Eastchurch

Chatham

Dover

Hawkinge

Folkestone

Lympne

Dungeness

Eastbourne

Brighton

Newhaven

Ford

Westhampnett

TANGMERE

Thorney Island

Lee-on-Solent

Gosport

Southampton

MIDDLE WALLOP

Foreword

The German invasion of Britain in the summer of 1940 never happened but it was one of the most important turning points of the Second World War. It represented the first occasion on which Hitler and his all-conquering *Wehrmacht* had been checked, perhaps defeated would not be too strong a word. It also marked the entry of Britain into the war as a serious contender rather than as a semi-detached ally of the French. It is true that before the end of May, 1940, the United Kingdom had contributed fourteen divisions to the Western Front (where the French had one hundred and fifteen divisions), that the Royal Navy was fully stretched in keeping command of the seas and that the Royal Air Force had a substantial number of aircraft, many of them obsolete, in France to support the Expeditionary Force. For the sailors and some of the airmen there was action enough but for the army and the great mass of the British people the situation combined most of the inconveniences of war without the excitements which make war at least interesting.

The nine months which followed 3 September, 1939, are today usually referred to as the Phoney War, a phrase coined in the United States and little current at the time in Britain where it was commonly referred to as the Bore War. Very little happened and when something did occur it was usually favourable to the enemy. To be sure the *Graf Spee*, after a most gallant action with smaller ships, had been hounded into scuttling herself while her tender, *Altmark*, with her cargo of British seamen, had been cut out while violating Norwegian neutrality. These incidents could not compare with the torpedoing of the battleship *Royal Oak* inside the Home Fleet's base at Scapa Flow or the sinking of the aircraft carrier *Courageous* in the Western Approaches. Moreover, what confidence could be placed in Britain's command of the sea when,

I

with apparent impunity, the Germans could land troops in Norwegian ports closer to the Home Fleet's bases than to their own, a spectacular defeat for Britain which the subsequent land operations, marked by unpreparedness and muddle, did nothing to redeem?

By the first week of May, 1940, the mood of Britain was one of apathy and inertia somewhat lightened by the inherited belief that we would probably muddle through in the end. Had this mood persisted until mid-June when France, regarded since 1914 as Britain's sure shield on land, collapsed ignominiously, it is most unlikely that the country would have found the energy or the enthusiasm to fight on. Fortunately in the second week of May occurred two events of supreme importance – Churchill came to power and Britain became obsessed with the idea that the Germans were going to invade her. The second of these events marginally preceded the first since Anthony Eden's famous wireless appeal for Local Defence Volunteers had been drafted for Chamberlain's uninspiring Secretary for War, Oliver Stanley. In his first speech as Prime Minister Churchill had made no reference to invasion. It was not until five days after Eden's broadcast that he foretold that once the front in France had been stabilized there would follow 'the battle for our Island – for all that Britain is, and all that Britain means' and called on the people to 'Arm yourselves'.

The invasion scare was not Churchill's invention. It arose spontaneously from a combination of misinformation and a sudden onrush of the totally unexpected. Churchill used it to shake the nation out of its indifference. Without it there would have been nothing against which he could have directed the country's new-found energy and determination. The possibility of landings which bulked so large in May and June in Britain's thinking and so small in Germany's was an ideal goad with which to galvanise the nation. It was a threat comprehensible to everyone – no one in the United Kingdom lives far from the sea and for those inland there was the possibility of airborne invasion. Nothing could have suited Churchill's purpose better.

The result was a phenomenon. Nobody who was more than ten years old at the time will ever forget the sudden switch from boredom to intense excitement, from depression to exhilaration. In June Britain's situation was arguably worse than at any time since 1066 and yet, in the words of A.J.P. Taylor,

> Anyone looking back must confess that the summer of 1940 was not only the most exciting, but also the gayest, time of his life.

2

Margery Allingham, living near the vulnerable Essex coast, vividly expressed the feelings of almost everybody in those early months:

> The whole tenor of life had altered and become simpler and in a way much easier. There was more than a touch of the address before Agincourt in the air, a secret satisfaction that if it was coming we were to be the chosen, we few, we happy few, and all the other happy few round the coast of an impregnable island. All this looks childish written down but it was a direct and childish time, quite different but more entirely satisfying than any other piece of life which I at least have ever experienced.

This direct and childish simplicity is the key to the British reaction to the dangers that the British believed threatened them. The perils were recognized, indeed they were greatly exaggerated, but there was an unreality which removed the terror from them. As Peter Fleming remarked, 'For the British their predicament retained to the end a story book quality.'

My own most vivid memory of the time is of a June night when I was about two weeks past my eighteenth birthday. As a Local Defence Volunteer I was set to guard a T-junction in the middle of a small Northamptonshire town. My orders were to stop any vehicle that passed and establish the identity of the occupants. For this task I was equipped with a heavily shaded torch and a rifle into the magazine of which I had, under orders, inserted ten rounds of live ammunition. My turn on duty started at midnight and for more than an hour only a few vehicles passed, all of which stopped obediently at the flash of my torch. Then a car appeared, coming fast from the market square. It ignored my signal and, unhesitatingly, I worked the bolt, got a round into the breech and brought the rifle to my shoulder, intending to fire at the tyres. Never a remarkable shot, I might have hit almost anything in that narrow street but, in the event, my marksmanship was not put to the test. The driver, who was, I think, somewhat the worse for drink, realized his mistake, braked heavily and backed up to apologize. Such incidents were being repeated all over the country and not a few innocent if inattentive civilians were actually shot in similar circumstances. Life was like that at the time.

The reality, unknowable at the time, was that it was not until four weeks after that incident that Hitler issued so much as a warning order to prepare for a possible invasion and a further two weeks before a somewhat hesitant executive order followed. Meanwhile the head of the German Navy, on whom the business of launching an invasion would chiefly fall, viewed the prospect with a dismay he was not always able to conceal and the commander of the German Air Force refused to take the possibility of a landing seriously. The only enthusiasts for the operation were the Army who were wilfully reluctant to understand the problems involved in transporting them across the intervening water.

This book is therefore the story of a non-event but the fact that the Germans did not invade makes the happenings of that summer no less important than many famous battles which appear as Battle Honours on the Colours of famous regiments. In May and June the British did their best to obey Churchill's biblical injunction to 'Arm yourselves and be ye men of valour' to combat a menace which did not exist. By doing so they gave themselves the courage to face a war which, on any logical premises, they had no hope of winning and which, for at least two more years, was to be almost uniformly unsuccessful. They also convinced themselves, and most of the world, that they had outfaced Hitler and his vast military machine. Hitler faced his first defeat, and a very serious one, when, on 17 September, 1940, he approved the order,

Sealion. Postponed until further notice.

Four previous works on the projected invasion have been of great help in writing this book. These are Ronald Wheatley's *Operation Sealion*, Walter Ansel's *Hitler Confronts England*, Telford Taylor's *The Breaking Wave* and Peter Fleming's delightful *Invasion 1940*. The first three of these deal almost exclusively with the German side of the operation, the fourth very largely with the British. In this book I have tried to bring the two points of view together, to present the picture as a whole as it developed on both sides of the Channel.

As an appendix I have attached a very simplified diagram of the German command structure which may need a word of explanation. The nearest approach in Germany to a combined headquarters was the *Oberkommando der Wehrmacht* (OKW), since strictly the *Wehrmacht* (defence force) comprised all three armed services. In practice OKW was entirely dominated by soldiers and *Wehrmacht* was commonly used to denote the German Army. I have used it in this sense to distinguish the Army from the *Kriegsmarine* (Navy) and *Luftwaffe* (Air Force).

The high command of the Army was known as *Oberkommando des Heeres* (OKH). I should add that the term *Oberkommando der Luftwaffe* (OKL) was not officially adopted, in place of a very lengthy Germanic acronym, until 1944, but it seems convenient to make use of it earlier. Equally the famous Messerschmitt aircraft were not, in 1940, officially referred to by the well-known (at the time) abbreviation Me but as Bf (*Bayerische Flugzeugwerke*).

In another of my most valuable source books, *The Right of the Line*, John Terraine refers to 'a general lack of statistical consistency'. Most of the figures given in this book are subject to minor variations according to the authority consulted. All that can be hoped is that if the figures I have used are not precisely correct they are correct enough to make no difference.

Prologue

On 4 June, as the evacuation from Dunkirk was in its final stages, Winston Churchill made his most famous speech in the House of Commons, ending with the words,

> We shall defend our island, whatever the cost may be. We shall fight on the beaches, we shall fight on the landing grounds, we shall fight in the fields and in the streets, we shall fight in the hills; we shall never surrender.

On the same day it was decided in Berlin that the campaign against England would be a matter of siege warfare conducted by the *Kriegsmarine*, the German Navy, and by the *Luftwaffe*. With that in mind, priority in manufacture would be given to U-Boats and the new Junkers 88 bomber.

A month earlier not one in a hundred of the population of the United Kingdom would have believed in the possibility of an invasion being launched against them. Over the centuries the Spaniards and the French had made occasional attempts to invade, only to be thwarted by the Royal Navy or the weather or a combination of the two. In the popular consciousness the matter had been finally settled when Nelson destroyed the Franco-Spanish fleet off Cape Trafalgar, a belief which overlooked the fact that when the Combined Fleet had sailed from Cadiz on that occasion their destination had been Naples. Half a century later there was a brief moment of panic at the sabre-rattling of Napoleon III which resulted in the raising of a plethora of ill-organized Volunteer units and the expenditure of much public money on redundant fortifications on the south coast. Between the two World Wars the matter had seemed so far-fetched that the Staff College had not considered the possibility of invasion.

The last occasion on which foreign troops had landed in the United

Kingdom could be considered a favourable omen in 1940. On the night of 22-23 February, 1797, a French force, 1,200 strong, had disembarked at Pencaern, a few miles west of Fishguard. The country was already in an edgy mood. In the previous December the French had shipped 18,000 troops to Bantry Bay in the hope of seizing a more than usually disaffected Ireland. The Royal Navy's attempts to intercept them had been wholly ineffective and only the perversity of the weather stopped the force from landing. On 20 February, 1797, Fort Cumberland at Portsmouth signalled that an invasion fleet was approaching and the few warships available hastily put to sea. It was soon discovered that the Fort had flown the wrong signal and that only a single French lugger was off the port. The country, and especially the City of London, was nevertheless alarmed.

It was only two days later that the actual invasion force came ashore in Wales. It was a makeshift affair composed of released convicts and galley slaves and commanded by an American, Colonel Tate, with one French and three Irish officers, one of whom, Joseph Wall, had been in the British service but had fled to France in 1784 to avoid a court martial for illegally flogging a sergeant to death. The Irish nationalist, Wolfe Tone, who had thrown in his lot with the French Republic, described the expeditionary force as a collection of 'unmitigated blackguards' and those who saw them in Wales said that they had

> not the least appearance of soldiers in their air or dress, which consists of a brown sort of jacket, trowsers of various kinds, and woollen caps of different colours, and [with] no difference between the common men and those called officers except that the latter wear hats.

The French Navy transported them in two frigates, a corvette and a lugger and Tate's orders were to sail up the Avon, burn Bristol, re-embark and land again near Swansea with a view to marching on Chester and Liverpool. In fact he restricted his activities to burning a few coasting vessels off Ilfracombe before rounding St David's Head and landing at Pencaern. It is not clear what he had in mind but in London it was assumed that he intended to liberate the 128 French prisoners of war held in Pembroke Castle.

Wales was barely garrisoned and, apart from some militia at Pembroke, no regular or even second-line troops were in the Principality, and the Duke of York, as Commander-in-Chief, hastily ordered the General Officer Commanding the Severn District to take charge of the situation. The forces under his command consisted of three troops of Sussex Fencible* Cavalry and five companies of Bucks Militia at Bristol who were sent forward to Brecon where they were to be joined by the Romney Fencible Cavalry, who were in detachments stationed at Worcester, Gloucester, Ludlow and Ledbury, and by half a battalion of Staffordshire Militia from Shrewsbury. In addition the company of Cardiganshire Militia at Pembroke handed over their prisoners of war to the townspeople and, on their own initiative, marched towards Fishguard.

As it happened this hastily assembled force was not required, for the Lord Lieutenant of Pembrokeshire, Lord Milford, assembled his available forces which consisted of 'The Pembrokeshire Gentlemen and Yeomanry', the Pembrokeshire Volunteers, the Fishguard Volunteers and a party of seamen from Fishguard who brought with them two 9-pounder guns. Under Lord Cawdor of the Yeomanry this motley force took up a position on the high ground above Pencaern where they were joined by

> innumerable numbers of colliers, peasantry, farmers, laborers, in short neither age nor sex restrained anyone from all the exertions they were able to make to meet and attack the invaders. . . . Two or three of the enemy were killed by the country people who fired upon them with common fowling pieces.

At Lord Cawdor's suggestion the array on the hills was swelled by a number of Welsh women who, in their traditional red cloaks and tall black hats, looked at a distance like infantrymen.

The invaders were anxious only to surrender. According to the French Commissary for Prisoners:

> On their departure from Brest they understood they were destined for Dunkirk [and] they were entirely ignorant of the place where they were landed.

Except for Joseph Wall, who was hanged, the officers were kept as prisoners of war while the rank and file were shipped back to France since they were more likely to do harm to France than to Britain.

This futile foray left two marks on British history. The Pembrokeshire Yeomanry were, after a delay of fifty-seven years, awarded the

---

* Fencibles were regular troops enlisted for home service only.

Battle Honour FISHGUARD, the only such honour for an action on British soil. The other result was more permanent. The news of the landing, increased in the following week by a rumour of another in Glamorgan, started a panic in the City. As William Pitt wrote to the King,

> The alarm (very disproportionate to the occasion) which has lately taken place in different parts of the country from the supposed possibility of invasion has led to a demand for cash from London which has produced the greatest difficulties. . . . The only possible remedy appears to be to restrain the Bank [of England] from paying in ready money till the impression has subsided. There might otherwise in a short time not remain enough money to satisfy the indispensible demands on Government for the Army and Navy.

The country therefore abandoned the gold standard and introduced bank notes. The former was resumed in 1819 but bank notes continue to this day.

'Has the Government
not prepared any plans?'

The idea that the Germans might land in the United Kingdom was first publicly aired on 7 May, 1940, in the memorable parliamentary debate which led to the fall of the Chamberlain Government. Colonel J.C. Wedgwood, Labour MP for Newcastle-under-Lyme, who had won the DSO at Gallipoli, asked:

> Has the Government not prepared any plans to combat the invasion of this country? The invasion of Norway took us so completely by surprise because all the military experts in the past have pointed to the extraordinary difficulty of landing an armed force on a hostile coast. . . . At present I think the fleet can save us from starvation but not from invasion. I think that is proved by what has taken place in the Skagerrak. If our naval superiority had been able to prevent the Germans from going to Norway, we surely would have acted, whatever the risks. The fact that we did not makes it easy to imagine a similar thing happening on the coast of Lincolnshire and the Wash – the same sort of coast and the same sort of distance.

He went on to suggest that civilians should be trained in the use of rifles.

> We should use them like *franc-tireurs*. They would no doubt be shot if they were taken, but they would be able to harass any small invading forces and not wait until some regular troops came up to help.

The next speaker was Sir Roger Keyes, wearing the uniform of an Admiral of the Fleet, his medal ribbons headed by that of the VC which he had won at Zeebrugge in 1918. He referred to 'the irresponsible musings of my Rt. Hon. and gallant friend.' Harold Nicolson noted in his diary,

> Wedgwood makes a speech which contains everything he ought
> not to have said. He gives the impression of being a little off
> his head.

Next day extracts from Wedgwood's speech were being copied into
the War Diary of the Operations Division of *Oberkommando der Marine*
(OKM), the high command of the German Navy.

OKM had a keen interest in the problem of invading Britain, not
because they thought it a practical proposition but because they feared
they might be required to undertake it. At their head was Grand
Admiral Erich Raeder, a talented staff officer with an ambivalent
view of his Nazi overlords. Like many other German officers he
admired Hitler for restoring Germany to her rightful place among
the great powers but mistrusted his judgment, not least his selection
of men to fill high offices. In particular he mistrusted Hermann
Goering who, among other appointments, was Commander-in-Chief
of the *Luftwaffe*. His confidence in Hitler had not been increased
by the latter's assurance, repeated as late as September, 1938, that
there would be no war with Britain until 1944–45. The expansion
of the *Kriegsmarine* had been geared to this date and under Plan
Z the fleet at the beginning of 1945 would have consisted of ten
battleships, three pocket battleships, seven heavy cruisers (with four
more building), nine light cruisers (thirteen building), two aircraft
carriers (two building) and 172 submarines (95 building). Such an
armada would have given Germany a fair chance of disputing the
supremacy of the North Sea with the Royal Navy, whose large fleet
would have world-wide commitments and a high proportion of elderly
ships.

In the event the outbreak of war in September, 1939, found Raeder
with a very inadequate navy consisting, apart from two obsolete (1906)
pre-dreadnoughts, of two battleships, three pocket battleships, two
heavy cruisers, six light cruisers, twenty-three destroyers and fifty-
seven U-Boats, of which only twenty-six were suitable for operations
in the Atlantic. As Raeder remarked,

> The surface forces are so inferior to the British fleet that, even
> at full strength, they can do no more than show that they know
> how to die gallantly.

The first six months of the war depleted even this meagre fleet. A
nearly complete heavy cruiser, *Lützow*, was handed over to the Soviet

Union, the pocket battleship *Graf Spee* was forced to scuttle herself off Montevideo, the light cruisers *Nürnberg* and *Leipzig* were torpedoed by HM Submarine *Salmon* and put out of action until May and December, 1940, respectively and, further deepening Raeder's dislike of Goering, the Luftwaffe bombed and sank two German destroyers in February, 1940.

It was against this background that in November, 1939, the Grand Admiral instructed his staff to make a study of the invasion of Britain. The working party replied with a paper that opened by laying down four essential pre-conditions for any landing – British air power must be eliminated, the Royal Navy must either be eliminated or sealed off from the landing areas and its approaches, any warships within that area must be neutralized, British submarines must be kept at bay. If all these conditions could be fulfilled it was recommended that, since the Low Countries were still neutral, the best landing area would be between the Tyne and the Thames. Everything, however, would depend on the early capture of a sizeable port and this should be achieved by an airborne attack, thus passing a major part of the problem to the *Luftwaffe*, who controlled all airborne troops.

This was not an encouraging document and suited Raeder admirably. He was implacably opposed to invading Britain under any foreseeable circumstances and was determined to have all the relevant facts marshalled in case the Führer, possibly encouraged by the Army or the Air Force, should propose invasion. The study was forwarded to *Oberkommando der Wehrmacht* (OKW), the supreme headquarters of all the German forces, with Raeder's recommendation that the war against Britain should be pursued by a blockade enforced by submarines and the Air Force. OKW, after a cursory reading, sent copies to the Army and the Air Force.

The comments of *Oberkommando des Heeres* (OKH), the high command of the Army, set a precedent for all future invasion planning by ignoring all maritime considerations such as tides, weather, moonlight, the availability of transport and the strength of the *Kriegsmarine*. They proposed an invasion force of seventeen divisions of which four would be armoured and two motorized. The initial attack would be made by such airborne troops as were available – five understrength parachute battalions and one air-landing regiment – who were to seize Yarmouth and Lowestoft immediately before a landing was made nearby by an infantry division and a brigade of cyclists. Simultaneously

13

another division would land south of Dunwich to guard against a counter-attack from the Ipswich area. If possible a third division should go ashore at Cromer to secure the northern flank. As a diversion two divisions should land north of the Humber and strike at the industrial region around Leeds. A second wave, a corps consisting of two panzer, one motorised and one infantry division, would land at Yarmouth and swing south-west to isolate London while two more air-landing regiments, using the same transports as the first attack, should be landed near Cambridge while the cyclist brigade pedalled up to the area of King's Lynn. The first two waves should sail from German ports but the third, two panzer, one motorised and three infantry divisions, should, for preference, embark from harbours in Holland and Belgium.

Patiently the Navy, while sketching in the problems of tides and landing beaches, pointed out that their entire strength would be required to escort the main force to Yarmouth so that the flank and diversionary attacks would have to sail unprotected. They added that transport for seven divisions would require, apart from many smaller vessels, four hundred 'medium-sized steamers', twice as many as Germany actually possessed. To clinch the matter they added:

> The British Home Fleet will always be able to appear in greater strength than our own fleet, if the will is there.
> It can neither be assumed or considered as probable that a major part of the enemy fleet will be incapable of action while our own forces are deployed to cover the landing. As our naval building programme develops, we should be able to maintain the ratio of naval forces between the two fleets but not to improve it.

This broadside left the Army as unenthusiastic about invasion as the Navy had been and Goering's opinion on behalf of the *Luftwaffe* was uncompromising.

> A combined operation to land in England cannot be considered.
> It would only be considered as the *coup de grâce* in a war already won since otherwise the preconditions could not be met.

There the matter rested for the next six months.

The British War Cabinet had discussed the possibility of invasion even before Raeder had begun his staff study. At the outset of the war several diplomatic and secret service reports had indicated that the Germans were considering a landing and late in October, 1939, a cable was received from Sir Ronald Campbell, Minister at Belgrade, outlining a plan said to have been leaked from OKH. The Germans, it was alleged, planned to use 5,200 aircraft in four divisions, the first of which would transport 12,000 parachutists. Two more groups would neutralize the Royal Navy and the RAF respectively, while the fourth would escort a convoy of small merchant ships carrying 23,000 men including armoured detachments. A second convoy bearing 45,000 men would follow twenty-four hours behind the first and, as a feint, a strong assault would be launched against the Maginot Line.

The Air Staff having confirmed, erroneously, that the Germans had 12,000 'trained parachute infantry' and 5,200 aircraft 'if all types are taken into account', the Cabinet had a lively debate on the subject, the lead being taken by Winston Churchill, then First Lord of the Admiralty, who gave it as his opinion that,

> The Germans were faced with the necessity of undertaking some great operation, either against ourselves or against the French. They might shrink from sacrificing vast numbers in an attack on the Maginot Line whereas they might well gamble on a hazardous venture against Great Britain which, if it succeeded, might well cause us great loss and confusion and, if it failed, would only entail the loss of 80,000 men.

He undertook to strengthen the naval guard in the North Sea and recommended that arrangements be made to bring back British divisions from France should the need arise. Lest parachutists should land in London he procured a stock of arms for the Admiralty so that every sailor stationed there could be issued with a rifle and bayonet. His colleagues, less impressed with the danger, decided to refer the problem to the Chiefs of Staff.

The rest of the Cabinet believed that invasion was one of the many bees in Churchill's bonnet. In 1934 he had proposed that 20 or 30,000 of the unemployed should be put to work building earthworks for the defence of airfields. Two years later he asked the Minister for Co-ordination of Defence what would happen if 200 German aircraft, each carrying fifty men, were discovered 'making towards (say) Newcastle', with a further hundred aircraft following with stores and ammunition. Having consulted the Air Ministry, the Minister replied that the Germans would be more likely to attempt a high level of bombing attacks than an airborne invasion but, if such an attempt was made, 'the Territorial Force* would be ready to move quickly to any threatened point'. Churchill replied,

> Surely four Territorial divisions in their present state of training and equipment could not make head against a quarter of their number of trained and regular storm troops. If they were raised to full strength and given three months training in each year, and mechanized to a high degree, they would be an effective deterrent.

As they considered the possibility of invasion late in 1939 the Chiefs of Staff were influenced by the situation in the North Sea where British naval supremacy was far from complete. After the *Royal Oak* had been torpedoed in Scapa Flow, the aircraft carrier *Courageous* sunk in the Western Approaches and there had been an ineffective but unopposed air raid on warships at Rosyth, the Home Fleet had been withdrawn to the west coast of Scotland where they remained until March, 1940. The German battleships *Scharnhorst* and *Gneisenau* had taken this opportunity to make a foray into the Atlantic and had returned without being detected. This being the case, the Chiefs of Staff considered that the enemy might make a raid on Britain but that the danger of invasion was not sufficiently serious to justify withdrawing troops from France. They did, however, rule that 'a suitable proportion of troops that would normally be at home should be disposed within easy reach of the east coast'. General Sir Walter Kirke, Commander-in-Chief Home Forces, was therefore instructed to implement Plan *Julius Caesar* under which nine infantry divisions, none of them sufficiently trained or equipped to be sent to France, should be deployed on the coast between Berwick and Sussex. In reserve would be two armoured divisions (mustering between them 25 cruiser and 267 light tanks) and a horsed division. Should an airborne invasion take place, the invaders were to be cordoned off by such troops as were available until the armour or cavalry could arrive to deal with them. Garrisons were to be established in all ports and the RAF undertook to make two squadrons of light bombers available to Home Forces should the Germans land.

The British public knew nothing of these alarms and would have

---

* The term Territorial Force had been abolished seventeen years earlier and replaced by Territorial Army.

been unlikely to be much interested if they had been better informed. They had gone to war in a mood of resignation, believing that something must be done to stop Hitler rampaging round Europe. They had been warned to expect devastating air raids and the probability of widespread gas attacks. Nothing had happened. Poland, on whose behalf Britain had declared war, had been swallowed up without a western hand raised to help her. Germany appeared to have acquired a powerful ally in the Soviet Union, which had promptly indulged in an aggressive war of her own, against Finland. Nothing could be done to help Finland. After a brief, illusory flurry of movement on the Western Front, the war communiqués had stagnated into a daily repetition of *Activité des patrouilles*. In the air, where so much had been anticipated, both sides kept largely to themselves. The RAF launched some attacks on the German fleet which, though widely publicised in a film entitled *The Lion has Wings*, were quickly abandoned having achieved nothing at prohibitive cost. The *Luftwaffe* attacked Scapa Flow and killed a rabbit. The first British civilian was not killed until 16 March, 1940, and that was in the faraway Orkneys. Meanwhile the all-pervasive blackout caused many casualties and many were unable to see why they should suffer the inconvenience of darkened streets when there seemed no chance of an air raid. The inconveniences took many forms and in December, 1939, *Reynolds News* reported that

> West End solicitors, who before the war netted five figure incomes from divorce cases, have been heavily hit by the blackout. In the winter months at any rate private inquiry agents are helpless. Adultery cannot be proved because identification is impossible in pitch darkness.

Matters were not improved when the first two months of 1940 turned out to be the coldest for forty-five years. On 20 January the temperature dropped below zero Fahrenheit in parts of Hertfordshire and Kent and 1,500 miles of railway were blocked with snow. For three weeks sea traffic out of the Humber was blocked by ice.

Although most of the cinemas and theatres had reopened, the blackout, to say nothing of the cold, militated against venturing out for public entertainment and boredom became a real enemy, not least to the thousands of men scattered in small detachments in isolated anti-aircraft and searchlight sites who had no occupation but endless drills. This would have been a golden opportunity for BBC radio but the Corporation, preparing for a war of heavy bombing, had cut its services to the bone. Between September, 1939, and February, 1940 only one programme was transmitted, offering insipid fare and dominated by frequent news bulletins at a time when there was no news and the broadcasting of what there was was hampered by an unimaginative censorship. The alternative was listening to the enemy's English language broadcasts from Hamburg, Bremen, Cologne and Zeesen. The British tuned to them in large numbers in the hope of gleaning something of interest or something that might have been kept from them by the British authorities. They found little of interest and even less that was true and the veracity of German radio was much impugned by the repeated claims, the first being on 27 September, 1939, to have sunk the aircraft carrier *Ark Royal*, which in fact survived until November, 1941. Nevertheless many people derived much entertainment from this long-running cabaret during the dreary winter, it being officially estimated in October, 1939, that six million adults listened regularly to German broadcasts while eighteen million listened occasionally.

There was no hindrance to listening to these broadcasts, the wavelengths and times being published in even the most reputable newspapers, but their impact was much diminished when one of the newsreaders became a national figure of fun. Lord Haw Haw became a standby for musical hall comedians and even had a variety show named after him. His utterances, and even his reputed utterances, were passed round the country. There was, however, great confusion about his identity. His nickname was bestowed on him by a columnist in the *Daily Express* who wrote on 14 September, 1939:

> A gent I'd like to meet is moaning periodically out of Zeesen. He speaks English of the haw-haw, damit-get-out-of-my-way variety, and his strong suit is gentlemanly indignation.

That newsreader was Norman Baillie-Stewart, a former captain of the Seaforth Highlanders who had been cashiered under the Official Secrets Act in 1933 and had subsequently taken German nationality.

The man identified as Lord Haw Haw by millions of listeners was a very different personality, William Joyce, an Irishman of Welsh extraction whose father had acquired United States citizenship only to let it lapse when he returned to Ireland. William Joyce repeatedly claimed British nationality and believed himself to be an ardent patriot. In his youth he had acted as an informer for the Black and Tans during the Irish Troubles and, early in 1922, had enlisted in the Worcestershire Regiment, only to be discharged because he was under-age. He took a BA degree at London University in 1927 and devoted himself to politics, joining first British Fascists Limited and later Mosley's British Union of Fascists, of which he became Director of Propaganda. He was an effective rabble-rousing orator but became increasingly out of sympathy with Mosley whom he considered insufficiently anti-Jewish and under the influence of Mussolini rather than Hitler. When the BUF could no longer afford to pay his £300 a year salary, he was not sorry to leave and to found the National Socialist League.

Joyce was a man of talent but was totally devoid of judgment. He had made approaches to Berlin radio for employment at the time of the Munich crisis of 1938 and in the following year, with war imminent, went to Germany. Even then he had second thoughts and tried unsuccessfully to leave the country. German radio was very reluctant to employ him but eventually engaged him since they were desperately short of native English speakers and felt they had to ignore the unattractive grating voice, so different from the P.G. Wodehouse-type accent which was to earn him his nickname, fame and eventual death sentence. He had made his first, unsuccessful broadcast only three days before the *Daily Express* 'haw-haw' item was published.

The Lord Haw Haw who became a cult figure in the winter of 1939–40 was a composite character made up of several voices who regularly read the German news in English while Joyce, although he frequently broadcast, made his greatest contribution by editing bulletins and excising many, though not enough, of the solecisms written into the scripts by Germans. In the early months of the war listening to Lord Haw Haw was a national pastime but, like an oft-repeated joke, the appeal wore thin. In January, 1940, a BBC report estimated that

> A typical 9 o'clock BBC news bulletin is listened to by 16,000,000 people, over 50 per cent of the listening public. If this is followed by a talk, this will be heard by 9,000,000 people. Of the other 7,000,000, 6,000,000 switch over to Hamburg, while the remaining million choose either some other programme or switch off.

The calculation that some 20% of the adult population tuned to Germany regularly may have been an underestimate. The Ministry of Information's figures for January put the proportion at over 26% but, two months later, they found that it was only 15.7% and in May, when Germany attacked in the west, it was down to 13.3%. The Anti-Haw Haw League sponsored by the *Daily Mirror* was wound up that July.

Discontent was widespread in the first wartime winter. The Minister of Information, Sir John Reith, reported a passive, negative feeling of apathy and boredom and the Home Secretary commented:

> At the present moment public opinion is only too ready to discount risks of large scale air attack, merely because no such attacks have yet been delivered.

He recommended 'active steps . . . to counter this spirit of false optimism', but the taking of active steps was not the style of the Chamberlain Government. As a senior public servant wrote at the time, the Prime Minister was 'costive, dull and talks of endurance and victory in the most defeatist terms'. As Chamberlain wrote to his sister:

> You don't need offensive forces sufficient to win a smashing victory. What you want are defensive forces sufficiently strong to make it impossible for the other side to win except at such a cost to make it not worthwhile.

As he privately admitted in September, 1939, 'I was never meant to be a war minister', and few of Chamberlain's colleagues gave the nation much inspiration. Most pinned their faith on a blockade of Germany that was wide open on the enemy's southern and eastern frontiers, a leakage which did not prevent the Minister for Economic Warfare, R.H. Cross, from declaring in January, 1940, that the first four months of war had caused the German economy as much difficulty as the first two years of the Great War. Lord Halifax, the Foreign Secretary, could only cheer Britain up by saying 'Time is on our side' and the Ministry of Information fired martial ardour with a leaflet which declared:

> We do not have to defeat the Nazis on land, but only to prevent them from defeating us.

It was illogical of the British to feel aggrieved when, having been promised a rain of high explosives, no one bothered to bomb them. They had been conditioned by Stanley Baldwin's declaration to the House of Commons in 1932:

> I think it is as well for the man in the street to realize that
> there is no power on earth that can prevent him from being
> bombed. Whatever people may tell him, the bomber will always
> get through. The only defence is offence, which means you have
> to kill more women and children more quickly than the enemy
> if you want to save yourselves.

This vision of the war of the future had its roots in inter-service rivalry. In his determination to preserve the RAF as an independent service, Sir Hugh Trenchard, Chief of the Air Staff, had set about convincing politicians that an independent RAF would be an efficient and, more important, an economical part of the nation's defences. In doing so he conjured up a vision of wars in which large (and expensive) armies would be superfluous since the matter could be quickly and cheaply settled by an air force. In 1923 he told the Committee of Imperial Defence:

> In a democratic country like ours, power rests ultimately with
> the people and war cannot be continued unless the bulk of the
> people support it. If the people are subject to sufficient bombing
> they will compel the government to sue for peace.

In this campaign Trenchard had as allies the newly fashionable military gurus. J.F.C. Fuller wrote in 1923:

> Picture if you can what the results will be: London for a few days
> will be one vast raving Bedlam, the hospitals will be stormed,
> traffic will cease, the homeless will shriek for help, the City will
> be in pandemonium. What of the government at Westminster?
> It will be swept away by an avalanche of terror. The enemy
> will dictate his terms which will be grasped like a straw by a
> drowning man.

He was supported two years later by Basil Liddell Hart:

> Provided that the blow be sufficiently swift and powerful, there
> is no reason why either within a few hours, or at most days, the
> nerve system of the country should not be paralysed.

Trenchard's formula for averting this chimera lay not in building up defences against enemy bombers but in carrying the war to the enemy.

> To win the war it will be necessary to pursue a relentless offensive
> by bombing the enemy's country, destroying his sources of aircraft
> and engines, and breaking the morale of his people. . . . It would

21

be better to have less fighters and more bombers to bomb the
enemy and trust to their morale cracking first.

To bolster this line of argument Trenchard and the disciples who
succeeded him at the head of the RAF greatly exaggerated the effects
of bombing. When in 1924 the Government began to consider devising
a policy for Air Raid Precautions, the Air Staff asserted that every ton
of bombs dropped on a city would cause fifty casualties, and that one
third of those casualties would be fatal. From this they calculated that
should the French (then regarded as the only potential aggressor)
attack London at their full strength there would be 5,000 casualties
on the first day, 3,750 on the second and 2,500 in every subsequent
period of twenty-four hours. By 1937, with Germany identified as
the probable enemy, the Air Staff raised their estimate, asserting
that 6,000 tons of more effective bombs would be dropped every
day causing 200,000 casualties a week of which 66,000 would be
fatal.*

Even if the British were not being bombed and could find little to
exhilarate them on the radio or in the newspapers, they could find
plenty to grumble about, especially after rationing started with bacon,
butter and sugar on 8 January, 1940. Meat followed in March with
an allocation of 1/10d worth (9p) for an adult and half as much for
a child. *The Hereford Times* advised its readers,

> Don't expect deliveries on the day you order. Ask for afternoon
> delivery if you cannot take your order with you.
> Give an alternative when ordering.
> Treat offals as non-procurable for the time being.
> Remember that there is a very large proportion of coarse meat
> to prime meat in every carcass, and accept your share.

It was clearly going to be a long and tiresome war but there were com-
pensations. The wages of agricultural workers were increased to fifty
shillings (£2.50) a week, women workers in the armament industries
were to receive 35/- (£1.75) a week if they were over twenty-one years
old, a bottle of Drambuie could be obtained for 22/- (£1.10), Canadian

---

* Between 1939 and 1945 the enemy dropped an estimated 64,393 tons of bombs on Britain,
killing 51,509, seriously injuring 61,423 and slightly injuring about 150,000. In the heaviest raid
on Coventry, a very concentrated target, 500 tons of bombs (and 900 incendiary canisters) killed
544 and seriously injured 865 people. The British experience was that a ton of bombs killed
or injured about four and a half people.

fresh salmon (middle cut) was being advertised at two shillings (10p) a pound and a fortunate bidder bought a picture by Fra Filipo Lippi for £360 at Sotheby's.

As spring began to appear in England the Nazis won a notable victory. In the early hours of 9 April German troops attacked Oslo and all the main ports of Norway, being successful at every point. They also overran Denmark. It was a humiliating defeat for the Royal Navy that the Germans could carry out landings at points further from their own bases than those of the British. A small and hastily assembled expeditionary force, consisting largely of ill-equipped Territorial troops failed to achieve any effective counter-thrust. This evidence of impotence in the North Sea came as a shattering shock to the British but it may have been a blessing in heavy disguise since it induced them in the following month to dismiss Chamberlain's turgid Government and replace it, in the nick of time, with Churchill's more lively administration.

The Norwegian enterprise also reduced the *Kriegsmarine* to a remnant. The Norwegian shore defences sank the heavy cruiser *Blücher* in Oslo fiord and at Bergen immobilized the light cruiser *Königsberg*, enabling her to be sunk by the Fleet Air Arm. Her sister ship *Karlsruhe* was sunk by HM Submarine *Truant* and the heavy cruiser *Admiral Hipper* sustained a great gash in her side when rammed by the sinking destroyer *Glowworm*. Ten German destroyers, half her flotilla strength, were sunk in the two battles in Narvik fiord and eight U-Boats were lost. A torpedo damaged the pocket battleship *Lützow* (formerly *Deutschland*) and the battleship *Scharnhorst* needed dockyard repairs after her engagement with HMS *Renown*.

If Grand Admiral Raeder had ever nursed serious thoughts of invading Britain, this wholesale reduction in his naval strength would have put an end to them. The Norwegian campaign was essentially his triumph, designed to break the British stranglehold on his fleet bases, but he had always recognized the risks involved. A month before the landing took place he had written:

> The operation in itself is contrary to all principles in the theory
> of naval warfare. According to this theory it could be carried out
> only if we had naval superiority. We do not have this; on the
> contrary, we are carrying out this operation in the face of the

23

vastly superior British fleet. Despite this, I believe that, given
that surprise is complete, our troops can and will be transported
successfully to Norway.

Raeder's courage was justified by a remarkable success, but there was
another side to the coin. Not only did Norway cost him most of his
fleet but the ease with which the troops were landed gave the German
Army the notion that the Navy, if it set its mind to it, could achieve
the impossible. When, some three months later, the *Wehrmacht* set its
heart on crossing the comparatively narrow English Channel, they
expected the *Kriegsmarine* to produce a miracle.

'Arm yourselves
and be ye men of valour'

Even before the war started, measures had been initiated which would be useful if invasion came, though the reason for taking them was that London and other great cities might be made untenable by bombing. The country had been divided into twelve regions each with a Commissioner who was empowered to administer his region should central government break down. In May, 1939, a possible removal of the central authority, 'the Black Move', had been planned and authorized. The War Cabinet would be housed at Hindlip Hall, near Worcester, Parliament would sit at Stratford-on-Avon, while the Admiralty, War Office and Air Ministry would move to Malvern, Droitwich and Worcester respectively.

Churchill's return to the Admiralty at the outbreak of war renewed his interest in the possibility of invasion. On 7 October, 1939, he minuted:

> Why do we not form a Home Guard of half a million men over forty (if they like to volunteer) and put all our elderly stars at the head and in the structure of these new formations? . . . If uniforms are lacking, a brassard would suffice and I am assured there are plenty of rifles.

Two weeks later he wrote to the First Sea Lord:

> It might be as well to consider what would happen if, for instance, 20,000 men were run across and landed, say, at Harwich, or at Webburn Hook [Weybourne, near Sheringham], where there is deep water close inshore. . . . Have any arrangements been made by the War Office to provide against this contingency? . . . I do not think it likely, but it is physically possible.

The German coup in Scandinavia brought him back to the subject and, unimpressed by the *Julius Caesar* scheme, he urged the War

Cabinet to bring home from France 'at least one highly trained division . . . to meet a German landing'. It was agreed that two brigade of 5 Division (the third brigade was in Norway) should be ordered to England. It seems that the War Office had anticipated this decision since on the previous day, 30 April, the Chief of Staff to the Expeditionary Force had noted in his diary:

> We have to part with the 5th Division. They are sick at home of not having an effective reserve.

The order, however, was rescinded for, on 4 May, the Chief of Staff wrote:

> I have succeeded in getting the removal of 5th Division stopped, or at least postponed . . . At present there is a Home Defence flap on, started by Winston, and the S of S, who is not a courageous man, is very excited at the alleged lack of trained troops in the country.

Invasion was back before the Cabinet on 9 May when they considered a paper from the Chiefs of Staff based on the assumption that, determined to win the war in 1940, the Germans might launch an air offensive against Britain and follow it up with a landing. The German attack on the Low Countries on the next day showed that this apprehension was at least premature.

The part in that invasion attributed by the newspapers to airborne troops immediately fired the public imagination and on 11 May the Liberal National MP for Fife East asked the Secretary of State for War

> Whether, in order to meet the imminent danger of enemy para-chutists landing in this country and to avoid displacing regular troops, he will consider the immediate formation of a voluntary corps of older, responsible men to be armed with rifles and Bren guns and trained for instant action in their own localities in case of raids?

Anthony Eden, the new Secretary for War, replied that the matter was under consideration whereupon W.J. Thorne, Labour Member for Plaistow, shouted, 'Let us arm everybody! Let us all have arms!'

Private enterprise had already taken some steps in this direction. In Herefordshire Lady Helena Gleichen had organized seventy men from her estate and the surrounding countryside even before the war broke out. Naming them the Much Marcle Watchers, she demanded arms for them from the county regiment and, being refused, armed them with pikes, halberds and flintlocks hanging on the walls of her ancient house. The coasts of Dumfriesshire were regularly patrolled by cyclists as early as April. In Essex the Bishop of Chelmsford had warned his diocese of the danger of invasion and, as he told *The Times*,

> In the Romford area there had actually been a company of about
> 100 strong guarding vital spots and watching for parachutists.
> They had run it with money from their own pockets and had
> continually asked for recognition and the necessary arms.

All this was regularized when, on 14 May, Anthony Eden broadcast for 'large numbers of men in Great Britain, who are British subjects, between the ages of seventeen and sixty five' to join the Local Defence Volunteers. He went on to say:

> The purpose of the parachute attack is to disorganize and confuse,
> as a preparation for the landing of troops by aircraft. The success
> of such an attack depends on speed. Consequently the measures
> to defeat such an attack must be prompt and rapid. . . . This
> appeal is directed chiefly to those who live in country parishes,
> in small towns and in less densely populated suburban areas.

At this stage all thoughts were concentrated on repelling landings from the sky, the result of exaggerated reports of the numbers and capabilities of German parachutists. It was the Italians who had first trained parachute troops and had had two battalions of them as early as 1930. The Russians took up the idea and in 1935 demonstrated a mass drop by a whole battalion to the Military Attachés stationed in Moscow. Only the Germans followed this example but their development of the idea was hampered by typical inter-service wrangling, both the army and the air force claiming to control them. It was not until July, 1938, that the two existing battalions were brought together under a *Luftwaffe* officer, Colonel Kurt Student, who was instructed to expand them into 7 *Flieger Division*. Thanks to this late start the coming of war found them with only five incomplete battalions with anti-aircraft and anti-tank detachments.

One of these battalions took part in the Scandinavian campaign and got off to a very successful start. The important Vordingbord road bridge, south of Copenhagen, was captured by dropping a platoon at either end without firing a shot. Another platoon seized the two airfields at Arlborg in north Denmark enabling the *Luftwaffe* to use them within two hours of their capture. In Norway things were more difficult due to the weather, but, after the ground defences had been beaten up from the air, a parachute company managed to grab Sola airfield near Stavanger and, despite heavy loss, hold it until reinforcements arrived. Two companies and battalion headquarters took part in the attack on Fornebu airfield outside Oslo, but the visibility was so abominable that, after two transport planes had collided, the force was recalled to base. Nevertheless the battalion commander, seeing a patch of clear weather, decided to press on and the defenders, surprised and bemused, withdrew. Reports of these actions lost nothing in the telling, but no reports reached Britain of a further attack on 14 April which was an unmitigated failure. The intention was to cut off the retreat of the Norwegian forces in the south by seizing the Dombaas Pass in their rear. In more bad weather several Ju52 transports flew into mountains and those parachutists who did land were quickly rounded up.

Four weeks later, in the small hours of 10 May, the Germans carried out the most spectacular of all airborne feats, the capture of Ford Eben-Emael. No parachutists were used but eighty-five specially trained engineers were launched towards their target in eleven gliders which were released at 8,000 feet over German territory to plane down over the Maastricht appendix to land on the roof of what was probably the most formidable fortification ever built. Standing on an artificial cliff above the Albert Canal, the fort measured 900 yards by 700 and mounted a dozen guns, having a battalion of infantry apart from gunners as garrison. It would have been unassailable to ground attack but the glider-borne sappers blew in the gun turrets with hollow charges except in the case of the heavier guns where they pushed explosives down the barrels. Fort Ebel-Emael, the lynch-pin of the allied defensive line, fell to the Germans at a cost of six dead and fifteen wounded.

A few hours later 7 *Flieger Division* and a new formation, 22 Air Portable Division, landed in Holland. Most of the parachute battalions dropped successfully to capture three bridges over the Maas river and completed their 'airborne carpet' by landing a dozen seaplanes, each carrying ten men, beside the bridge on the Rotterdam waterfront. Simultaneously a single parachute battalion and 22 Division, landing in Ju52s, attempted to seize The Hague with Queen Wilhelmina and her Government. Warned by events in Denmark and Norway, the Dutch command had kept reserves well back and the German force was almost destroyed.

Apart from the débâcle at the Hague, the German airborne forces had done spectacularly well in the Low Countries but the cost was high. 22 Division required complete reconstruction and 7 *Flieger*, which had gone into action only 4,000 strong and short of trained reinforcements, had suffered heavily in killed and wounded, among the latter being General Student, who was incapacitated for the rest of the year. One hundred and eighty-four transport aircraft were lost, as were most of the parachutes used, a serious business since parachute silk was in very short supply in Germany and occupied Europe had to be combed for fresh supplies.

None of this was apparent in the west and the wildest stories quickly circulated. Prince Bernhard of the Netherlands reported, on reaching England, that 'The Germans sent about 12,000 troops by parachute', though he added that the Dutch had killed 10,000 of them. According to *The Times* a Dutch Minister told a press conference that Germans had landed 'disguised as nuns, Red Cross nurses, monks and tram conductors.' The notion of parachuting nuns became a great favourite in Britain and the *Daily Express* improved on it:

> On the first day of the invasion parachutists dropped out of the sky like a vast flock of vultures. Most of them were disguised in Allied or Dutch uniforms, others came down in the uniform of Dutch policemen and began to direct the population in the streets and mislead the army. One 'policeman' told a group of isolated Dutch troops that their friends were round the corner. When the Dutch troops turned the corner, German troops, barricaded across the road, slaughtered them. . . . But, most fantastic of all, the steward of an English ship said that he and the crew had watched parachutists descend in women's clothing. They wore blouses and skirts and each carried a sub-machine gun. The steward could not tell if they were women or men disguised as women. Several eye-witnesses in the boat confirmed it and said that others had come down disguised as priests, peasants and civilians.

On 17 May the *Evening Standard* reported:

> Parachutists near Ostend are said to have had transparent parachutes and sky-blue uniforms to make them semi-invisible during their descent.

29

In fact the Germans dropped no parachutists in Belgium or France, although both countries seethed with stories of their landings in the guise of priests or of staff officers who issued misleading orders. In Belgium 'all clergymen were suspected of being parachutists in disguise', while a story circulated that among the Dutch refugees were SS men in ringleted wigs and false beards, posing as orthodox Jews from Amsterdam. The Mother Superior of the Breton convent of St Nicholas was twice arrested as a parachutist and a young French officer told the correspondent of the *New York Times*, 'We simply shoot all officers we do not know.' For allied airmen, baling out behind the lines became a proceeding of great danger.

In Britain the first official manifestation of the parachute scare came on 10 May, the day the Netherlands were invaded, in the form of a misleading letter from the Air Ministry addressed to all RAF home commands, copies being sent to the Admiralty, War Office and Ministry of Home Security.

> Information from Norway shows that German parachute troops, when descending, hold their arms above their heads as if surrendering. The parachutist, however, holds a grenade in each hand. These are thrown at anyone attempting to obstruct the landing. To counter this strategem, parachutists, if they exceed six in number, are to be treated as hostile and if possible shot in the air. The largest crew carried by any British bomber is six persons.

It might have been supposed that someone in the Air Ministry would be sufficiently conversant with parachutes to know that anyone descending on one has to keep his hands above his head to grasp the cords by which the contraption is controlled and that to attempt to hold a primed grenade at the same time would be, at best, a risky proceeding.

A day or two later *The Times* commented:

> It would not be correct for country gentlemen to carry their guns with them on their walks, and to take flying or running shots as an opportunity is offered. Such action would put them in the position of *franc-tireurs* and should be avoided.

A letter to the *Manchester Guardian* made an ingenious suggestion:

> In many areas it should be possible to fix standardised armoured crows' nests on the tops of electricity pylons. Two men with a

machine gun in such a post would be a formidable obstacle to a landing party.

The *Daily Telegraph* of 13 May reported:

> Existing precautionary measures against attempts at sabotage in the country by enemy airborne troops have been greatly strengthened by the Home Defence authorities.
> The formation of mobile military columns, equipped with rifles, light machine guns and hand grenades, has been completed. These detachments have been posted at convenient centres, ready to proceed to any locality in a specified area where enemy troops are reported to have landed or are likely to land. Road patrols have also been established to stop cars, motor coaches and other vehicles suspected of carrying soldiers of whose identity they are in doubt. . . .
> It is realised that any attempt by the enemy to land air-borne troops would be carefully planned. Deception would be practised to the extent of sending detachments with a knowledge of the English language and wearing uniforms of a British pattern. The areas thought most likely to be threatened are those within easy reach of airfields. At each of these the guards have been strengthened. The assistance of the public, it is emphasised, is of vital importance. The presence of strange aircraft, parachute dropping or unusual movements of men, whether in uniform or not, should be reported immediately to the nearest police station.

A week later the same paper cast doubt on the adequacy of such precautions:

> A former British Army officer, who has just escaped from Holland, told me that in his opinion Britain must at once prepare to deal with Nazi parachute troops and that infantry armed with rifles would not be sufficient to deal with them.

By the second week in May there were few people in Britain who doubted that at any moment parachutists 'would drop out of the sky like a vast flock of vultures'. On 12 May a housewife near Coventry confided to her diary:

> My mind runs on parachute troops today – we are hearing so much of them in Holland and Belgium.

A week later a Londoner was writing:

> Even the hitherto unbelievable fact that this isn't really an island any more wasn't unbelievable after a bit.

Naturally the Germans were quick to exploit such fears and on 19 May a senior official in the BBC noted:

> Last night the Nazis broadcast a statement to the effect that they had ten thousand aeroplanes waiting to drop a hundred thousand troops in England.

On 11 May a letter to the *Telegraph* opened with the sentence 'The Government is rightly alive to the danger of parachute raiders who may be let loose over the countryside at any moment', and proposed that the task of rounding them up should be entrusted to the British Legion. Two days later a correspondent from Chandler's Ford suggested that the job could safely be left to the Legion of Frontiersmen.

It was against this background that on 14 May the country heard Eden's appeal for Local Defence Volunteers and, within minutes, police stations were besieged with volunteers. In a few days a quarter of a million men had been enrolled and the numbers went on swelling. About three-quarters of the recruits had seen service between 1914 and 1918 and, as a battalion commander noted, 'Military experience . . . varied from the Scots Guards to the Zhob Levies.' Men who had fought in the Great War were not necessarily much above forty years old but there were some notable veterans. Field-Marshal the Earl of Cavan, Colonel of the Irish Guards, served as an NCO and a man whose services had been refused in 1914, on the grounds that he was over-age, was enlisted as a private in Caernarvonshire. The *Kent Messenger* reported that one of the earliest applicants at Sevenoaks was eighty-three. He was turned away but elsewhere Alexander Taylor of Crieff, a seventy-eight-year-old ex-sergeant-major of the Black Watch, who had seen service with the Gordon Relief Expedition in 1885, was enrolled. In East Anglia, 'The Bishop of Norwich wishes to make it known that any of the clergy who desire to join the Local Defence Volunteers are at liberty to do so.' The Bishop of Truro, who had won the MC in the previous war, joined as a private soldier.

The clergy also passed information to the LDV. In Shropshire:

> A clergyman returning home about midnight saw a parachute descending and immediately reported the incident which, on investigation by the LDV, proved to have been a swan alighting on the adjacent lake in broad moonlight. The matter was thus satisfactorily cleared up, but not until a lorryload of RAF personnel, who had been sent to investigate it, inadvertently put a bullet through the huntsman's window at the local kennels.

As the London Correspondent of the *New Yorker* reported, the British were

> Flocking to enlist in a local defence corps formed to deal with
> what a BBC announcer referred to in an absent-minded moment
> as American, instead of enemy, parachutists.

A verdant mythology has grown up about the early shortage of arms for the LDV and it is true that at first there were rifles for only about a third of the volunteers so that many resorted to ingenious expedients. Members of the staff of the British Museum who were caring for exhibits evacuated to Drayton Hall in Northamptonshire proposed acquiring bows and arrows which they would fire at invaders from the crenellations on the house's roof. The Museum authorities disapproved and ordered the senior official present to seek out any German officer and tell him what was in the house, adding that he would hold the German authorities responsible for the safety of the collection. In Kent several units armed themselves with rifles and even Bren guns abandoned on the quays by soldiers evacuated from Dunkirk. They were affronted when the Army insisted on the return of these weapons, but 'a great deal of ammunition was kept and was very useful in teaching the men to shoot'.

In that part of the world some units had less trouble with arms. On Friday, 17 May Eastern Command telephoned the Kentish Zone Commander,

> and told me I must have 1,500 armed men on patrol on the
> following night and that I could draw 1,500 rifles and 150,000
> rounds of ammunition. . . . By 9 p.m. on Saturday 18 May 1,500
> men were on patrol.

This was almost certainly the first LDV patrol in the country but the *Daily Telegraph* sparked off a lively correspondence by reporting that the first patrol was sent out from Chatham on 21 May. Burnham-on-Crouch responded that they had been on duty on 19 May but were surpassed by Babraham, Cambridgeshire, who claimed that their men had been patrolling on 18 May 'armed and in uniform'.

The men of Babraham were probably armed with shot guns but the provenance of their uniforms is a mystery. In his broadcast Eden had said that uniforms would be provided but it was many weeks before anything more than an armband and a forage cap was forthcoming. There was an exception in the West Riding of Yorkshire where Sir

Montague Burton furnished barathea battle dress for every member of his local battalion. This would not have found favour with a *Telegraph* reader from Kingston Hill who wrote:

> Surely the enemy will quickly attire his parachuters with copies of [LDV] uniforms so that invaders and defenders will be indistinguishable. Could not volunteers in each district or county be provided with a type of uniform peculiarly its own?

It may have been with this in mind that in June tailors were forbidden to supply uniforms to members of the LDV, the War Office ruling that 'Uniforms can only be supplied through regular channels'.

The provision of uniforms was a serious matter, since it was important that any LDV captured should not be treated as a *franc-tireur*, a point quickly seized upon by German radio:

> The British Government is committing the worst crime of all. Evidently it permits open preparations for the formation of murder bands. The preparations which are being made all over England to arm the civilian population for guerrilla warfare are contrary to the rules of international law. German official quarters warn the misled British public and remind them of the fate of Polish *franc-tireurs* and gangs of murderers. Civilians who take up arms against German soldiers are, under international law, no better than murderers, whether they are priests or bank clerks.

The problem was acute in Northern Ireland. Fears that arms might fall into the hands of the IRA ensured that the province was not included in the first appeal for volunteers but, with the deteriorating military situation, the authorities changed their mind. Since there was already the nucleus of a home defence force in the armed Special Constabulary, it was decided that recruits for the Ulster Defence Volunteer Force would be enrolled as special constables and that military control of them would be exercised through the Inspector General of Special Constabulary. They were issued with green uniforms which would have been black but for an error in the dye. It was then pointed out that the use of policemen as soldiers was unquestionably contrary to the Hague Convention and the 26,000 volunteers had to be reattested as soldiers and re-dressed in khaki.

The Government did nothing to discourage even the more extravagant apprehensions of German intentions and capabilities and Churchill

34

lost no opportunity of suggesting that invasion was not only possible but probable. On 18 May he wrote to President Roosevelt that 'We must expect . . . to be attacked here on the Dutch model before very long and we hope to give a good account of ourselves'; five days later he cabled to the Prime Ministers of Australia, Canada, New Zealand and South Africa that 'an early heavy attack' on Britain was expected.

> We are preparing, and we hope that our naval defences will be
> effective against large bodies, and that our land defences will
> deal with any sea-borne survivors after some rough work.

In his first broadcast as Prime Minister on 19 May he told the nation:

> We must expect that as soon as stability is reached on the Western
> Front, the bulk of the hideous apparatus of aggression . . . will
> be unleashed on us. . . . After this battle in France abates, there
> will come the battle for our island – That will be the struggle.
> . . . Centuries ago words were written to be a call and a spur to
> the faithful servants of Truth and Justice. 'Arm yourselves, and
> be ye men of valour, and be in readiness for the conflict; for it
> is better for us to die in battle than to look upon the outrage of
> our nation and our altar.'

The combination of Churchill's words and the realization of imminent danger changed the atmosphere in Britain. On 21 May the American broadcaster Ed Murrow told his audience, 'To me it seems that this country is ten years younger than it was ten days ago.'

Churchill saw his first task to be rousing the British people from the indifference and uncertainty that had gripped them for the first nine months of the war. He saw that, whatever happened in France – and he was already expecting the worst – Britain had a long ordeal in front of her although it might consist largely of ruthless bombing. Unless the people were keyed up to withstand an identifiable danger their morale would be at the mercy of any threat. The prospect of invasion was ideal for his purpose – anyone could visualize German soldiers storming into their village, town, city or suburb, even if they might not visualize it with much accuracy – and soon more than a million men in the LDV were convinced that they were playing their part in resisting 'the hideous apparatus of aggression'. Whether the Prime Minister seriously believed that a German invasion was a practicable operation is another question. He had a lively appreciation of the difficulties which would beset a landing force trying to make its

35

way across the treacherous waters of the North Sea or the Channel in the face of the Royal Navy and the Royal Air Force and there was a reasonable chance that even the remnants of the army still in England could deal with whatever seasick and disorganized survivors might struggle ashore. It may be that Churchill hoped that invasion would be attempted since its repulse would be the only victory against Germany to which Britain could look forward in the immediate future. A partial victory would be won if Hitler could be shown to be making preparations for an invasion and be induced to abandon them.

As it happened, the Germans had no thought of invasion at that time. On 21 May, the day on which it became known that the *Wehrmacht* had reached the Channel and cut the main Anglo-French armies from their base, Admiral Raeder sought an interview with Hitler at his headquarters in the Eifel mountains. His aim was to forestall any thought of a landing in England.

> There was a danger that the obvious proposal would be put
> forward by some irresponsible quarter and taken up by Hitler,
> who might suddenly make impossible demands on the Navy.
> From my knowledge of Hitler's temperament I realised that
> it was always advisable in such cases to let him know my
> views promptly before some uninformed person had a chance
> of influencing him.

The Admiral therefore explained the Staff study that he had initiated in the previous November and gave the conclusion that 'a landing would be very difficult and dangerous'. He added his opinion that preparations should be made for a long-term siege war against Britain. The Führer agreed and ruled that, once operations in France were completed, priority should be given to the construction of submarines and bombers. He added that, while it would be prudent to prepare for a long war, he believed that England would be reasonable and agree to make peace. Raeder was relieved by Hitler's reaction but was not convinced that it would last. As a precaution he gave orders for a survey to be made of the shipping resources of the conquered countries. This was to list the number of ships 'suitable for shorter sea-crossings in the North Sea and Channel' and was to include inland craft – tugs, motor boats and barges – which could be used to cross the Channel. Details of size, cargo space, landing facilities and requirements for crew were to be available by the end of June.

Simultaneously the study carried out in November was resurrected

36

and the head of OKM's Operations Division, Rear Admiral Karl Fricke, produced a memorandum *Studie England* dated 27 May. This postulated a very obstinate defence since 'the ancient fear of invasion has again manifested itself and has grown into an almost hysterical anxiety'. Expecting strong beach defences and a speedy commitment of British reserves, he advocated a very powerful assault wave of troops but pointed out that even this could not succeed unless the basic preconditions – grounding of the RAF, mine barriers on the flanks of the invasion corridor, silencing of British anti-aircraft guns and a prolonged period of good weather – had all been met.

Given these preconditions, he considered two possible landing areas – the stretch between Portland Bill and Yarmouth and that from the Thames to the Tyne. From a naval point of view the former was preferable since the crossing would be shorter, air cover more easily available, the flanks more easily sealed with mines and, for part of the front, artillery support would be available from heavy guns mounted in the Pas de Calais. He also pointed out reasons for preferring the northern area where the landing beaches were easier and more numerous, where the country behind them was less heavily populated and less easy to defend. Moreover, an invasion fleet aiming for the east coast of Britain could be prepared in harbours between Denmark and the Scheldt where it would have more security from British bombing and aerial reconnaissance.

Fricke's final paragraph contained the words:

> Our small fleet cannot and will not be able to achieve much. . . . Nevertheless, as in the case of Norway, it should be possible to put personnel ashore quickly. The remaining naval vessels, with auxiliaries in the form of merchant ships and fishing boats, will be able to carry out the landing over short distances.

Studie England is an excellent example of the *Kriegsmarine*'s attitude to invasion throughout the summer. No senior naval officer wished to undertake such a 'difficult and dangerous' operation, but all realized that it would be impolitic to assert that the project was impossible. Such an assertion must come from someone else, preferably the Führer. On the face of it the paragraph quoted above states that a landing in England could be carried out, but closer reading suggests the opposite. Personnel could be put ashore but nothing is said above the landing of heavy equipment – tanks and artillery – without which the army could not hope to succeed. Nor is anything said about supplying the men ashore, though the reference to the need to silence British anti-aircraft guns suggests that this might have to be done by air. At the time that *Studie England* was issued, no one commented on these evasions since the *Wehrmacht* and the *Luftwaffe* were fully occupied with the French campaign and Hitler was confident of a negotiated peace with Britain.

Although the Germans had barely started contemplating a landing, the British Intelligence services were constantly prophesying invasion. By 10 May so many reports of invasion had been submitted that the last Cabinet over which Chamberlain presided laid emphasis on the need to instruct troops in Britain on the action to be taken 'against parachute troops attempting to land in this country'. It also decided to move out of the vulnerable Dover area a Pioneer battalion composed of German refugees. On the same day the Chiefs of Staff set up the Home Defence Executive, presided over by Commander-in-Chief, Home Forces and consisting of representatives of the Admiralty, the active commands of the RAF – Bomber, Fighter and Coastal – and the Ministry of Home Security. Their main task, apart from tactical co-ordination, was to prepare 'the commercial and domestic fabric of the nation for the shock of invasion by air or sea'.

On 24 May the Joint Intelligence Committee (JIC) drew attention to the difficulties that the Germans would encounter in using Calais and Boulogne, then being fought over, but suggested that the allied withdrawal from Norway might encourage the enemy to attack from that direction. They expressed the opinion that the *Luftwaffe* would require two weeks after the end of the French campaign to regroup for invasion. Next day an intercepted message from the Japanese Minister in Budapest reported that, in the opinion of the Hungarian Prime Minister, the Germans had a plan for invading Britain. On 30 May the First Sea Lord reported increased German activity off the Norwegian coast and the assembly of motor boats at Bremen and Hamburg. On that day the JIC warned that they were unlikely to be able to give prior warning of an invasion attempt. Neither the JIC nor the Chiefs of Staff doubted for a moment that Germany would have prepared plans for an invasion and, on the day before he ceased to be Chief of the Imperial General Staff, General Ironside wrote in his diary:

> Obviously, when one considers how the Germans have worked
> out their plans for the conquest of all the other countries, they

must have considered how to get at us. Parachutes, troop-carrying aeroplanes, tanks in flat-bottomed boats and the like.

Meanwhile the military situation in France and Belgium was deteriorating at an unimaginable rate. The Germans reached the sea at Abbeville on 20 May, took Boulogne on 24 May and Calais three nights later. It was clear that no offensives would be able to break through the encirclement of the northern armies and *Operation Dynamo*, the embarkation of the BEF and of such Frenchmen as could be induced to sail with them from the remaining bridgehead between Dunkirk and Nieuport, was authorized on 26 May. Even the most optimistic estimate at that time did not contemplate the evacuation of more than 45,000 men and it was obvious that all heavy equipment must be lost.

On the day that *Dynamo* was approved the Cabinet asked the Chiefs of Staff to consider Britain's chances of being able to continue the war alone and, in particular, 'Can the Navy and the Air Force hold out reasonable hope of preventing serious invasion?' The conclusion was:

> While our Air Force is in being, our Navy and Air Force together should be able to prevent Germany carrying out a serious sea-borne invasion of this country.
> Supposing Germany gained complete air superiority, we consider that the Navy could hold up invasion for a time, but not for an indefinite period. If, with our Navy unable to prevent it, and our Air Force gone, Germany attempted an invasion, our coast and beach defences could not prevent German tanks and infantry getting a firm footing on our shores. In the circumstances envisaged above our land forces would be insufficient to deal with a serious invasion.
> The crux of the matter is air superiority. Once Germany has attained this she might attempt to subjugate this country by air attack alone.

Apart from the assumption that the German plans for invasion were already cut and dried, this assessment was based on two misconceptions. The first was that, in the air, 'the Germans have a superiority of four to one', a calculation that roughly doubled the effective strength of the *Luftwaffe*. The second was that, as has been seen, the expectation was that only a small proportion of the BEF could be rescued from Dunkirk and that those saved would be from the rear echelons of the army – clerks, storemen and drivers – while the fighting troops would have to be sacrificed to cover the embarkation. Thus only the nine under-equipped Territorial divisions involved in *Julius Caesar* would be available for the defence of Britain.

Although these calculations were unknown to the public at large, it was clear that the war was coming closer to home. On 17 May drivers were told that they must immobilize their cars between dusk and dawn by locking them in garages and by removing the distributor covers or sparking plugs*. Three days later Londoners saw preparations for the defence of Whitehall with road blocks. A machine-gun post was established on top of the Admiralty Arch. On 28 May an order was made that 'No person shall display or cause or permit to be displayed any sign which furnishes any indication of the name or situation or the direction of, or the distance to any place.' The arms were removed from signposts, place names were painted out or, in the case of war memorials, gouged out with chisels. It was recommended that 'Heavy milestones should be removed beyond the fence of the road or to some nearby place where they would be hidden from view.' A letter from Sevenoaks to *Picture Post* proposed that:

> With a view to misleading airborne invasion I suggest a scheme of 'adopting' the name of one town by another town in a different locality. For example, all civilians in, say, Coventry, if met by a parachutist and asked the name of the town would at once reply 'This is Bristol'. All residents in the same town would give the same reply.

On 16 May the sugar ration was reduced to eight ounces a week and butter to four ounces. Catering establishments were forbidden to serve more than one tenth of an ounce of sugar with any meal, the same amount being permitted with a hot drink.

By 20 May the Ministry of Information survey reported that 'many people have envisaged the possibility of invasion'. By the end of that month the finding was that the public were 'facing up to the possibility of invasion and many speak of it as certain'. The survey also revealed a strong belief in ultimate victory.

---

* This order was later strengthened so that no unattended vehicle could be left at any time without being immobilized. Milk delivery vehicles were permitted a few minutes' grace.

3

'Novel Methods will be adopted'

German parachutists were not the only danger that obsessed the British public in the early summer of 1940. They were equally convinced that they were to be plagued by the Fifth Column, a supposed organization of native traitors and aliens who would assist the invading forces. The phrase had been introduced by the Spanish General Emilio Moro (though *The Times* attributed it to General Franco) in October, 1936, when, referring to the four Nationalist armies converging on Madrid, he declared, 'We have a fifth column in Madrid itself'. His intention had been to spread confusion among the capital's defenders and, in fact, there was no Nationalist organization in Madrid, so that the only result was to encourage the extreme Republican elements in the Government's forces to conduct a bloody purge of those who might be thought to be deviationists.

This types of psychological warfare had an immediate appeal to Hitler who was reported to have said early in 1939:

> When I wage war in the midst of peace, troops will suddenly appear, let us say, in the streets of Paris. They will wear French uniforms. They will march through the streets in broad daylight. No one will stop them. Everything has been thought out to the last detail. They will march to the headquarters of the General Staff. They will occupy the ministries, the Chamber of Deputies. [The country] will be robbed of its leading men. An army without a General Staff. All political leaders out of the way. The confusion will be beyond belief. But I shall long have had relations with the men who will form a new government – a government that will suit me. We shall find such men, we shall find them in every country. We shall not need to bribe them. They will come of their own accord.

These words, recorded in Herman Rauschning's *Hitler Speaks*, which went through three English editions in 1939, were well known in Britain and when war came it was assumed that such tactics would be employed here. The early months of the war confirmed this assumption. In Poland the *Wehrmacht* received help from the *Volkdeutsche*, the million Germans who had arbitrarily been made Poles by the Treaty of Versailles. In Denmark there were 30,000 Germans living in North Schleswig which had been ceded to Denmark in 1920. These potential traitors might well have assisted the invaders had the Danish armed forces been able to put up any kind of effective resistance.

In Norway things were reported to be different. The Scandinavian correspondent of the *Chicago Daily News*, who was in Oslo when the Germans arrived, wrote:

> Norway's capital and great seaport were not captured by armed force. They were seized with unparalleled speed by means of a gigantic conspiracy which must undoubtedly rank among the most audacious and perfectly oiled political plots of the past century. By bribery and extraordinary infiltration on the part of Nazi agents, and by treason on the part of a few highly placed Norwegian civilians and defence officials, the German dictatorship built its Trojan Horse inside Norway. . . . Absolute control by only a handful of key men in administrative positions and in the Navy was necessary to turn the trick and everything had been faultlessly prepared.

Since this was precisely what the world expected, this despatch, and many others describing a similar state of affairs, was accepted as truth throughout the allied and neutral world.

In fact the German occupation owed nothing to the activities of traitors. Vikdum Quisling, the former Minister for War who was to give his name to this specialized form of treachery, was unquestionably disloyal but he was wholly ineffective. Since December, 1939, he had made three visits to Berlin offering to engineer a *coup d'état* in favour of Germany but no one took him seriously except the racial theorist Alfred Rosenburg, who carried little weight but introduced Quisling to Hitler. The Führer expressed a benign but vague interest in his plans and gave him sterling to the value of 100,000 marks (c£8,400) to build some kind of National Socialist organization. On the other hand Admiral Raeder mistrusted him and Halder, the Army Chief of Staff, considered that 'he has no one behind him', so he was told nothing of the invasion plans and even his name was unknown to General von Falkenhorst, who commanded the German forces. In the immediate confusion Quisling managed to seize the radio station, announce himself as Prime Minister and declare that the mobilization orders were cancelled. For this he was almost arrested by von Falkenhorst, who described him as 'a dreamer of fantasy' and Goebbels forbade any mention of his 'government' in the German media. It was not until 1942 that he was allowed to describe himself as 'minister-president'. His followers, such as they were, were equally ineffective although it was believed after the war that the garrison commander at Narvik had surrendered over-hastily and the same was claimed against a handful of other officers, most of whom were thought to have been misled by the cancellation of mobilization. For all that they achieved, Quisling and his followers might as well have spent 9 April, 1940, in bed.

In Holland there was a substantial number of German residents and a small but vociferous Dutch Nazi Party (*National Socialistictche Beweging*), but they had no prior warning of the invasion on 10 May and could do nothing to help. Nevertheless the abortive airborne attack on The Hague caused great scope for confusion as isolated parties from 22 Division tried to gain their objectives or defended themselves as best they could. This resulted in a flood of false reports of shooting by supposed Fifth Columnists and on 11 May the Dutch military command stated that Germans living in The Hague had tried to march on the centre of the city but had been beaten back. On 13 May both *The Times* and the *Telegraph* reported that more than a hundred German civilians had been killed in street fighting while the *Daily Express* contributed,

> As machine guns came out of the sky like unnatural lightning peppering the streets below, the Fifth Column crept out of their homes in their German uniforms, heavily armed. Holland had combed out the Fifth Column for weeks before but as the doors opened at 3 a.m., the men who had been proclaimed anti-Nazis and refugees from Germany held rifles.

Investigations after the war established that nothing of the kind occurred.

In Belgium the Germans obtained some minor help from members of the *Heimattreue Front* in the frontier districts of Eupen and Malmédy, which had been ceded by Germany in 1920, but in the rest of the country the myth of the Fifth Column had already resulted in so many arrests that anyone who could be suspected in even the remotest fashion was already in custody. The same could be said of France where the High Command was more than capable of creating as much confusion as any enemy could wish. The country was rife with stories of treachery – the cry of *Nous sommes trahis* is never far from French lips in times of defeat – but very few of them were true and the legend of the Fifth Column got a substantial boost on 21 May when the Prime Minister, Paul Reynaud, stated publicly that the bridges over the Meuse had been betrayed when the fact was that they had been lost through incompetence.

Since the British believed that the Germans had perfected their plans for the conquest of the island, it followed that such plans must include a substantial role for the Fifth Column. As early as 3 March the *Sunday Express* had asserted that the enemy had laid the foundations of such an organization and from then on many papers claimed that the public was anxious that something should be done to curb the danger. Events in Norway swelled this disquiet and on 1 May the *Daily Telegraph* reported that

> Seventeen enemy aliens engaged in ARP work in Marylebone have been dismissed 'in the interests of public safety'. Alderman W.W. Dean, who brought the matter before the Borough Council, said yesterday, 'Useful information can be obtained in the Civil Defence Services where aliens are employed. The idea of Germans taking charge of Britons in an air raid is grotesque.'

The London County Council dismissed all Germans in its employ in the first week of June.

There was a good deal of vagueness about the activities of home-grown traitors. The British Union of Fascists was an obvious target, but, apart from its talented leader, it was correctly regarded as a small collection of anti-semitic thugs. Sir Oswald Mosley was detained on 23 May and his organization wound up, among the lower ranks of those detained being Frank Joyce, Lord Haw Haw's younger brother. The most significant detainee was Captain A.H. Ramsay, Tory MP for Peebles and Midlothian. He was in fact anti-Nazi, though the *Daily Express* of 14 June reported that he had been nominated as *gauleiter* for Scotland, but he had a fanatical hatred of Jews and Freemasons which involved him with an organization known as the 'Right Club' where he became friendly with Anna Wolkoff, the daughter of a White Russian admiral. She in her turn was an associate of Tyler Kent, a cypher clerk at the United States Embassy, who, for American political purposes, was making copies of the secret cables between Churchill and

Roosevelt. These he showed to Miss Wolkoff who passed copies of some of them to an even closer friend, an Assistant Military Attaché at the Italian Embassy. She was already under observation by the security services who knew that she had written with advice to Lord Haw Haw by way of the Romanian diplomatic bag. She and Tyler Kent, whose diplomatic immunity was waived, were arrested on 18 May.

There were few other indications of native treachery. On 16 May there was a report that Scotland Yard were searching for two men dressed respectively as a group captain and a squadron leader, who had been making enquiries at airfields. Their youth suggested that they might not be entitled to the ranks they claimed and, when challenged by a sentry, 'they entered a large American-type car and drove away at high speed'. Four days earlier there had been consternation when the BBC, acting on a telephone call, broadcast a call-up order for some classes of RAF reservists. Three hours later a disclaimer had to be issued since the Air Ministry denied all knowledge of the order. It may not have been coincidence that on 23 May the Policy Committee of the Ministry of Information expressed disquiet about 'a considerable alien element in the BBC'.

On the whole the British, inherently xenophobic, preferred to believe that foreigners formed the mainstay of the putative Fifth Column and there was no shortage of foreigners. At the outbreak of war two hundred suspected spies had been rounded up and tribunals had investigated the cases of 74,000 German nationals, a term which then included not only Austrians but Czechs. Six hundred further internments resulted while 6,800 more were placed in Category B, 'absolute reliability uncertain'. Of the remaining 66,000, who were assessed as Category C, 'reliable', 55,000 were either Jewish or political refugees but the worsening war situation revived public clamour against aliens and certain areas of particular sensitivity were declared out of bounds to all foreigners without special permits. On 8 May,

> Frederich Schweitzer (33), German, who plays the saxophone and clarinet in Jack Hylton's band, pleaded guilty at Portsmouth to entering a prohibited area without permission. He has been in the country since 1933 and has applied for his naturalisation and has been granted exemption from all special restrictions. His case was dismissed on payment of 4/- [20p] costs.

On the following day the Home Secretary, at the request of the Chiefs of Staff, issued directions for the internment of all male aliens between the ages of 16 and 60 living in a coastal strip from the Moray Firth to the Isle of Wight, an operation which put some five thousand men behind barbed wire. In the view of the *Daily Telegraph* on 13 May:

> Although this decision is a change of government policy and recognised as a drastic step, it is necessitated by military considerations arising from the extensive use by the enemy of parachutists and troop carriers. It is the view of the military authorities, with the example of Norway and Holland before them, that if an attempt were made to land troops in this country by these methods, we could not afford the risk of having our counter-measures hampered by alien spies.

Reports from Holland added to the pressure on government to intern more and more Germans. This pressure was increased when Sir Neville Bland, just returned from serving as British Minister in The Hague, attributed the collapse of Holland to a close collaboration between the Fifth Column and German parachutists. He quoted a story of a detachment of invaders being guided to a vital bridge by a German maidservant. He was in no doubt that, when the moment came, the Fifth Column in Britain would 'at once embark on widespread sabotage and attacks on civilians and military indiscriminately. . . . Every German or Austrian servant, however superficially charming or devoted, is a real and grave menace.'

Ministers were opposed to taking harsh measures against aliens, most of whom were innocent and well-disposed to the allied cause, but recognized that firm steps were expected of them. On 15 May Churchill minuted:

> Internment would probably be much safer for all German-speaking persons themselves since, when air attacks develop, public temper in this country would be such that such persons would be in great danger if at liberty.

It is probable that he had in mind the anti-German riots that broke out after the sinking of the *Lusitania* in 1915 in which 257 people were injured when the populace turned on the German residents of Liverpool and West Ham. On 16 May all males in Category B were ordered to be interned, a decision generally approved, the headlines in the Liberal *Manchester Guardian* being 'No Half-Measures Will Do' and in the Labour *Daily Herald* 'Country Saved from Fifth Column Stab'. The *Daily Mail* and *News Chronicle* demanded that Category B women should also be interned and this was ordered before the end of the month. The pressure for internment still mounted and the London Correspondent of the *New Yorker* reported 'a general feeling that the government hasn't gone far enough with its internment of aliens'. In Gloucestershire the inhabitants of Ashton Keynes protested against the continuing freedom of a refugee community called the Cotswold *Bruderhof* to whom the Home Secretary had promised immunity.

There were other restrictions. On 20 May aliens of all nationalities were forbidden to possess firearms, ammunition or explosives without a permit and, before the end of the month, they were deprived of 'bicycles, motor vehicles, sea-going craft and aeroplanes'. On 5 June a curfew between midnight and 6 a.m. was declared for all aliens and stateless persons and on the same day the Ministry of Information's Intelligence report noted that 'Fifth Column hysteria is reaching quite dangerous proportions'. At Marylebone police court a Category C German asked to be interned since his accent meant that he could not obtain employment. According to the *Daily Express*, the Magistrate told him, 'The way we do things in England, I cannot shut you up even if you want to be shut up.'

On 1 June the Archbishop of York appealed for fair-mindedness in dealing with aliens, but he had heavy competition from the Ministry of Information which published a leaflet which declared:

> There is a Fifth column in Britain. Anyone who thinks there isn't, that 'it can't happen here', has simply fallen into the trap laid by the fifth column itself. *For the first job of the fifth column is to make people believe that it does not exist.* In other countries the most respectable and neighbourly citizens turned out to be fifth columnists.

Earlier the *Daily Telegraph* had quoted the Ministry as asserting that Fifth Columnists were making signals to German aircraft 'by, for example, setting fire to haystacks or spreading sheets, or even newspapers on the ground' to give them directions. On 5 June General Sir Edmund Ironside, recently appointed C-in-C Home Forces, told a meeting of LDV commanders, 'We have got examples of where there have been people quite definitely preparing aerodromes in this country.'

Despite apprehensions of clouds of parachutists, of widespread sabotage and treachery and of obliterating bombing, the news that almost

47

200,000 British troops had been rescued from Dunkirk sent a wave of triumph through the country to such an extent that, in his 'Fight on the Beaches' speech on 4 June, Churchill felt obliged to draw the country's attention to the fact that the campaign had been 'a colossal military disaster. . . . Wars are not won by evacuations'. He went on to promise that the French would be reinforced by every available soldier, although, as he pointed out, the Germans with their advanced posts on the Somme, had the option of completing the conquest of France or of turning their attention to the invasion of Britain.

> I would observe that there never has been a period in all those long centuries . . . when an absolute guarantee against invasions, still less against serious raids, could have been given to our people. . . . There was always the chance, and it is that chance which has excited and befooled the imaginations of many Continental tyrants. . . . We are assured that novel methods will be adopted, and when we see the originality of malice, the ingenuity of aggression, which our enemy displays, we may certainly prepare ourselves for every kind of novel stratagem and every kind of brutal and treacherous manoeuvre. I think that no idea is so outlandish that it should not be considered and viewed with a searching, but at the same time, I hope, with a steady eye. We must never forget the solid assurances of sea-power and those which belong to air power if it can be locally exercised.
>
> I have, myself, full confidence that if all do their duty, if nothing is neglected, and if the best arrangements are made, as they are being made, we shall prove ourselves once again able to defend our island, to ride out the storm of war, and to outlive the menace of tyranny, if necessary for years, if necessary alone.

On the day after Churchill made this speech, one 'brutal and treacherous manoeuvre' was proposed in Berlin. General Ernst Milch, deputy to the Commander-in-Chief of the *Luftwaffe*, suggested to Goering that the key airfields in south-eastern England should be seized by an airborne *coup de main* but Goering, who resented Milch as a cleverer and better informed airman, refused to take the idea seriously*. Milch, however, raised the matter again on 27 June, adding his view that such an attack would cause such chaos in England that a seaborne force could be rushed across the Straits of Dover against minimal opposition. This time Goering passed the

---

* According to some accounts Milch did not make this proposal for the first time until 18 June.

1. A Pillbox disguised as bathing huts, Sandgate, Kent.

2. Building an anti-tank obstacle near Hythe, Kent.

3. Local Defence Volunteers covering a road.
Note bombing post in the right background.

4. Civil Servants from the War Office under instruction
as Local Defence Volunteers. The sergeant is holding a Ross rifle.

suggestion to Hitler who dismissed it as hazardous and unnecessary. Britain, he believed, would make peace.

Several German authorities, among them the commander of *Luftflotte* II, General Kesselring, and the commander of airborne forces, General Student, have gone on record as believing that this plan offered Germany the best chance of defeating Britain. The Air Staff in London would have agreed with them. In early June they estimated that 5,000 parachutists would be enough to seize the seven vital sector stations and thus rip the heart out of Fighter Command. If simultaneously there were heavy bombing raids, they would provide sufficient diversion to cover the arrival of reinforcements in transport planes. In the opinion of the Air Staff, the Royal Navy would not be able to prevent the transport of 20,000 men with tanks across the North Sea provided they had 'special landing craft'. The new Commander-in-Chief, Home Forces, wrote in his diary:

> As regards air-borne expeditions, the Bosches have sufficient aircraft to transport 9,750 lightly equipped men in one flight. The number of flights per day will vary from $1^1/_2$ per day for East Anglia to 3 for Kent. Taking into account air opposition and ground opposition, it is thought that the numbers can be calculated upon the basis of 10,000 for East Anglia and 20,000 for Kent. . . . Sea-planes and gliders may add to these numbers.

The probability is that Hitler and Goering were right in rejecting the idea of a *coup de main*. They knew the forces available and these were far less formidable than the British estimated. Apart from a handful of experimental models, there were no 'special landing craft' and the *Luftwaffe* could not muster 5,000 parachutists. A month earlier they had been able to use less than 4,000 trained men, who were without reserves, for the Dutch operation where they had suffered heavily. It is doubtful whether, during June, they could have fielded more than 2,000 men in 7 *Flieger Division* even if sufficient parachutes could have been found for them (see p 29). 22 Air Portable Division had been wrecked and was being reconstituted. Aircraft were in short supply. On 29 June there were only 357 serviceable Ju52s each of which could transport twelve parachutists or eighteen men for landing operations. One hundred and sixty-six aircraft would be required to lift 2,000 parachutists, leaving the capability of lifting 3,200 air-landing troops provided that none of the aircraft were required for equipment or re-supply. One hundred and fifty gliders, capable of transporting

49

1,200 men were available but the towing aircraft could only come from the available Ju52s. It could be added that the Germans had identified neither the location nor the purpose of the sector stations.

This scale of attack would scarcely have been sufficient to overcome the less than formidable defensive arrangements available in June. The divisions which returned from Dunkirk did not start to reassemble until the end of June and until they were, as far as possible, re-equipped the defence of the United Kingdom depended on fifteen infantry divisions of which four were no more than training formations. There was also the embryo 2 Armoured Division which had 160 light tanks representing their establishment of 300 cruisers. Eight of the infantry divisions were deployed for coast defence 'with the rear elements deployed to deal with airborne attack'. The coast from the Wash to Selsey Bill was guarded by five of these divisions.

All these formations were under strength and short of weapons of all kinds, in particular of heavy weapons. Each division should have had seventy-two field guns but the five on the invasion coast had only one hundred and one between them. Of these only thirty-one were the makeshift but relatively up-to-date 18/25-pounder while the rest were 18-pounders (24) and 4.5-inch howitzers (48), both pieces dating from 1918. The position was even worse with anti-tank guns. Each division should have had forty-eight 2-pounder A/T guns but they had only twelve between the five while only one of the five had more than 15% of its establishment of that dubious asset, the Boyes anti-tank rifle.

The reserve of three infantry divisions were somewhat better supplied. They were deployed in a line from Aldershot (52 Division) to Northamptonshire (1 Canadian) with 53 Division between them and in East Anglia there was also 2 London (later 47) Division, a second-line Territorial division with a dozen antique field pieces. South of London there were forty-eight field guns belonging to a division of which the infantry had been destroyed on the Somme. 2 Armoured Division was stationed in Lincolnshire since the War Office, the Admiralty and the Intelligence services being unanimous in believing that the German attack would be made against East Anglia, an opinion they continued to hold until the end of August.

Inadequate as this array was, it was soon weakened. The two best of the reserve divisions were sent to France to bolster the French front, 52 (Lowland) disembarking at Cherbourg on 8 June and 1 Canadian starting to go ashore at Brest a few days later. Since the Chiefs of

Staff no longer believed that the remnant of the French army could hold its ground, this could only be a political gesture. They agreed, however, that something must be done to convince the French that they were not being incontinently abandoned. A gesture of solidarity might rescue the French fleet, if no more, from the coming *débâcle*. As they wrote:

> The despatch of any forces at this juncture must further increase these risks [to the security of the United Kingdom] to a dangerous degree. Nevertheless the military disadvantages of a flat refusal [to help the French] must lead us to the conclusion that we must accept the additional risks involved in assisting our ally.

On 5 June the Germans launched *Operation Red* against the French line which included the remains of 1 British Armoured Division, 51 (Highland) Division and an improvised formation amounting to another weak division. The onslaught was wholly successful, the Germans advancing continuously until France asked for an armistice on 17 June. By that time two brigades of the Highland Division had been forced to surrender and the armoured division had managed to extricate only fourteen cruiser and a dozen light tanks. In all 114,171 British servicemen and 20,000 Polish soldiers were evacuated from France south of the Somme. By 20 June the British, with the Commonwealth and Empire, were standing alone to face not only a triumphant Germany but Mussolini's Italy which declared a supposedly opportunistic war on 10 June.*

This unexpected and perilous isolation produced an illogical stimulation for the British people. King George VI wrote to his mother, 'I feel happier now we have no allies to be polite to & to pamper', and a Hampstead reader of *Picture Post* wrote:

> Too many people seem to regret that we have not got Russia and America as allies. 'So much the better,' say I. 'A nation without allies is a nation with no one to let them down.'

Air Chief Marshal Sir Hugh Dowding, AOC Fighter Command, remarked 'Thank God we're alone now.' His relief was understandable since he would no longer have to use his exiguous strength of Spitfires

---

* It is pleasant to record that one small state freely declared war on the Axis Powers at this unpromising stage of the war – the Emirate of Transjordan, now the Kingdom of Jordan.

and Hurricanes in fighting over the continent, but even so unmilitary a figure as Leonard Woolf wrote:

> We had that strange sense of relief – almost of exhilaration – at being left alone, 'shut of' all encumbrances, including our allies – 'now we can go it alone' in our muddled, makeshift, empirical English way.

There was a sudden simplification of the issues and in eastern Essex Margery Allingham wrote:

> It has resolved into the [problem] which is often put to individuals by their doctors in the most civilised of worlds: 'Will you have a dangerous operation now, which may easily kill you, or will you just die by inches, slowly and painfully, in the next few months or years.'

There was a tiny minority of doubters. An old man in a Gloucestershire village was heard to remark, 'Oh well, if the Germans win at any rate I've got my pension', while a trainee fighter pilot (who was soon to die in action) wrote home:

> I can't believe that there's much help for us, at any rate in Europe. Against a ferocious and relentless attack, the Channel's not much of an obstacle and with an army presumably unequipped, I don't give much for our chances.

A Gallup Poll in June revealed that only 3% of the population believed that we might lose the war.

This irrational optimism was attributed by Liddell Hart, himself in a defeatist phase, to the 'sublime stupidity' of the British people. Others found it puzzling. Mollie Panter-Downes wrote for the *New Yorker*:

> It would be difficult for an impartial observer to decide today whether the British are the bravest or merely the most stupid people in the world. The way they are acting in the present situation could be used to support either claim. . . . Perhaps it's lack of imagination.

The American correspondent, Quentin Reynolds, just back from France, wrote:

> After I had seen with my own eyes what the military men were calling their 'defences' on the beaches at Dover and Brighton, I marvelled at their confidence. Except for some mangy barbed-wire barricades and some concrete anti-tank constructions, I saw little that would delay an invader. Yet the military spokesmen

kept reassuring me (so they thought) with such comments as 'We still have our Navy, Mr Reynolds' and 'The Channel will stop Hitler' – the Channel that a month before had not stopped a thousand English small boats from bringing the beaten armies to safety. Hearing what I heard, seeing what I saw, I found time to wonder at British sanity.

Insane or sublimely stupid, the British had got their second wind and were full of confidence. The phrase 'We're in the final and we're playing at home' was much heard. The weather was fine, only a few scattered bombs fell on the island and they were uplifted by Churchill's speeches which, with astonishing accuracy, struck a chord in almost every heart. They were also being encouraged in less responsible ways. On 8 June Hugh Dalton, Minister for Economic Warfare, told them on the wireless that 'Already streaks of shortage are spreading like weals across the economic body of Germany'. On the same day Edward Hulton, founder and proprietor of the immensely popular *Picture Post*, told his readers:

> Before the start of the present battle Germany had not more than three months' reserves of steel. Her oil resources cannot last six months at the present rate of consumption. In such vital necessities as fats she is still more deficient.

In fact the British were too busy to be seriously worried about the enemy's problems. Wearing their LDV brassards and armed with shotguns or loaded clubs, they were spending their time guarding vulnerable, or supposedly vulnerable points, an occupation more dangerous to their fellow countrymen than it was likely to be to their enemies. On 9 June there was a report that two motorists who failed to stop at a checkpoint were shot by a sentry and a few days later a correspondent from Oxford complained:

> When motoring to London, travelling with as much speed as I could muster down an arterial road, I heard a faint shout and at the next moment hurtled into a barbed-wire entanglement. When I had finished cursing the soldiers on duty, they announced that there was a warning on and they had no means of warning motorists except by shouting.

They were also digging trenches or erecting obstacles on any open spaces on which aircraft might attempt to land and working harder than they had ever worked before producing aircraft and tanks, the latter, for the most part, models of most dubious value.

When not at the work bench or on guard duty, life went on much as usual. Fêtes were held on vicarage lawns and at Dover, within sight of German-held Cap Gris Nez, marquees were being advertised for sale or hire. In nearby Folkestone the Deputy Mayor voiced 'strong criticism of people of leisure and position who could have stayed to steady the public nerve but have left the town.' For those who stayed in Folkestone the Majestic Gardens Hotel was advertising,

Come and Meet Cheerful People

Jitterbugs, Chatterbugs and Conchies Not Welcome

Not far away 100,000 sheep were being evacuated from Romney Marsh to safer pastures. Rationing was being tightened. Tea was restricted to two ounces a week; margarine and cooking fats were controlled. To make the most of what meat was available the Ministry of Food recommended that scrag end of mutton be boned and made into a compact cut that would be found 'as tender as a chicken'.

On 8 June the *Daily Telegraph* commented sourly on the news that members of BBC staff, other than members of orchestras, were exempt from military service, but cheered up five days later when a hundred of the staff were to be released. Car radios were banned and it was pointed out that it was technically illegal to put a wireless set, unless it would work only on mains electricity, in the back of the car to take it to be repaired. From 16 June the ringing of church bells was forbidden except to sound the alarm that the enemy was landing. Though widely known, the issue of this order seems to have been bungled and as late as 1 August the Archdeacon of Chester was complaining that 'We have never been told officially on what occasions the bells are to be rung.' Campanologists were scornful of the ability of soldiers to pull bell ropes but north of the Wash Lt. Gen. the Hon. Harold Alexander had the matter in hand and issued an order to I Corps:

> As regards the ringing of church bells as an alarm signal, it is pointed out that nearly everybody who rings a bell for the first time pulls the bell too hard and, finding that the bell does not ring, pulls it harder. The result is not to make the bell ring, but to carry the ringer up to the roof. The Archbishop of York is kindly arranging that there should always be a competent person available.

On 15 June many newspapers carried what must have been the most unfortunate advertisement of the month*

---

* Almost as unfortunate was that in the *Daily Express* of 7 June, LOVELY GUERNSEY FOR A RESTFUL HOLIDAY. The island, after having been bombed, was occupied by the Germans on the last day of the month.

For a Peaceful Holiday or Extended Stay
Travel to the ISLE OF MAN

Already many people had gone to the island for an extended stay against their will since it was the main place for keeping interned aliens and their numbers were swollen when, on 27 June, pressure of public opinion* induced the Government to round up Category C aliens, those adjudged to be wholly well-disposed to the war against Hitler. It was a step which caused vast suffering among men, women and children, most of them whole-heartedly loyal to the country which had given them refuge and conditions on the island were made worse since, inevitably, no proper arrangements had been made to accommodate this vast influx of internees. At least on this occasion the authorities exempted Czechs from the status of enemy aliens.

Precautions were being taken to prevent interference with military movements. On 20 June a strip of land twenty miles wide from Rye to the Wash was declared a Defence Zone which could not be visited by anyone, British or foreign, without a permit and, nine days later, the same restriction was extended to the whole of the east coast. On 3 July all beaches from Brighton to Selsey Bill were closed to the public. The authorities' obsession with a landing in East Anglia was underlined when all aliens, not only those of enemy origin, were instructed to seek special permission if they wished to remain in Buckinghamshire, Hertfordshire, Middlesex or Northamptonshire. They were also forbidden to possess cameras, telescopes or nautical charts, while on 5 July they were ordered to hand over to the police all guide books and maps on a scale of more than twelve miles to the inch. Since 21 June officers of the armed services had been forbidden to employ enemy aliens as domestic servants or in any other capacity.

1,769 British subjects had been detained of whom 763 were members of the British Union of Fascists and among the others was Admiral Sir Barry Domville, a former Director of Naval Intelligence. Any remnants of the Fifth Column were clearly lying very low because there was little evidence of traitorous activities. There was a minor rash of notices stuck on lamp posts or inside telephone boxes giving the wavelengths of German broadcasts in English, information which could more easily be obtained from the newspapers. On 11 June there

* On 17 June a reader writing to the *Telegraph* had expressed surprise that Germans in Britain were permitted to speak to each other on the telephone in their native language.

was a report of a woman arrested in Bath who had been distributing the same information on postcards and for being in possession of two documents signed respectively by Unity Mitford and Dr Goebbels. Two days later a domestic servant was charged with possessing matter which might be of value to the enemy – a map of some docks, some fascist literature and a simple code. A mess waiter on a balloon site near Sheffield was arraigned for showing a German leaflet to an airman and for remarking, 'We should be better off under a Nazi government than any other.'

On 13 June the Ministry of Information put out a leaflet entitled *If the Invader Comes* which, in part, read:

> If the Germans come, by parachute, aeroplane or ship, you must remain where you are. The order is 'Stay Put.' . . .
> Do not believe rumours and do not spread them. When you receive an order, make quite sure it is a true order and not a faked one. Most of you know your policeman and your ARP warden by sight, you can trust them. If you keep your heads, you can tell whether a military officer is really British or only pretending to be. If in doubt ask the policeman or ARP warden.
> Keep watch. If you see something suspicious, note it carefully and go at once to the nearest police station or to the nearest military officer.
> Do not give the Germans anything. Do not tell him anything. Hide your food and your bicycles. Hide your maps. See that the enemy gets no petrol. . . . Remember that transport and petrol will be the invader's main difficulties. Make sure that no invader will get your car, petrol, maps or bicycles. . . .
> Be ready to help the army in any way. Do not block roads until ordered to do so by the military or LDV authorities.
> In factories and shops, all managers and workmen should organise some system by which a sudden attack can be resisted.
> Think before you act. But think always of your country before you think of yourself.

This muddled and uninspiring document was the work of the Director of the National Gallery (though the authorship was claimed by Harold Nicolson). It is not clear why, in the fourth sentence of the second paragraph, he should have assumed that members of the population had more than one head each. The initial exhortation to 'Stay Put' was later changed to the more inspiring 'Stand Firm' but not before the Ministry had issued a further leaflet entitled *How shall I prepare to Stay Put?* As to the problem of 'whether a military officer is really British

56

or only pretending to be' the answer was less simple than might appear. Britain and Northern Ireland contained a large number of officers from allied countries – French, Polish, Dutch, Belgian, Norwegian, Danish and even a few Luxembourgois – whose colourful uniforms added variety to the scene.

4

'Failing to discover
the Undiscoverable'

It was natural that the British should feel concern about the possibility that the Germans might make an indirect approach to Britain through their undefended back door, neutral Ireland. It was the way by which revolutionary France had twice tried to circumvent Britain's guard and Bonaparte had frequently considered invading Ireland, though he had never actually despatched troops there. As early as 24 May, 1940, readers of the *New Yorker* were told:

> Since many people believe that Eire is on the Nazi map as a jumping off place for the attack on England, those who evacuated their families to the west in September are wondering if they picked such a safe spot after all.

The Commander-in-Chief, Home Fleet, gave it as his opinion that a German invasion of Ireland was quite possible.

In early June the garrison of Northern Ireland was scarcely impressive. It consisted principally of 53 (Welsh) Division whose Bren guns had been taken from them to equip the troops in France and replaced with Lewis guns of Great War vintage. The battalions had at most one carrier (a lightly armoured tracked vehicle) and their transport consisted of requisitioned commercial vehicles. They were soon reinforced by 61 Division which was even less trained and less well equipped. So meagre was this garrison that, late in June, the War Office decided to send 3 Division, the only more or less fully equipped formation in England, to defend the province. This move was blocked by Churchill, although he had his own fears in that direction, having written to President Roosevelt on 15 May:

> We have many reports of possible parachute or airborne descents in Ireland. The visit of a United States squadron to Irish ports, which might well be prolonged, would be invaluable.

Quentin Reynolds heard that the editor of the *Daily Express* was sending two reporters to Dublin to cover a possible invasion of Ireland. He recalled that Lord Beaverbrook, proprietor of the *Express*, was a member of Churchill's Government and decided, 'If Lord Beaverbrook . . . figured the Germans might pull another Norway in Ireland, it was time for me to move. . . . We took the boat from Liverpool the same day.' What Reynolds discovered in Dublin was that 'neutrality was the one issue on which the Irish were united', a view echoed by every other observer of the Irish scene. In a private interview with De Valera he learned that Eire was prepared to fight anyone who invaded her borders and that the Taoiseach believed that her army and air force would be able to repel any attacker. Since the army was small and ill-equipped (and could scarcely be much enlarged since Irishmen of military age were flocking to join the British forces), Reynolds found this hard to believe and, as for the Irish Air Force, 'the planes lined up on the field – all twenty four of them . . . looked to me suspiciously like left-over bi-planes from World War I days.'

In London the War Cabinet discussed the Irish situation on 20 June when Neville Chamberlain urged taking a firm line with Dublin to ensure that the Royal Navy should have the use of the Atlantic ports (which he himself had incontinently handed back to the Irish four years earlier), that British troops and aircraft should be permitted to enter the country before any invasion started and that 'all leaders of the IRA still at large should be interned'. In return he proposed that the British Government should declare their support for a United Ireland after the war. Foreseeing infinite trouble in Ulster should such an undertaking become known, Churchill refused to countenance such a suggestion, commenting that it would be better if Germany rather than Britain should violate Irish neutrality. A leader in the *Daily Telegraph* of 26 June remarked:

> An Irish expedition [by Germany] might encounter less resistance
> *en route* and on arrival, but Hitler would also find that he
> had achieved something hitherto beyond the power of British
> statesmanship to accomplish, that of unifying Ireland.

The Irish Government took some steps to ensure their security. They appointed Regional Commissioners on the British model and interned many of the disaffected. On 17 June de Valera told the people that 'the nation is in imminent danger' and one of his ministers broadcast that 'the next great battle of the war may be fought out on Eireann territory' but, although the *Luftwaffe* was anxious to acquire Irish airfields for the attack on Britain, the *Kriegsmarine* was flatly opposed to any attempt to move troops there by sea.

Hitler agreed with Churchill that 'a landing in Ireland can only be attempted if Ireland requests help' and in June Hitler did not favour undertaking any overseas operations. He hoped, and confidently expected, that Britain would make peace and was prepared to offer her easy terms for a prompt settlement. He realized that no government headed by Churchill would contemplate peace talks but assumed that, since Britain could no longer look for victory, a compromise government would be formed and open negotiations. He did not expect a government of Quislings although some neutral observers thought this a possibility. William C. Bullitt, US Ambassador in Paris, had reported to Washington in June:

> The British intend to conserve their fleet and air force and their army, and either before a German attack or shortly afterwards, to instal eight Fascists trained under Mosley, and accept vassalage to Hitler.

The Führer was sufficiently realistic to understand that, apart from Mosley, there were not enough competent British Fascists to run a borough council and he knew that forcing a Mosleyite government would be too open a humiliation for a country for which he continued to nurse a sneaking admiration. What he wanted was an Anglo-German alliance on his own terms. Under certain limitations he wished Britain to continue as a world power believing that she, like the Catholic Church, was one of the cornerstones of western civilization. More than that, he appreciated that the beneficiaries of the disintegration of the British Empire would be not Germany but Japan, the United States and the Soviet Union.

He assumed that, faced with a hopeless war, British public opinion would compel a change of government through normal political processes and the inclusion of Chamberlain and Lord Halifax in Churchill's Government gave him hope that 'appeasement' might surface once more. The appointment of Sir Samuel Hoare, former Foreign Secretary and noted appeaser, to the British Embassy in Madrid was taken to indicate that he would be used as a channel for peace talks with General Franco as intermediary. What Hitler totally failed to grasp was the all but unanimous determination of the British to continue the fight. Few of them could see how ultimate victory was to be obtained but, in their 'sublime stupidity', they could not see that this was any reason for throwing in the towel.

In the more reactionary reaches of the Conservative Party there had been some who had seen Nazi Germany as a bulwark against Communist Russia, but the Nazi-Soviet Pact of 1939 had made this a difficult belief to sustain. It was true that in the same ranks were men who distrusted Churchill's judgment and who resented the 'gang of adventurers' – Beaverbrook and Bracken – whom he had brought to office. It was noted that the bulk of the Tory Party had been reluctant to cheer the new Prime Minister when he appeared in the House of Commons and this might have given the false impression that some of Chamberlain's more extreme supporters might favour a compromise peace until, on 4 July, the entire Tory party in the Commons rose as one man to cheer Churchill.

On the other flank, six Labour Members of Parliament had declared their opposition to the war from the outset and in November, 1939, twenty-two of them, supported by seventy Labour constituency parties, had signed a manifesto calling for an armistice to be followed by a world conference to agree peace terms. Since that time the experience of Denmark, Norway, Luxembourg, the Netherlands and Belgium had not encouraged even the most purblind pacifist that Hitler was likely to abide by any pledge he gave. There were a few men who believed, like Professor Joad, not yet a popular broadcaster, that 'The ordinary person in England would be less unhappy after a Nazi victory than if he or she lost their sons, lovers or husbands', an opinion not susceptible to proof. It was also true that the number of conscientious objectors was three times as high as it had been in 1914–18 but it still amounted to only 1.3% of men liable to military service and Bertrand Russell, a conscientious objector in the earlier war, declared that, had he been young enough, he would have fought against Hitler. The Chief Rabbi condemned Jewish conscientious objectors saying, 'There is no basis for such a claim in Judaism, which ranks defence of country among the supreme duties.'

Some reports of defeatism may have reached Berlin through diplomatic channels. The US Ambassador, Joseph Kennedy, constantly reported to Washington his conviction that Britain would be defeated, a view that his Military Attaché did not share. Stanley Bruce, the Australian High Commissioner, was another pessimist. Before Dunkirk he wrote a seven-page memorandum urging an international

61

conference 'to formulate a peace settlement [since] the shedding of further blood and the continuance of hideous suffering is quite unnecessary.' In the margin of this paper Churchill wrote 'Rot' and the British public would have agreed with him.

To Hitler the best hope for a compromise Prime Minister seemed to be David Lloyd George. Despite his seventy years and the dubious dealings of his last administration, the 'Welsh Wizard' still retained some of the prestige of having led the government which won the Kaiser's war and, in his egocentric *War Memoirs*, he had done Germany the service of undermining Britain's faith in her military leaders. As early as 20 September, 1939, he had shown signs of defeatism, remarking in the hearing of Harold Nicolson,

> If our chances are 50/50, then it might be worthwhile organising the whole resources of the country for a desperate struggle. But if the chances are really against us, then we should certainly make peace at the earliest opportunity, possibly with Roosevelt's assistance.

Believing that such an appointment might be popular, Churchill had offered him the Ministry of Agriculture in May, 1940, but he had refused 'because he thinks the country is in a hopeless position and is generally despondent'. To a friend he remarked that asking him to join the Government 'was like calling in a specialist when the patient's case was well-nigh hopeless'. Although as late as 24 July Hitler was still speculating on the possibility of his return to power, Lloyd George was a burnt-out volcano, useless alike to his country and her enemies.

The one gleam of hope that the British attitude might be weakening came from the Foreign Office whose chief, Lord Halifax, had been prepared to contemplate Italian mediation when France was *in extremis*. His Under-Secretary, R.A. Butler, had been bitterly opposed to Churchill's advent to power, saying to John Colville,

> that the good clean tradition of English politics, that of Pitt as opposed to Fox, had been sold to the greatest adventurer of modern political history. . . . He believed that this sudden coup of Winston and his rabble was a serious political disaster and an unnecessary one.

These strong feelings did not move him to resign his Under-Secretaryship.

On 17 June, as France started suing for peace, Butler was walking back to the Foreign Office through St James's Park when he met an old friend, Björn Prytz, the Swedish Minister, whom he invited back to his office. As Butler reported their talk:

> Mr Prytz made it clear that it was in the interest of the neutrals to see an end to the war. I reminded him that if we were to negotiate we must do so from strength, and that force must be met with force.

This was not the Swede's understanding of their conversation and that afternoon he cabled to Stockholm:

> Mr Butler's official attitude will for the present be that the war should continue, but he must be certain that no opportunity should be missed of compromise if reasonable conditions could be agreed and no diehards would be allowed to stand in the way. He was called into Lord Halifax and came out with a message that common sense and not bravado would dictate the British Government's policy. Halifax said that he felt that such a message would be welcome to any Swedish Minister but that it must not be taken to mean peace at any price.

The Swedish Ministry of Foreign Affairs passed this message in confidence to their Parliamentary Foreign Affairs Committee who seem to have had little sense of security, since, on the following day, the British Minister, Sir Victor Mallet, learned its contents from a British journalist who understood the gist of the message to be that 'Britain would only continue to fight if certain of ultimate victory.'

Meanwhile Stockholm cabled Prytz to ask if it was his view that Halifax and Butler intended their sentiments should be passed on to Berlin and, after consulting Butler, the Minister replied that the remarks should not be taken to represent the views of the British Government. By this time Churchill, alerted by the legation in Stockholm (and probably by radio intercepts), was making enquiries. He commented that 'Butler held odd language to the Swedish Minister and certainly the Swede derived a strong impression of defeatism' and sent instructions to Mallet to make a firm statement to the Swedish Government that the British had no interest in peace talks. The Swedes, however, had already passed Prytz's message to their Minister in Berlin who, possibly on his own initiative, gave it to Ernst von Weizsäcker, State Secretary [Permanent Under-Secretary] at the German Ministry of Foreign Affairs. As a result Victor Mallet was approached on 25 June by a Swedish businessman who enquired about Britain's willingness to start negotiations and suggested Lord Halifax as a plenipotentiary. Mallet merely undertook to forward the question to London. There was no direct reply but, in view of an offer of mediation from the Papal Nuncio, the Foreign Office sent a circular to all overseas posts forbidding diplomats to entertain any enquiries about peace with Germany.

Although Churchill accepted Butler's explanation of his talk with Prytz, his indiscretion was greeted with great warmth in Berlin. On 23 June Hitler told the Commander-in-Chief, von Brauchitsch, 'The British are coming down a peg' and on the same day Goebbels told his daily departmental conference:

> This week will bring a great swing in Britain. Churchill, of course, cannot hold on. A compromise government will be formed. We are very close to the end of the war.

Four days later he told the same gathering 'The first reports about British peace feelers are available.'

Hitler's illusions about Britain's willingness to make peace stemmed largely from a problem that was bedevilling both sides – almost total ignorance of what was going on on the other side of the Channel. Germany had two intelligence agencies in increasingly bitter competition with each other. One was the intelligence arm of the Supreme Command (OKW), the *Abwehr*, under Admiral Wilhelm Canaris; the other was the *Sicherheitsdienst* (SD), a part of the Nazi party apparatus. Both organizations, like the Navy, had been misled by Hitler's assurance that there would be no war with Britain before 1944–45 and the outbreak of war found them without an adequate network of agents in the United Kingdom. Most of their existing spies were rounded up in September, 1939, and the rest were neutralized by the extension of internment in May and June. The intelligence position was made worse by Germany's spectacular victories. The overrunning of Denmark, Norway, Holland and Belgium obliterated the most convenient bases from which supposedly neutral agents could be infiltrated into and withdrawn from Britain. From June onwards espionage had to be conducted through such faraway neutral countries as Sweden, which was isolated, and Portugal. Eire was much closer to Britain and had a border which was more or less open with Ulster but the German Legation, which continued to operate throughout the war, proved astonishingly unfruitful for intelligence gathering. 'It seems incredible,' complained Hitler, 'that we do not have a single informant in Great Britain,' words echoed by the Italian Foreign Minister. In July Goebbels could not make up his mind whether to jam British broadcasts 'or to use them as a source of information, since frequently they are the only source of news available to us.' On 21 June OKW, trying to make up for lost time, instructed Canaris to undertake a crash course for twenty agents to be sent to Britain and Ireland. Hastily recruited, the new agents were of uniformly low quality and their training necessarily hurried. Meanwhile Germany was dependent for information about Britain on what they could glean from BBC broadcasts, from British and neutral newspapers, from aerial reconnaissance, from a handful of neutral diplomats in London and, since wireless security in the British army was abysmal, from such indiscretions as could be intercepted from military radio sets.

One clandestine operation was in progress at the time of the fall of France and it seems to have been initiated directly by OKW without reference to the *Abwehr*. In January, 1940, a fifty-year-old reserve officer of the *Luftwaffe*, Dr Wilhelm Goertz, who claimed to be a specialist in private international law, was transferred to the Operations Division of OKW and asked to volunteer to go to Ireland, a country in which he had spent a holiday nearly twenty years earlier. He spoke good English and had contacts with the IRA which he had acquired in Maidstone gaol where he served most of a four-year sentence for spying on RAF airfields and from which he had been released in February, 1939. The IRA, who had representatives in Berlin, was proposing that Germany should occupy Ulster and the task offered to Goertz was that of liaison officer between the *Kriegsmarine* (who do not appear to have been told of the plan) and the 'Irish Independence Group'.

> I enquired about the support I could expect . . . and it was
> assumed that the IRA would be sufficiently equipped for a start.
> Later I could expect small arms, especially light automatics [to
> be sent]. . . . Finally I was told I was master of my fate.

It had been intended to drop him by parachute near a farm in County Tyrone in Ulster but on 5 May he landed south of the border, wearing *Luftwaffe* uniform and with his First World War medals in his pocket. The canister with his radio set and other equipment went astray and could not be found. He set out to walk to an alternative

65

rendezvous, a house in Laragh, County Wicklow, where he had spent his holiday years before, which was seventy miles from his landing place and, since he expected the bridges to be guarded, he felt obliged to swim the River Boyne. This ruined his invisible ink and induced him to discard his tunic but he retained his medals and his uniform cap which he used as a drinking vessel. His discomfort was increased because, apart from a large sum in dollars, he had only been supplied with British money and failed to realise that it was acceptable in Eire.

From Laragh a 'mysterious Irishman' guided him to Dublin where he started talks with the IRA who told him that they had insufficient arms for serious action. They suggested that he establish himself on an uninhabited island to which a U-Boat could deliver arms. His preferred plan was to buy a yacht but in the event neither plan was adopted.

> I had the greatest difficulty in working with the IRA who sought every conceivable opportunity of embroiling me in their ridiculous street shootings. They had no code, no discipline, no military training. . . . I used them when necessary to help me but I lost all hope of them being useful as an organised force. . . . I was building up my organisation in Eire and the Six Counties independently of them.

The organization he established, if it ever existed, remains a mystery and seems to have produced neither results nor information and it seems probable that, like Goertz himself, it was being manipulated by two or more IRA factions.

What is certain is that when he attempted to get to France in a fishing boat his plan was betrayed to the authorities and he was fortunate to escape arrest. After two more attempts to leave Ireland he decided to send a message to the Irish Government offering German help to liberate Ulster and offering to act as a go-between if they would provide an aircraft to get him to France.

In November, after nineteen months in Ireland, he was arrested and interned for the rest of the war.* It is hard not to be sorry for Wilhelm

* When released in 1945 Goertz was to be deported to Germany but was eventually permitted to remain as an alien. He was given a message that 'The Irish government knows what you have to expect from the Allies and the present German administration'. This is most unlikely to have emanated from the Dublin authorities who knew that there was no 'present German administration' at that time and that he was no war criminal. Nevertheless the message so frightened him that he took poison and, in May 1946, died. He left an account of his mission which was published in the *Irish Times* in the following year.

66

Goertz, anxious to help his country, who was sent on an ill-conceived mission only to be deprived of his communications and plunged into a morass of internecine feuds in the IRA.

The British suffered many of the same frustrations as their German counterparts. Their intelligence services were even more fragmented and, if they were somewhat less mutually antagonistic than the *Abwehr* and the SD, had suffered appallingly from the economies imposed on the armed services between the wars. In the Army the post of Director of Military Intelligence had been abolished in 1922 and the Intelligence Corps disbanded in 1929. The Air Ministry did not establish its Intelligence department until 1936 and, although the Directorate of Naval Intelligence had a continuous existence, many of its Directors before 1938 had not been of the highest quality and one of them, as has been seen, was interned in May, 1940, for pro-German activities.

Co-ordination between the three services was imperfect, the Admiralty being particularly reluctant to pool information and none of them worked at all closely with either the Industrial Intelligence Centre or with the Government Code and Cypher School (which was renamed Government Communications Headquarters (GCHQ) in 1942). The latter was financed by the Foreign Office which, apart from being the paymaster for the Secret Intelligence Service (SIS), kept an exclusive grip on anything that could be described as political intelligence. The Foreign Office also played a key role in the transmission of intelligence and it was unfortunate that the diplomatic service had little sense of security. A not atypical case can be found in the Embassy in Rome where in 1936 the Ambassador asked for an investigation into the theft from his wife of a diamond necklace. Since the Foreign Office had, until 1946, no security department of its own, a senior SIS officer was sent out and uncovered a very lax state of affairs. While he could not make out a legally watertight case, he was convinced that the culprit was an Italian chancery servant (who, it was later revealed, had been passing documents to the Italian secret service since 1922). He had been suspect since, thirteen years earlier, his brother had been dismissed after the theft of two code books. The diplomats, however, could not be persuaded of the guilt of so devoted a member of their staff. He was retained until the Embassy was closed on Italy's declaration of war when he was found a post in the British mission to the Vatican.

The performance of the Intelligence services in the years before the war did not give much grounds for confidence. They failed to forecast either the German reoccupation of the Rhineland or the invasion of Austria and, while they predicted a German invasion of Czechoslovakia, they dated it for May, 1938, three months before the occupation of the Sudentenland. In the following six months they gave warning of twenty major moves by the Axis powers but only two of these – the German absorption of Czechoslovakia and the Italian seizure of Albania – actually occurred, so that the authorities, perhaps naturally, refused to believe these predictions. These two events, however, resulted in the establishment of the Joint Intelligence Committee (JIC), the Foreign Office taking the chair, which was charged with 'the assessment, the co-ordination of intelligence received from abroad'.

This new régime took time to get into its stride and to gain the confidence of the user departments. Their prediction of the Nazi-Soviet Pact in August, 1939, was unanimously rejected by the Foreign Office and all the service departments. Up to the morning of 1 September the Permanent Under-Secretary at the Foreign Office could not be persuaded that Germany was going to invade Poland. Confidence was not much increased when, soon after the war began, two senior SIS officers, lured by false information, let themselves be kidnapped near the Dutch frontier at Venlo, an event that was widely exploited by the German propaganda machine and which infuriated the Dutch whose neutrality had been compromised. With some accuracy the Joint Intelligence Committee forecast the German invasion of Norway, only to be disbelieved by the Admiralty.

The overrunning of the Low Countries and France and the entry of Italy virtually destroyed the network of agents that had been established in western Europe and, until resistance cells could be built up and supplied with wireless sets, such intelligence as could be gathered on the ground had, for the most part, to be transmitted through the highly insecure radios in the few remaining embassies in neutral countries. In the summer of 1940 very little intelligence was forthcoming and what was obtained was largely misleading, if not actually untrue. Things were, however, beginning to improve. The Government Code and Cypher School at Bletchley Park began to be able to read *Luftwaffe* messages sent through the Enigma cypher machine. This did not give quite the advantage that might be supposed since in mid-June the war entered a static phase in which there was no need for *Oberkommando der Luftwaffe* (OKL*) to send radio messages when they could send them more securely by invulnerable land lines. Fortunately Goering took a delight in sending orders over the air, thus leaking valuable information. On 28 June Bletchley Park intercepted an Enigma message calling for all anti-aircraft units in France to be issued with maps of Britain. Under the German system anti-aircraft guns belonged to the Air Force, but why this particular message should have been sent remains a mystery since Goering's general order to the *Luftwaffe*, which was issued on the following day, ignores the possibility of invading Britain.

This interception was a boon to the British intelligence services who, for more than a month, had been working on the assumption that invasion was imminent, but had been unable to find any evidence to support the belief.† This was a natural result of the fact that nothing *was* being done to prepare for invasion. The Intelligence services came to the conclusion that, although preparations were being made, they had been unable to detect them. In the words of the Official Historian:

> Unearthing no evidence – failing to discover the undiscoverable – they suspected their sources rather than questioning their assumptions.

* The term *Oberkommando der Luftwaffe* was not used officially until 1944 but it is convenient to employ it for this earlier period.
† In the third week of June Intelligence secured copies of German-English phrase books for the German forces and these were taken as evidence of invasion preparations. In fact the books were produced for the occupation of the Channel Islands which had been demilitarized as indefensible. The occupation started on 30 June. According to the *Manchester Guardian* the phrases supplied included,
'Are you the mayor?'
'Where is the cash?'
'I confiscate all this money.'
'I have the stomachache; give me opium.'

5

'Incomparably more
Powerful Military Forces . . .'

Thanks to what General Ironside called 'the complete blank wall of Intelligence' Germany and Britain were like two ill-matched boxers in separate but contiguous rings trying to achieve a knock-out in darkness. Germany was a lithe and active heavyweight with the European championship under his belt. Britain, though game, was no more than a welterweight who had taken a severe mauling in the opening rounds. Though they knew very little of each others' condition, it is essential to assess the capabilities of each at this crucial stage and such an assessment must start at the top.

A single commanding figure stood at the head of each of the contestants. Both, in their different styles, were inspired orators. Both worked largely by instinct rather than logic. There the resemblances stopped. Adolf Hitler, a rabble rouser, was a visionary who saw the world as he wished it to be, who forced facts into a mould of his own design. In terms of days spent under fire he had probably seen more active service than Churchill, since, except when incapacitated by wounds or gas, he had spent four years on the Western Front between 1914 and 1918. Yet, even towards the end of that war, when Germany was desperate for experienced men as NCOs, no one had thought to promote him above the rank of corporal. Since obtaining power in 1933 his excursions into military command had been uniformly successful. He had overridden the nervousness of the High Command to make peaceful victories in the Rhineland, Austria and Czechoslovakia and had driven them, against their will, to conquer Poland. He had adopted Raeder's plan, considered insanely hazardous by the soldiers, for occupying Norway and had scored a triumphant success. For the even greater success in France he had imposed on the *Wehrmacht* a scheme devised by a junior general and had proved to be right. It is true that both in Norway and in France he had had moments of doubt when he had tried to halt successful gambits only to be thwarted by the zeal of commanders on the spot, but, by mid-June 1940, with a string of victories ascribable to his boldness, he had come to see himself a military genius. The fact was that he was a gambler on a lucky streak and his victories owed more to the incompetence of his adversaries and the professional skills of his subordinates than to any solid military skills of his own. He knew nothing of naval matters and confessed himself afraid of the sea. His estimate of the capabilities of air power was derived from his political associate, Herman Goering, whose comprehension of the subject was suspect.

Like all dictators, Hitler suffered from the fear of 'the porpoise close behind me', the idea that someone or some combination of his subordinates might rival him in power. In particular he feared that the heads of his armed services might conspire to usurp his position. This was unreasonable since the Army took little account of the Navy and both the older services despised and disliked the Air Force which was more permeated with Nazism than they were. The idea of General von Brauchitsch, Grand Admiral Raeder and Marshal Goering conspiring to overthrow their Führer was unrealistic to everyone except Hitler, but it ensured that he kept them compartmentalized, seldom seeing even two of them together. Such co-ordination as did exist was provided by *Oberkommando der Wehrmacht* (OKW), presided over by the subservient General Wilhelm Keitel, little more than the manager of Hitler's military office, but containing several highly competent staff officers, notably General Alfred Jodl, the head of the Operations Division. The concept of combined operations was shunned by Hitler on political grounds and discouraged by the three services through professional isolationism. It was a poor basis for undertaking a cross-channel operation.

Winston Churchill made no claim to military genius but he had considerable military expertise and experience. He had served as a junior officer or as a war correspondent (and sometimes as both) in minor wars in many parts of the world and had charged the Dervishes at Omdurman with the 21st Lancers. In the Great War he had briefly but competently commanded a battalion of Royal Scots Fusiliers on the Western Front; he had studied military history widely and had, at different periods, been the political head of all three service departments. Although he had led the demand for rearmament in the years before 1939, his judgment was widely considered to be unsound. The failure of the Gallipoli campaign in 1915 hung like an albatross round his neck and, as First Lord of the Admiralty in 1940, his conduct during the Norwegian campaign has been described, not unfairly, as 'hot-headed, muddled and interfering'.

He was to continue to make serious misjudgments after he came to power in May, 1940, but he took steps to minimize such errors. Although he had access to more power and influence than any Prime Minister in British history, he considered himself, with perfect sincerity, to be the servant of the House of Commons and was scrupulous in accounting to them for his actions as far as security would permit. By taking on the role of Minister of Defence, a post hitherto unknown, he took upon himself the whole responsibility for the conduct of the war – a most unappetising task in May, 1940 – but insisted on conducting it through a committee. To guard against his own impetuosity, every move was debated by the three Chiefs of Staff. Admiral Sir Dudly Pound, General Sir John Dill and Air Chief Marshal Sir Cyril Newall may not have been the most conspicuous stars in their respective services but they were all highly competent professionals who could restrain the rashness of their chief as he, without doubt, intended they should. He bullied them, taunted them and made their lives hideous with his aggressive schemes, many of them wholly impractical, but he never went against their advice. It was the antithesis of the German system and, in the long run, forced the three services into a co-operation which did not come naturally to them.

In June, 1940, the German Army, the *Wehrmacht*, was at its peak. In six weeks it had achieved a feat that the previous generation had failed to accomplish in more than four years of desperate fighting. It had utterly defeated France and driven Britain from continental Europe. Its command structure appeared impeccable and its ten panzer divisions were the admiration of the world. The *Wehrmacht* was indeed a magnificent instrument of war but things were not as good as they appeared. The Mark I and Mark II tanks, comprising more than half the armoured force, were, like the British and French light tanks, all but useless. The larger models, Marks III and IV, and the Czech-built Praga, had been proved serviceable and reliable, but far from perfect. The outstanding German tank leader, General

72

Heinz Guderian, believed the French Somua was the best tank of the 1940 campaign and the British Matilda Mark II, few as were available, had greatly impressed the Germans by its invulnerability. It was recognized that all German tanks needed thicker armour and more efficient guns.

By British standards the *Wehrmacht* was, for the most part, old-fashioned. Outside the ten panzer divisions and the handful of motorised formations, not only the first-line transport but the field artillery was horse-drawn, a serious drawback if amphibious operations were to be contemplated. Not that the *Wehrmacht* was contemplating anything of the kind. Before the French had asked for an armistice it had been decided to demobilize thirty-nine divisions so that men could return to agriculture and industry and on 26 June von Brauchitsch, the Commander-in-Chief, expressed the opinion that the Army's part in the war was complete, since the business of compelling the British to surrender was a task for the Navy and the Air Force. The naval liaison officer with *Oberkommando des Heeres* (OKH), the Army High Command, reported to Raeder:

> OKH is not concerning itself with the question of England as
> they regard invasion as impracticable. Assuming that the English
> have twenty divisions, it would require forty divisions to subdue
> the island. They also question whether absolute air supremacy
> is obtainable. They reject the whole operation.

The Army had given some attention to the problem. In June they had appointed a study group, a colonel and two lieutenant-colonels, to study the possibilities and they had submitted a plan for landing three divisions somewhere between Ramsgate and Hastings, treating the operations as a river-crossing on a large scale. Their superiors rejected the scheme as inadequate. Amphibious operations were unknown territory to the *Wehrmacht*. In the war of 1864 they had made a short seaborne hook into Denmark and in 1917 they had combined with the Navy to land a force, against minimal opposition, on a Russian island in the Baltic. Between the wars combined training with the Navy had been confined to one or two signal exercises. No doctrine for amphibious operations existed, but, as June passed, the Army began to realize that something might have to be done. On 26 June Franz Halder, the Chief of Staff, noted in his diary, 'It is not impossible that we shall be compelled to land in England.' In the weeks that followed, Army enthusiasm for invasion grew steadily, but their attitude remained that they would be glad to conquer England provided that someone else would transport them and their equipment to such landing areas as they, the Army, would designate for purely Army considerations.

On the other side of the Channel the British Army was in no doubt that invasion was coming and was far from certain that the Germans could be stopped once they got ashore. There was a great shortage of equipment and fighting troops. On 4 June Churchill had told the Commons that 'We have got for the time being in this island incomparably more powerful military forces than we have ever had at any moment in this war or the last.' It would have been more accurate if he had substituted the word 'numerous' for 'powerful'. Although 338,491 British servicemen had been brought back from France, a high proportion of them were not immediately serviceable. Leaving aside the vast number of clerks, storemen and other administrative personnel (including those of the RAF), there were the drivers of the 63,679 vehicles that had been left behind and who, for the most part, had nothing to drive. Even gunners and troopers were of only marginal value since most of them could not be provided with guns to fire or tanks to crew. The men who would have been most immediately valuable would have been trained infantrymen since they could have been re-equipped and ready for action in a relatively short time. In the infantry units of the BEF (including machine-gun, motor-cycle and pioneer battalions) there had been only about 125,000 men and it was they who had suffered the bulk of the 65,000 'permanent' casualties, the killed and missing. Many of the regular battalions, the seed corn for rebuilding the infantry, had been all but obliterated. At Calais two regular Greenjacket battalions had been wiped out. On the retreat to Dunkirk the 1st Battalion, Royal Welsh Fusiliers had, after recovering rear parties, men on leave, on courses and in hospital, been reduced to five officers and 263 other ranks. The 1st Battalion, Gordon Highlanders returned from St Valery with six officers and 107 other ranks, mostly first reinforcements. Men were available to fill the gaps, but they were barely trained and wholly without experience.

On the equipment side the situation was even worse. The French campaign had cost the army 880 field guns, 310 heavier artillery pieces, 500 anti-aircraft guns, 650 anti-tank guns, 6,400 anti-tank rifles, 11,000 machine guns and nearly 700 tanks, beside many thousands of tons of ammunition. Since all available stocks had been sent across to equip the BEF, the reserves of equipment were meagre. In the whole United Kingdom, whether on issue to units or in store, there were only fifty-four anti-tank guns, barely more than enough to equip one division, and 2,300 Bren guns, enough for one division and one brigade. There were 420 field guns, most of them obsolete, with 200 rounds a gun, 153 medium and heavy guns each with 150 rounds. It could be said that there were 963 tanks in Britain, but 132 of them were the old Vickers Medium Mark II which the Army had belatedly discarded in the early thirties. Most of the rest, 110 'Infantry' tanks, 103 cruisers and 618 light tanks, were obsolete designs scattered in training units. A Mark IV 'diamond' tank of 1917 formed part of the force guarding the Dorset coast. The only formed units early in June were 2 Armoured Division, with 180 light tanks, and 8th Battalion Royal Tank Regiment with fifty Mark I Matildas, each mounting a single machine gun and capable of moving at 7 mph on a good surface.

The supply situation was unpromising. The combined production of 'Infantry' and cruiser tanks was 113 in May, 115 in June and somewhat above 120 a month thereafter. To arm them with 2-pounders, a weapon already being viewed as inadequate, would require all but thirteen of the monthly production in May and fifty-four in June, meaning that the anti-tank gun strength must grow very slowly. The production of 25-pounder field guns was forty-two in June, sixty in July and over seventy thereafter. Each infantry division required seventy-two of them.

Inevitably there could be little mobile reserve and General Ironside, C-in-C Home Forces from late May, decided that his only course was to devote his main strength to holding the enemy on the beaches while doing his best to establish a number of 'stop lines' inland to check a breakthrough. At this time he was correct for, as Lt. Gen. Claude Auchinleck, commanding the corps which held the coast between Selsey and Portland Bills, wrote on 26 June:

> Two divisions on a hundred-mile front. . . . The lack of mobile reserves is serious. At the moment we have all our goods in the front window which, in my opinion, is the right policy, as our lack of equipment and transport does not make it possible to fight a mobile battle in the interior. . . . Until he can get his heavy stuff *ashore* the enemy cannot do much. Therefore he must be prevented by all possible means from getting it ashore.

The mobile reserve, which on 25 June was stationed near Oxford, consisted of 1 Canadian Division (less one brigade which had lost its transport in France) with two understrength tank units. As the Divisional Commander explained to his subordinates,

> We . . . may have to operate anywhere in Great Britain from the south coast to Scotland, or in Wales.

He went on to tell them that the main German assault from the sea was expected to take place in the area of the Wash with diversionary landings to the north and south. There was expected to be a small airborne landing in the Isle of Ely and, somewhat later, a major airborne assault in the quadrilateral Birmingham – Wolverhampton, Shrewsbury – Ludlow.

In the next few days the mobile reserve was split into two with one section, 2 Armoured and 43 Infantry Divisions, north of the Thames to reinforce East Anglia and, for the support of south-east England, a second corps around Aldershot. This comprised the Canadian Division, the New Zealanders (two infantry brigades) and the hastily re-equipped 1 Armoured with 81 cruisers and 100 light tanks.

As, towards the end of June, the Dunkirk divisions were reassembled or reformed, the number of troops both on the forward defences and in reserve increased. The strongest and best equipped of these was Bernard Montgomery's 3 Division, which had been intended to return to France before the end of the month. A number of roles were contemplated for it and, between 21 and 28 June, it was successively briefed for operations in the Azores, the Cape Verde Islands and, should the Germans invade Eire, for the seizure of Cork and Queenstown (Cobh). Then it was ordered to Ulster but, before the end of the month, it was put in charge of the coast between Brighton and Bognor. Montgomery's ruthless energy was much in evidence and the War Diary noted:

> The Divisional Commander said that we had got to the stage where we must do as we liked as regards upsetting private property. If a house was required as an HQ it must be taken. Any material required to improve the defences must be taken. On matters of this kind unit commanders must decide for themselves. . . . Kindness, firmness and politeness was all that was required.

Behind the Army stood the Local Defence Volunteers, staunch but barely organized, possibly fit for guerrilla warfare but far from capable of holding their ground against trained German regulars. Their numbers continued to expand, passing the million mark in

June, but this meant that there were fewer weapons to go round. The *Daily Express* launched a campaign for 'A hand grenade dump by every village pump', insisting that every schoolboy who could throw a cricket ball could hurl a grenade. Here the shortage of grenades greatly contributed to the public safety. Great ingenuity was displayed in devising weapons. A railway workshop constructed a version of the Roman *ballista* for hurling explosives and a letter to *Picture Post* suggested:

> What about using the services of British and Norwegian sailors who have worked on whaling ships? A harpoon can be fired with sufficient accuracy to penetrate the vulnerable chinks in a tank's armour.

The most popular improvisation was the Molotov Cocktail, a bottle filled with petrol and fitted with a wick (or, if available, a fuse) which could be manufactured anywhere and, given an unusually gallant thrower, was said to be effective against tanks. These undoubtedly dangerous devices may have caused some alarm in Germany where Goebbels thought it worth drawing the attention of the English language broadcasters to 'the manufacture of home-made Molotov Cocktails [which] had been represented as a national duty. . . . Extreme nervousness must be aroused among all owners of such grenades as their devices might blow up at any moment.' Lord Haw Haw weighed in with:

> Suicide academies have apparently been set up all over Britain. The headmasters are cunning blackguards who teach their inmates how to make bombs at the modest cost of two shillings each, how to poison water supplies by throwing dead dogs into streams, and how to kill sentries noiselessly from behind.

Only the air forces of the two contestants were in regular contact with each other across the barrier represented by the Straits of Dover and they were more evenly matched than the armies or the navies. They also shared common illusions, both believing that air power alone could settle wars and that aircraft could deliver bombs accurately to their intended targets. In June the *Luftwaffe* had every reason to feel proud of its contribution to the victory in France. The dive bombers, the Ju87 Stukas in particular, had done much to clear the way for the free-ranging panzers by breaking the morale of the poorer class French troops. One French historian wrote of the effect of a Stuka attack on a Category C Division from Paris:

> Riflemen and machine gunners got up and fled, carrying off in their flight such artillerymen as had not beaten them to it, mixed up with fugitives pouring back from neighbouring sectors.

The dive bomber is unquestionably a most alarming weapon, but it can only achieve its full effect on two conditions – a faint-hearted enemy and the absence of strong fighter opposition. In France it had been able to operate almost unopposed since the French Air Force was outclassed and confused, while the small RAF contingent lacked the ground control apparatus which would have enabled it to intervene effectively. Much of the French Army did not have the stamina to resist the resulting attacks. Nevertheless, despite German domination in the air, the loss of Stukas amounted to a quarter of the planes employed.

The level-flight bombers had also done everything that could be expected of them and the single-engined fighter, Me109E, had shown itself at least the equal of any other fighter in existence. The whole French campaign had been tailor-made to suit the *Luftwaffe*'s capabilities, and its professional skills had won the admiration of the world, but it was not the kind of victory of which its chief, Marshal Goering, had dreamed, since its part had been largely that of supporting the Army. It was not only in Britain that men believed that wars could be won by bombing. In Italy General Douhet (who had also pioneered parachute troops), had written in 1931:

> A complete breakdown of the social structure cannot but take place in a country subjected to merciless pounding from the air. . . . The disintegration of nations . . . will be achieved by aerial forces.

Goering, according to one of his officers, 'swore by the doctrines of General Douhet, so far as he was capable of understanding them.'

Some of the more intelligent *Luftwaffe* officers were recognizing Goering as one of their most severe handicaps. In the First World War he had been an air ace and had succeeded to command of the Richthofen squadron. His view of air warfare had largely remained rooted in those heroic days and, it was said, his 'knowledge and capabilities remained fixed at the level of battalion commander'. His reputation and his close association with Hitler had given him the opportunity to oversee the creation of the reborn German Air Force, a great achievement, but he could not resist the temptation to boast. He had asserted that no enemy aircraft could reach Berlin, a claim disposed of as early as 1 October, 1939, when a British bomber dropped leaflets over the capital. He had claimed that by 1939 Germany would possess such air strength that the British fleet would not be able to use its home ports, but in fact his *Luftwaffe* never made serious efforts to deny Scapa Flow or even Rosyth to the Royal Navy. In May, 1940, he persuaded Hitler that the *Luftwaffe* alone would be able to prevent the BEF escaping from Dunkirk. He blamed the weather for that failure and remained confident that air power alone could settle the war against Britain.

Not all his subordinates agreed with him. In 1938–39 General Helmuth Felmy, commanding *Luftflotte* II, conducted a series of exercises and *kriegspiele* at his Brunswick headquarters to assess the feasibility of a knock-out blow against Britain. His conclusions were not encouraging. It was found that the main naval bases were beyond the effective range of the bombers and that the bombs available were ineffective against major warships. The evidence also suggested that attacks against fighter bases in southern England would be too costly to achieve their purpose. On the alternative strategy of breaking the morale of London by terror bombing, Felmy reported:

> It is doubtful whether a catastrophic effect can be produced on
> the capital. It seems more probable that the innate toughness
> of the English character will cause an unacceptable rise in the
> national will to resist.

Felmy was eased out of his command and Goering clung to his belief in the efficacy of heavy bombing.

It is impossible to know whether Goering appreciated the extent to which the *Luftwaffe* of 1940 was incapable of subduing Britain as a whole or the RAF in particular. The Stukas were soon seen to be too vulnerable while the level-flight bombers were too small. The Heinkel had, with full tanks, a bomb-load of only 2,134 lbs and the later Junkers 88 could carry 3,968 lbs, less than one-third of the bombload of the great allied bombers of 1944–45. The *Luftwaffe* had started work on a four-engined bomber in 1935 but its chief advocate, the *Luftwaffe* Chief of Staff, General Walther Wever, was killed in an accident in the following year and work on the prototype was stopped on the recommendation of Wever's successor Kesselring, who ironically was the man who was to need it most when he commanded *Luftflotte* II in 1940. To make matters worse, all the existing German bombers required fighter escorts to operate in daylight, so their range was conditioned by that of the Me109 which could reach only to the northern outskirts of London. Goering's favourite aircraft, the twin-engined Me110, with a longer range, proved to be no match for British fighters.

The *Luftwaffe* were also hampered by their lack of information about the opposition. They were even later than the RAF in setting up an intelligence branch and when they did so in January, 1938, its head was only a major (= squadron leader). The RAF branch had from the beginning rated an air commodore. They knew the location of many of the RAF airfields but not of their function (Bomber, Fighter, Coastal or Training Command or Fleet Air Arm). They were ignorant of the repair and maintenance facilities which the RAF had built up and of the location and function of many of the aircraft factories. While they knew that the British were developing radar, they arrogantly assumed that it could not be more advanced than their own more sophisticated but less effective system. Above all they failed to grasp the intricate command system established within Fighter Command to control the defences to which they had no equivalent. As Adolf Galland, one of their outstanding fighter commanders wrote:

> We had no radio fighter control at the time . . . and no way of
> knowing what the British were doing as each battle progressed.
> As a result, each German formation had to fly where it was
> ordered according to a carefully prearranged battle plan and
> had to depend on its own observations and initiative to assess
> the British reaction and take offensive measures.

As has been seen, the Royal Air Force had its own illusions about the self-sufficiency of air power. Trenchard's doctrine that the only defence against bombers was a larger bomber force of one's own died hard and even in 1937, when radar was a reality and the prototypes of the new fast fighters were flying, the Air Staff proposed an expansion scheme to give them ninety bomber squadrons and only thirty-eight of fighters. It was left to the civilian Secretary of State for Air to put the obvious counter-argument:

> At the outset of the war our first task is to repulse a knock-out
> blow within the first few weeks, trusting thereafter to defeat the
> enemy by a process of exhaustion.

5. 6″ gun overlooking the seafront at Hastings.

6. *Kanalkampf.* Attack on a coastal convoy, 14 July.

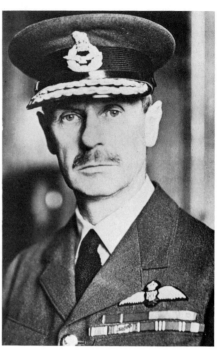

7. General Sir Edmund Ironside,
C-in-C Home Forces.

8. Air Chief Marshal Sir Hugh Dowding,
AOC Fighter Command.

9. Hitler with Grand Admiral Erich Raeder, head of *Oberkommando der Marine*.

Although the Air Staff characterized such a view as 'inadequate and defeatist', they were forced to scale down their demands for bombers and at the outbreak of war were aiming for a target of eighty-two bomber and fifty fighter squadrons.

The obsession with bombers would have been more excusable had the Air Staff paid more attention to the practicability of bombing. Shortage of money can be blamed for the dearth of suitable aircraft at the outbreak of war but, for a fraction of the cost of a single squadron, they could have provided effective bombs, accurate bombing sights, increased the defensive armament of bombers and developed navigation to a point where the crews could find their way to their targets. Only a month before war broke out AOC Bomber Command reported that 'over 40% of the force . . . were unable to find a target in a friendly city in broad daylight'. A series of daylight raids on the German fleet in September and December, 1939, resulted in minimal damage to the target and heavy loss to the attackers, so that Bomber Command had to fall back on night attacks where the crew could not find their targets, could not hit them if they should find them and were most unlikely to do serious damage to them if they should happen to hit them.

Fortunately Fighter Command under Air Chief Marshal Sir Hugh Dowding was the most efficient branch of the service. It had an excellent command and control system, good aircraft, highly professional pilots, a well-thought-out, if by later standards rudimentary, radar system and satisfactory co-ordination with the Army's Anti-Aircraft Command, the Royal Observer Corps and, for landline communications, the Post Office. It had a sophisticated and competent repair and maintenance organization. Late in June it suffered from two shortages, of aircraft and pilots. There were only 644 aircraft against an establishment of more than 800 and only 1,259 pilots instead of 1,456. Both these shortages were attributable to the campaign in France which had cost 67 Spitfires and 386 Hurricanes, most of the latter destroyed on the ground. Three hundred and sixty-two pilots had also been lost and these were more difficult to replace. New fighters were coming through at a satisfactory rate but the RAF training system was so excellent that it was inevitably slow. If Fighter Command was regularly to lose more than fifty pilots a week through death or serious injuries, the replacement situation would become very serious.

In late June the Command could deploy nineteen squadrons of

Spitfires and twenty-five of Hurricanes, apart from two squadrons of Defiants, a new two-seater fighter which had had a brief (and illusory) triumph over Dunkirk. There were also six squadrons of Blenheims which, it soon emerged, could only be used as night fighters. The Spitfire was, under all conditions, the equal of the Me109. The Hurricane was scarcely a match for the single-engine Messerschmitt but could play havoc with all types of German bombers and with the Me110 long-range fighter. Fighter Command would have to fight against numerical odds, but they had several advantages. German fighters would have to engage near the end of their effective range and any *Luftwaffe* pilot taking to his parachute would become a prisoner, while a British pilot, if uninjured, could, and frequently did, go straight back into action. Similarly, damaged British aircraft could forceland on friendly ground, while German aircraft in similar case would have to be nursed back across to France.

The Royal Navy, although many of its ships were elderly, was as superior to the *Kriegsmarine* as the *Wehrmacht* was to the British Army. At the end of June, when a large detachment had been made to Gibraltar, there were in home waters five capital ships, eleven cruisers and fifty-three destroyers, apart from twenty-three destroyers based on Liverpool for convoy duties, some of which would certainly be available in an emergency. Behind this imposing armada was the Auxiliary Patrol, a cloud of smaller craft, ranging from sloops, minesweepers, converted trawlers and drifters to motor boats. Two or three hundred of these craft were always at sea though the effectiveness of some of them may be doubted. A journalist joined the navy on 22 June and, since he had some experience in small boats, was immediately rated petty officer and given command of a forty-two foot motor cruiser at Lowestoft. There was a crew of three, armed with a Lewis gun, a rifle and a pistol. His orders were that:

> If they try to invade, we beat it out to sea with all the other ships in port and (in the captain's words) use our wits and make as much trouble as we can.*

* *Picture Post* readers were very fertile in devising ways of beating off the enemy at this time and one suggested: 'It has occurred to some of us who have done surfboarding behind speed boats that the sport might be adapted to war purposes. A lightly armoured man with an automatic weapon towed behind in some way would introduce an unexpected aspect into naval tactics.'

The only serious threat to the Royal Navy's supremacy in home waters was the *Luftwaffe*. Until the outbreak of war the Admiralty had been scornful of air attack, maintaining that anti-aircraft guns could deal with any such threat. Since September, 1939, they had been making increasing demands on the RAF for protection, the more so since the fighter aircraft of the Fleet Air Arm, reluctantly handed back to them in 1937, were incapable of dealing with Messerschmitts or even with German level-flight bombers. Dunkirk gave them less comfort that it might have done. Thirty-nine destroyers had taken part in the evacuation, an operation that entailed delicate manoeuvring in a small harbour and periods stationary against a jetty while troops embarked. Although the enemy had command of the air for long periods, the fact that the *Luftwaffe* had sunk only four destroyers (and more or less damaged twenty more), might have given them some measure of hope that aircraft would not do irreparable damage to a large force of destroyers moving at high speed to intercept slow-moving landing craft.

No one was more dubious of the *Luftwaffe*'s ability to keep the Royal Navy at bay than Grand Admiral Raeder. Although Hitler had reaffirmed on 4 June that the war against England would be pursued by sea and air blockade, the Admiral was convinced that, sooner or later, the *Kriegsmarine* would be expected to produce a miracle. He lost no opportunity of drawing attention to the difficulties of invading Britain, emphasizing the need for total air supremacy and asking that the *Luftwaffe* should carry out 'vigorous air action against British bases in order to destroy ships under construction and repair'. At a meeting with Hitler on 21 June he tried again to forestall any proposal for invasion:

> I declared that an essential preliminary for any successful landing
> was absolute command of the air over the English Channel.
> Germany's air supremacy must be so complete . . . that even
> if British naval intervention could not be prevented it would be
> impossibly costly. I said that unless this condition was met the
> risk of a landing operation would be so great that it should not
> be accepted.

Hitler made no comment except to say that no preparation for invasion should be made for the time being. He still believed that Britain would make peace and he had other matters on his mind. He told Raeder of the need to establish a new order in Europe, of reducing the size of the Army and of his plan to settle the Jews under French supervision in Madagascar. It might, he mused, be better to send them to Angola which, he believed, the Portuguese would be ready to exchange for Madagascar.

Undeceived by this rambling, Raeder pressed on with preparations for a landing. His study of possible beaches in south-east England was not encouraging. Convinced that frontal assaults on such desirable harbours as Dover or Folkestone would be lethally ineffective, he looked for alternatives. The information to be gained from the *Channel Pilot* was not encouraging. It wrote of the coast from Selsey Bill to Brighton that 'a vessel without local knowledge is recommended to take a pilot'. The narrow entrance was known to be fortified at Newhaven and the *Pilot* said bluntly, 'No vessel should attempt to enter without up-to-date knowledge.' Since the barges he might have to use would draw six feet it was no help to be told that there would only be two foot of water beside Eastbourne pier at low tide, that there were 'numerous rocky ledges' off Bexhill and that the anchorage at Hastings was 'not recommended except in fair weather'. At Rye, with its twisting approach and tricky currents the advice was unambiguous – 'Only vessels with local knowledge should attempt the entrance to the harbour'. Dungeness was protected by a succession of sandbanks which, at low water, were covered by between two and nine feet, a serious problem since, by *Kriegsmarine* calculations, transports would have to lie off for thirty-six hours while they were unloaded. Only the beaches on either side of Hythe looked practicable and it was obvious that the Army would need a much wider landing front than that.

By late June the registration of possible shipping was complete and an estimate made that some 750,000 tons would be required, mostly in cargo ships of up to 7,500 tons. Such an amount was hard to find. In 1939 Germany had possessed $4^1/_2$ million tons of sea-going shipping but of this one million tons was trapped in neutral ports and 350,000 tons had been sunk or captured, apart from 50,000 tons lost in the Norwegian campaign, and as much again had been modified as commerce raiders which were on the high seas. About 200,000 tons were represented by great liners, such as the *Bremen* and *Europa*, which were unsuited for inshore use in the Narrow Seas. Although the Army had overrun several countries with strong merchant fleets, few ships had been captured. The Polish trading ships, including the great liners *Batory* and *Sobieski*, were plying for the British as were more than a million tons of Norwegian shipping. On 11 May sixteen merchantmen were removed from Flushing and on the following three days HM Destroyer *Brilliant* had escorted out of Antwerp twenty-six merchantmen, fifty tugs and 600 other craft ranging from dredgers and barges to floating cranes. All her conquests had yielded only 200,000 tons. Of what remained to Germany, one and a half million tons was engaged in the vital Baltic trade which included the supply of iron ore from Sweden without which the armament industry would come to a halt, but, allowing for some ships to supply the isolated garrisons in Norway, it was clear that no invasion could be mounted without seriously disrupting the Baltic trade.

Shipping was only part of the requirement. To get troops, guns and tanks on to open beaches needed landing craft and the *Kriegsmarine* had none. Some experiments had been made between the wars with landing armoured fighting vehicles from lighters by means of ramps and, after the declaration of war, thirty-eight flat-bottomed pontoons, each capable of carrying one of the heavier German tanks, had been constructed. These had to be towed by motor boats. For the rest there were only barges from the canals some of which were self-propelled but underpowered for work in the open sea, so that, like the majority, they would be dependent on tugs. None of these were likely to take kindly to the treacherous waters of the Dover Strait. Experiments and improvisations were being made, one of which was later to evolve into the highly successful Siebel ferry, but none of them seemed likely to be available in the summer of 1940.

Above all there was the question of naval escort and there the cupboard was increasingly bare. The damage done by *Renown* to *Scharnhorst* had been quickly repaired, but on 20 June a torpedo from the submarine *Clyde* had sent her back to the dockyard where she joined her sister ship *Gneisenau*, torpedoed by the sinking destroyer *Acasta*. The pocket battleship *Admiral Scheer* was undamaged, but her engines gave constant trouble, as did those of the heavy cruiser *Admiral Hipper*, although the gap in her side had been patched. There remained the light cruisers *Emden*, launched in 1921, and the *Köln*, which was ten years younger, and, if all went well, ten destroyers. The effective U-Boat fleet was just over thirty strong. It was a very small fleet with which to challenge the Royal Navy in their home waters.

6

'One of the
Most Disagreeable Tasks'

During the Napoleonic wars, when invasion seemed imminent, Admiral Lord St Vincent, First Lord of the Admiralty, remarked, 'I do not say the French cannot come. I only say they cannot come by water.' In 1940 the British might have echoed these words but for one factor – the French fleet. In mathematical terms the British superiority was clear. Britain had eleven battleships, although only two, *Nelson* and *Rodney*, had been built since the Great War and no reinforcements could be looked for until the end of 1940 when two of the *King George V* class were due to come into service. There were also three battle-cruisers of which the newest, *Hood*, had been commissioned in 1920.

Information about the German capital ships was scanty and it was not known in London until late July that *Scharnhorst* and *Gneisenau** were both seriously damaged. Both of them were less heavily gunned than the British battleships, but they were considerably faster. Nor was it clear when the new battleship *Bismarck* would be ready for sea but there was no doubt that, once commissioned, she would be more than a match for any British ship until the *King George V* class were ready.†
More was known about the state of the Italian Navy which had six battleships of which two were new and the remainder extensively modernized. All these ships were built specifically for service in the Mediterranean and were unlikely to venture out into the Atlantic but, to keep them in check, four British battleships had to be stationed at Alexandria and more would have to move to Gibraltar to seal the

---

* The Germans called these two ships battleships but the British always referred to them as battle-cruisers.
† *Bismarck* was, in the event, not ready for sea until March, 1941. *King George V* joined the Home Fleet on 2 December, 1940.

western end of *Mare Nostrum*. Further to reduce the size of the Home Fleet it was found necessary for one of the older battleships to be used on Atlantic convoy duty.

The British margin of superiority over the possible strength of the *Kriegsmarine* was not, therefore, very considerable and the balance could be tipped if the Germans acquired the French fleet. This consisted of five battleships built between 1913 and 1917 but modernized in 1932–35. There were also two battle-cruisers, *Dunkerque* and *Strasbourg*, completed in 1937–38, which were comparable to the *Scharnhorst* and *Gneisenau*. Nearing completion were two battleships *Richelieu* and *Jean Bart*, which would be a match for *Bismarck*, whose sister ship *Tirpitz* was believed to be within measurable distance of coming into service. At the time of the French Armistice *Richelieu* had completed her sea trials and *Jean Bart* lacked only her main armament. If the Germans could have got their hands on these four capital ships they could have built up a Franco-German squadron greatly superior to anything the Royal Navy could have brought against them in home waters. In addition the French had a strong force of cruisers, destroyers and submarines.

Britain could not afford to ignore the possibility of a large hostile fleet in the North Sea and on 7 June, at a meeting between the Admiralty and the Foreign Office, fears were expressed that the Germans might insist on possession of the French ships as a condition of an armistice, possibly threatening to destroy Paris to ensure compliance with their demand. Pound, the First Sea Lord, expressed the view that 'the only practical way to deal with the matter was to sink the French fleet'. By this he meant that the French should be persuaded to scuttle their own ships so that they could not be used as a bargaining counter. Both then and when the Chiefs of Staff put the matter to the War Cabinet four days later it was decided that it would be impolitic to put the matter to the French since it would imply a lack of confidence in them that Whitehall was not yet prepared to admit.

When Paris fell on 14 June it was clear that the end was near and instructions were sent to the naval mission at French headquarters to approach Admiral Darlan, head of the French Navy, to give orders that the two incomplete battleships should be sailed to British ports, that the two battle-cruisers should go to Gibraltar and that all naval stores at Cherbourg, Brest and St Nazaire should be shipped to Britain. Meanwhile Churchill had gone to Briare on 12 June to meet the French ministers. At the end of the meeting he had said to Darlan, 'I hope you will never surrender the fleet.' The Admiral replied, 'There is no question of doing so; it would be quite contrary to our naval tradition and honour.'

On 15 June, when the French Cabinet decided to ask the enemy what terms they would offer, the Premier, Reynaud, signalled to Churchill a request that France might be released from her undertaking, given on 28 March, not to conclude a separate peace. On the following morning Churchill replied,

> Provided, but only provided, that the French fleet is sailed forthwith for British harbours pending negotiations, His Majesty's Government give their full consent to an inquiry by the French Government to ascertain the terms of an armistice for France. His Majesty's Government, being resolved to continue the war, wholly exclude themselves from all parts in the above-mentioned inquiry concerning an armistice.

Unfortunately this message was never put before the French Cabinet, being lost in the discussion which followed the abortive offer of Anglo-French unity, and in the night of 16–17 June, Reynaud resigned and his place was taken by Marshal Pétain who immediately asked for peace terms, telling the French people that he had done so on the morning of 17 June.

Admiral Jean Louis Xavier François Darlan continued in office as both Minister of Marine and Commander-in-Chief of the Navy, a force which was largely his creation and whose personnel were overwhelmingly loyal to him. Even after the land war had turned disastrously against France he had seemed not to be a member of the growing band of defeatists. On 28 May he had said to his Deputy Chief of Staff that if an armistice became necessary he would not consent to the surrender of the fleet but would order it to sail to British ports. He had said the same thing to General Weygand on 14 June, a day on which he had told an air force general that, if necessary, he would 'put the whole fleet under the British flag'. On 15 June he asked Edouard Herriot, President of the Chamber of Deputies, 'Is it true that those bastards Pétain and Weygand wish to conclude an armistice? If that is how things are, I am leaving with the fleet.' Herriot spoke to him again on the evening of 17 June, when the advent of Pétain was inevitable, and asked him if he was moving the government to North Africa and got the reply, 'No. A government that leaves never returns.' As Herriot commented, 'This Admiral knows how to swim.'

On the morning of 18 June Pétain's Cabinet resolved 'not to let the fleet fall into enemy hands in any circumstances. If its surrender were included in the armistice conditions they would be rejected out of hand, however grave the consequences of such a refusal.' They also decided that the ships would not be sent to British ports since it would not be proper for any part of the armed forces not to be doing its best against the enemy when the armistice terms were received. These decisions were sent to London and, on the same day, Darlan personally communicated them to his two British opposite numbers, the First Lord and the First Sea Lord. He gave an undertaking that the *Richelieu* would be sailed to Dakar and the *Jean Bart*, if it was possible, to Casablanca. If it was not possible, she would be destroyed at St Nazaire where she was completing. Both ships duly reached West Africa. All French warships on the Atlantic and Channel ports were ordered to sail, preferably to French African ports, and a number of small craft which were unfit for sea were scuttled.

With these definite assurances that the French fleet would not be allowed to fall into German hands, the British were left with two questions. Could they trust Pétain's Government to keep its word and could they trust Hitler to keep any arrangement he made with the French? They were provisionally prepared to believe in French honour, but they had no intention of trusting Hitler. As it happened the Führer had no designs on the French fleet. On 17 June the *Kriegsmarine* had put forward its *Military Demands of the Naval War Staff in case of a French Surrender*.

> French warships are to be recalled immediately to ports desig-
> nated by Germany and there secured. They are to remain under
> the surveillance of the German and Italian navies. . . . Such
> ships and vessels specified are to be handed over immediately to
> German commands. The future of remaining units of the fleet and
> the ships to be disarmed will be decided in the peace treaty.

On the face of it this was exactly what Britain had feared, the handing over to Germany of major French ships. In practice all Raeder had in mind was to replace the ships – three cruisers and ten destroyers – which he had lost in the Norwegian campaign with the addition of some smaller craft for escort duties. He recognized that it was wholly impracticable for the *Kriegsmarine* to man any more ships. Much as

Raeder would have liked to recreate a High Seas Fleet with modern French ships, he would have found it impossible to provide the officers and trained ratings to sail them.

In the event even these modest demands were not included in the armistice terms since Hitler was insistent that 'The result of the negotiations must not be jeopardized by making excessive demands on France' or as his Foreign Minister explained to his Italian counterpart:

> We must offer lenient terms, especially concerning the fleet; this is to avoid the French fleet joining the English.

Under the impression that Britain would quickly make peace, Hitler's chief concern was that the fifty French destroyers should not be available to strengthen the escorts to British convoys. In unwonted agreement with Admiral Pound, he remarked, 'It would be a favourable solution if the French fleet scuttled itself.'

The result was that when the German terms were handed to the French at Compiègne on 21 June, the naval section read:

> The French war fleet, with the exception of those vessels permitted to the French government for the protection of French interests in its colonial empire, is to be assembled in ports to be specified and is to be demobilised and disarmed under German or Italian supervision. The choice of these ports will be determined by the peacetime station of each ship.
> The German government solemnly declares to the French government that it does not intend to use for its own purposes in the war the French fleet which is in ports under German supervision, with the exception of those units required for coastal patrols and minesweeping. Furthermore they solemnly and expressly declare that they have no intention of making any claim to the French war fleet at the time of the conclusion of the peace. With the exception of the French ships, still to be determined, which are to represent French interests in the colonial empire, all war vessels which are outside French territorial waters are to be recalled to France.

The Pétain Government found nothing 'dishonouring' in these terms but asked that, after the fleet had been disarmed, it should be kept in African ports under German or Italian supervision so as to avoid British bombing. This was refused, although they pointed out that the Armistice Commission could modify the terms and might permit dispersal to African ports.

The terms, but not the French counter-proposals, were communicated to the British Ambassador at Bordeaux on 22 June and he spent that day trying to persuade the French to reject them. He received, from Pétain and Darlan, renewed assurances that the fleet would never be allowed to fall into German hands and, late that evening, was told that the armistice had been signed. On his own initiative he then sailed for England, taking with him the naval mission. This was unfortunate since it deprived London of its only link with the French, the more so since the French Ambassador in London resigned on 23 June in protest against his own Government's policies. Henceforward messages between the two Governments had to pass through very insecure cables by way of Spain and were liable to delays of up to three days.

The War Cabinet considered the terms, which they did not know the French had agreed, early on 23 June. Admiral Pound was of the opinion that Darlan 'had taken all possible steps to safeguard our interests', but Churchill countered that we could not afford to rely on one man's word:

> However good his intentions might be, he might be forced to resign and his place taken by another minister who would not shrink from betraying us. The most important thing would be to make certain of the two modern battleships *Richelieu* and *Jean Bart*. If those fell into the hands of the Germans, they would make a very formidable line of battle when the *Bismarck* was commissioned.

Three points disturbed the Cabinet and Churchill in particular. The first was the reliability of the French Government. On 13 June Reynaud, as Premier, had promised that the 400 German pilots, many of them shot down by the RAF, who were prisoners in France, would be sent to Britain. It was clear from the armistice terms that these men were to be shipped back to Germany to add to the strength of the *Luftwaffe*. The second was the stipulation, to which the French themselves had objected, that warships would return to their home ports. This meant that, among others, the two new battleships would be held at Brest and St Nazaire within the German occupation zone so that their security would depend entirely on German good faith, a factor on which the British declined to rely.

The third point was an illusion, an error in translation. In the naval terms it was stipulated that the ships were to be 'demobilised and disarmed under German or Italian supervision' but in the French version received in London the last word was *controle* which was translated as 'control'. This is an imprecise rendering of the French meaning which is given in a reliable French dictionary as '*Registre double que l'on tient pour la vérification d'un autre*', a double check that the French were doing what was intended rather than that the ships were under German or Italian control. It was a misunderstanding that was to distort the British view of the situation.

The defection of France forced the British to redispose their fleets to take into account the fact that Italy was now hostile and France, at best, neutral. Covering forces were stationed off Dakar and Casablanca to observe the unfinished battleships in case they attempted to return to France, and a powerful squadron, Force H, was assembled at Gibraltar. This consisted of the battle-cruiser *Hood*, the old battleships *Valiant* and *Resolution*, the aircraft carrier *Ark Royal*, two cruisers and eleven destroyers. Vice Admiral Sir James Somerville was appointed to the command on 27 June, hoisting his flag in *Hood* three days later.

By this time the operational units of the French fleet were widely dispersed. Two hundred small craft were in British ports, with the old battleships *Courbet* and *Paris* at Portsmouth and Plymouth respectively. There were cruiser squadrons at Toulon and Algiers, and the battle-ship *Lorraine* with four cruisers, three destroyers and a submarine were an integral part of the British Mediterranean Fleet at Alexandria. The main striking force, *Force de Raid*, was at Mers-el-Kebir, near Oran, and comprised the battle-cruisers *Dunkerque* and *Strasbourg*, the battleships *Bretagne* and *Provence*, a seaplane carrier and six fleet destroyers.

In the last days of June Anglo-French relations deteriorated sharply, the inevitable consequence of recriminations over their joint defeat. The French bitterly resented the announcement on 25 June that the British blockade would be extended to include France, British support for General de Gaulle, in Pétain's eyes no better than a mutineer, and Churchill's broadcast in which he said that he found it hard to believe that any French government 'which possessed freedom, independence and constitutional authority' could have accepted the armistice terms. The British were dismayed to hear on 23 June that Pierre Laval, known to be an Anglophobe and in favour of close co-operation with Germany and Italy, had been included in Pétain's cabinet.

They were also concerned when Darlan gave orders to the French ships in British-controlled ports to return to France. His trustworthiness became a key issue and his *volte face* on 16–17 June gave little grounds for confidence. He had always been considered as a devious character and in late June the French Embassy in London advised against trusting him. Inevitably the British decided that they could not rely on his word alone in a matter which so vitally affected their security, perhaps their survival.

This may have been an uncharitable judgment but, at the time, it was understandable. Like his Cabinet colleagues, he was convinced that Britain could not stand alone and on 1 July he remarked to the US Ambassador, William C. Bullitt, that he was 'certain that Great Britain would be completely conquered by Germany within five weeks unless she surrendered sooner.' The Ambassador commented that 'he seemed to regard this prospect with considerable pleasure.' Should this forecast prove correct the fleet would be the only bargaining counter that France held and Darlan was determined not to let it fall into foreign hands, German or British. He signalled to all senior officers on 24 June in a high security code:

> 1. The demobilized warships are to stay French, under the French flag, with reduced French crews, remaining in French metropolitan or colonial ports.
> 2. Secret preparations for scuttling are to be made so that an enemy or foreigner seizing a vessel shall not make use of it.
> 3. Should the Armistice Commission charged with interpreting the text come to a decision differing from that in para 1 above, as soon as action is taken on such a decision, warships are, without further orders, to be despatched to the United States or scuttled if no other action is possible to preserve them from the enemy. Under no circumstances are they to fall into the hands of the enemy.
> 4. Ships seeking refuge abroad are not to be used in operations of war against Germany or Italy without prior orders from the Commander-in-Chief of the French Navy.

A copy of this signal was sent to the French mission in London but only the first paragraph was communicated to the Admiralty.

Churchill found it inconceivable that the Germans would not do their utmost to secure a fleet that would make the seaborne invasion of Britain a practicable operation. He would have wished to have the ships under British control but he would have settled for any other solution – scuttling or internment in the United States – which would have kept them out of German hands. He was prepared to use force if it became necessary, particularly once he had heard that such a

93

course would be acceptable to the United States. Washington was as concerned that the French fleet should not come under German control since, with their own navy largely tied down by Japanese strength in the Pacific, the Germans might use the French ships to conquer Britain and leave the United States to face in the Atlantic a fleet composed of German, Italian, French and British warships. On 27 June the Assistant Secretary of State, Cordell Hull, told the French Ambassador that it was 'a matter of great importance to us if France hands Germany a cocked gun to shoot at us'. When the British Ambassador, Lord Lothian, made, on Churchill's orders, a confidential approach to President Roosevelt, he was told that the United States would warmly approve any steps that would keep the French ships out of German control. Lothian reported,

> I asked him whether this meant that American opinion would support forcible seizure of these ships. He said certainly. They would expect them to be seized rather than that they should fall into German hands.

On 30 June Churchill received a memorandum from the Chiefs of Staff recommending that the French ships should be secured as soon as possible.

> In the light of recent events we can no longer place any faith in French assurances, nor can we be certain that any measures, which we were given to understand the French would take to render their ships unserviceable before reaching French metropolitan ports, would in fact be taken. Once the ships have reached those ports we are under no illusions as to the certainty that, sooner or later, the Germans will employ them against us.

They recommended that 'the uncertainty surrounding the French fleet should be dissipated as soon as possible' so that ships could be brought home 'to meet the imminent threat of invasion'.

> We realize that the action contemplated may result in France becoming actively hostile to us. In weighing up the implications of this possibility we take the view that if we carry out our intention of including France in our blockade, it will only be a matter of time before France becomes, in any case, actively hostile.

They also pointed out that a large proportion of the French ships already lay under British guns in English harbours but that the crucial point was the *Force de Raid* at Mers-el-Kebir which not only contained the most important of the completed capital ships but would also be the most difficult to influence.

This memorandum from the Chiefs of Staff was agreed unanimously and they were supported by the Vice Chiefs, but outside that inner circle senior naval opinion was wholly opposed to the use of force at Mers-el-Kebir or elsewhere. There is no doubt that the Chiefs came to their conclusion with the greatest reluctance and the probability is that, as they told Somerville before he sailed for Gibraltar, they thought it unlikely that it would be necessary to use force, that the threat would be sufficient.

Meanwhile the War Cabinet, acting on the professional advice of their senior advisers, endorsed the plan to secure or neutralize the French fleet without delay. At 2.25 a.m. on 1 July orders were sent to Somerville telling him to deal with the *Force de Raid*. They were received with extreme distaste by all the officers charged with carrying them into execution and, as Force H steamed towards Oran, the Admiral received a personal message from Churchill.

> You are charged with one of the most disagreeable and difficult tasks that a British Admiral has ever been faced with, but we have complete confidence in you and rely on you to carry it out relentlessly.

Soon after 7 a.m. on Wednesday, 3 July the destroyer *Foxhound* sought and was refused permission to enter the harbour of Mers-el-Kebir. She therefore sent in her motor boat carrying Captain C.S. Holland, a former Naval Attaché at Paris. The commander of the French ships, Admiral Marcel Gensoul, refused to meet him but sent a member of his staff to speak to him in his barge anchored in the middle of the harbour. Holland handed over a letter from Somerville setting out the alternatives which he could offer the French:

> A. Sail with us and continue the fight for victory against the Germans and Italians.
> B. Sail with reduced crews under our control to a British port. The reduced crews will be repatriated at the earliest moment. If either of these courses is adopted by you we will restore your ships to France at the conclusion of the war, or pay full compensation if they are damaged meanwhile.
> C. Alternatively, if you feel bound to stipulate that your ships

95

should not be used against the Germans and Italians unless these break the Armistice, then sail with us with reduced crews to some port in the West Indies – Martinique for instance – where they can be demilitarized to our satisfaction, or be perhaps entrusted to the United States and remain safe until the end of the war, the crews being repatriated.

If you refuse these fair offers, I must, with profound regret, require you to sink your ships within six hours. Finally, failing the above, I have the orders of His Majesty's Government to use whatever force may be necessary to prevent your ships from falling into German or Italian hands.

Gensoul knew Captain Holland well and, if he had consented to see him, some accommodation might have been reached, but he was not a self-confident man and relied on a literal interpretation of his orders. He was less literal in his reports to Darlan and, after reading Somerville's letter, he signalled:

British force comprising 3 battleships, 1 aircraft carrier, cruisers and destroyers off Oran. Ultimatum sent: sink your ships within six hours or will force you to do so. Reply: French ships will meet force with force.

Three and a half hours later he amplified this by admitting that the British had made an alternative offer 'to join the English fleet'. At no stage did he report the proposal to take the ships to French West Indian or American ports, an option coinciding closely with Darlan's order to the fleet on 24 June (see p 95).

Negotiations through an intermediary dragged on through the morning and early afternoon before Gensoul consented to allow Holland to come to him on board *Dunkerque*. By that time it was too late as the French were raising steam for sea and the British, seeing this, mined the entrance to the harbour. In addition Somerville received an intercepted wireless message telling that four heavy cruisers and three divisions of destroyers were sailing from Toulon to reinforce the *Force de Raid*. Since Gensoul refused to accept any of the options, Holland was recalled and at 5.54 p.m., as soon as *Foxhound* was clear, Force H opened fire. *Dunkerque* was soon heavily hit and dropped anchor at the end of the harbour. *Bretagne* capsized with heavy loss of life, *Provence* was hit so heavily that she had to be beached and a destroyer had her stern blown off. Under cover of the smoke, *Strasbourg* with five destroyers broke out and, despite the mines and torpedo attacks by aircraft from the *Ark Royal*, reached Toulon unscathed. On 6 July a

Swordfish torpedo bomber finished off *Dunkerque* by hitting a small vessel loaded with depth charges anchored close to her. In all the action at Mers-el-Kebir cost the French navy 1,297 dead and 351 wounded. A few men were wounded in *Hood* and the crew of one Swordfish were lost.

Simultaneously boarding parties took possession of the French ships in British ports, the only casualties, three British and one French, occurring at Plymouth where there was resistance on board the giant submarine *Surcouf*.

At Alexandria there was a triumph of negotiation between Admiral Sir Andrew Cunningham and his opposite number, Vice Admiral Réné Émile Godfroy. The latter realized that his ships were under the guns of a greatly superior force, but that he had the possibility of making a vital harbour unusable by sinking his squadron in the navigable channel. Both Admirals were determined to avoid bloodshed and neither was averse to disregarding impatient signals from their respective Admiralties when to obey would have precipitated a clash. In the event, common sense prevailed and Godfroy agreed to disarm his ships and discharge his fuel oil. A similar solution might have been reached at Mers-el-Kebir had Gensoul not insisted until the last moment in dealing at arm's length.

Predictably the Vichy* Government, the French Navy and, above all, Admiral Darlan were infuriated by the action of Force H and things were made no better when a British submarine, acting under a misapprehension, sank a French escort vessel, a mistake for which the British speedily apologized and offered compensation. Darlan, who seems chiefly to have been incensed because the British had doubted his word, urged counter-measures which must have led to war between Britain and France. He was restrained by his colleagues, even Laval opposing him, and reprisals were limited to a half-hearted air raid on Gibraltar.

On 4 July Churchill reported the action at Mers-el-Kebir to the House of Commons, stressing the distaste that all concerned felt over an incident which was nevertheless regarded as unavoidable. He ended his speech by saying:

> I feel that we are entitled to the confidence of the House and that we shall not fail in our duty, however painful. The action we have

* Pétain's government moved to Vichy on 1 July.

already taken should be, in itself, sufficient to dispose once and for all of the lies and rumours which have been so industriously spread by German propaganda and Fifth Column activities that we have the slightest intention of entering into negotiations in any form and through any channel with the German and Italian governments. We shall, on the contrary, prosecute the war with the utmost vigour by all means that are open to us until the righteous purposes for which we entered upon it have been fulfilled.

The Commons received this statement with the greatest demonstration of unanimous approval Churchill had yet been given. The press was equally unanimous. The Liberal *News Chronicle* wrote, 'To be weak is to be destroyed' and the view of the Labour *Daily Herald* was, 'Every high and honest motive made our Government's decision inescapable. . . . We are proud of the British Government for its fearless and terrible decision, and of the Navy which carried out that decision.'

There was widespread approval abroad. When the French Ambassador gave President Roosevelt a message from Pétain deploring 'this hateful aggression', the President replied, 'Even if there was only the remotest possibility of seeing your fleet pass into German hands, the British Government had reason to act as it did. I would not have acted otherwise.' The American press took the same line and interpreted the action as a signal that Britain really intended to fight on to the end. The Turkish Foreign Minister expressed his sympathy for the British action and even *Krasny Flot*, journal of the Soviet Navy, commented approvingly on British common sense in depriving Germany of a weapon which would have been dangerous to Britain's survival.

Approval was not to be expected from the enemy nations and the German radio excelled itself in hypocritical horror at the attack. In Rome, however, the Foreign Minister wrote in his diary:

> It proves that the fighting spirit of His Britannic Majesty's Navy is quite alive, and still has the aggressive ruthlessness of the captains and pirates of the seventeenth century.

It was this demonstration of 'aggressive ruthlessness' that gave the real benefit to emerge from the brutal use of thirty-six 15-inch shells against an almost defenceless fleet which, little more than two weeks earlier, had been an allied force. It signalled unmistakably that Britain was not going tamely to submit, that if Germany intended to win the war, she would have to win it by conquest.

7

'I have decided . . .'

While the tragedy at Mers-el-Kebir moved towards its consummation, British Intelligence was garnering sufficient misinformation to keep invasion fears brightly alive. On 1 July Neville Chamberlain had written in his diary:

> All reports seem to point to invasion this week or next.

On the following day John Colville, in Churchill's private office, noted,

> Secret Service reports from Norway make it clear that invasion is being prepared there as well as from other quarters. It is suggested that Iceland* and the Shetlands may be among the first objectives, that a feint will be made against the East Coast, but that the real attack will be from the West.

The Director of Military Intelligence thought invasion probable since he had reports that two parachute units had been moved to Belgium to join picked detachments from divisions which had distinguished themselves in France and because aerial reconnaissance over Kiel had detected a hundred special rafts, thought to be 'intended for invasion purposes'. More immediately a Derbyshire battalion of LDV had been called out on a report that many parachutists had been seen landing. Regular troops were also summoned but after a thorough search of the district it was established that 'the alleged parachutists were really haycocks which had been picked up by a whirlwind to a tremendous height and gradually deposited over a wide area'.

In Germany thoughts were beginning to turn, reluctantly, towards

---

* The Germans had given some cursory attention to the possibility of seizing Iceland, an operation to which they had given the discouraging codename *Icarus*.

invasion. On 30 June Jodl, head of Operations at OKW, submitted a memorandum entitled *Continuation of the War against England*. He suggested that Germany was faced with a choice between two courses. The first entailed striking at the British Empire with the closure of the Mediterranean as a first step. Such a peripheral strategy entailed the close co-operation of Italy, Spain, Japan and the USSR, and he preferred the second option, a blockade by sea and air, 'allied to propaganda and periodic terror attacks, announced as reprisals'.

> This weakening of the system of food supply will *paralyse and finally break the will of the people to resist, and thereby force the government to capitulate.*

He regarded invasion as a last resort to be undertaken only when Britain was paralysed and 'practically incapable of fighting in the air'. Meanwhile 'the landing must be prepared in every detail as *ultima ratio.*' Calculating that Britain could field twenty divisions, he estimated that thirty German divisions would be needed for the task.

Also on 30 June the Army Chief of Staff, General Halder, remarked to a senior Foreign Office official, 'England will presumably need one more demonstration of our military power before she gives in.' Three days later Hitler issued a warning order not for invasion but for preparing the preparations for invasion. He doubted its necessity as it was his intention to make an appeal on 7 July to the British people over the heads of their Government since, in his view:

> England no longer fights for victory but only to retain her possessions and place in the world, there is every reason to suppose that she will agree to peace once she learns that it can be obtained at little cost.

This sanguine view was severely shaken on the following day by the news of Britain's Draconian action at Mers-el-Kebir. The speech offering peace was postponed.

This gave the warning order more importance, but it remained a document about a landing which was not expected to meet heavy opposition. It called for information about beaches and tides, about the availability of shipping, about the state of the British Army and about the chances of establishing air superiority.

> A landing . . . should not be undertaken for the purpose of overthrowing England *militarily*, which can be achieved by the *Luftwaffe* and the *Kriegsmarine*, but only to give the *coup de grâce*,

if necessary, to an England which is economically paralysed and impotent in the air. It cannot be expected that such a state of affairs can be achieved before late August or early September. ... All preparatory work will take into account that no decision to invade England has been taken and that all that is required is preparations for an eventuality which may not arise.

Clearly Goering was a main contributor to this paragraph. No one else would have claimed that Britain could be reduced to economic paralysis within two months and Admiral Raeder, who had recently told Hitler that the U-Boat fleet had suffered 46% losses since the beginning of the war, would have been the last to agree with such an estimate.

Britain's determination, as demonstrated at Mers-el-Kebir, to continue the war changed the whole situation. At last it started to become clear to the Germans that, unless they wanted a long war, they would have to invade Britain. It was a daunting prospect and Keitel, Jodl's chief at OKW, remarked on 7 July that invasion would be:

an extremely difficult operation which must be approached with extreme caution, the more so since the information available on the military state of the island is meagre and far from reliable. ... Moreover the British Air Force is known still to be extremely efficient.

It is clear from this comment that in the five days since the warning order was issued invasion had stopped being a vague mopping-up operation and become a dangerous possibility.

The lack of information about the 'military state of the island' applied chiefly to the British Army. The overwhelming strength of the Royal Navy was clearly appreciated, though sometimes overlooked. The estimates of the 'very efficient' RAF were not far from the mark, if lacking in detail, but there was a dearth of information about the Army. The *Wehrmacht* calculated that, at the end of June, Britain could field twenty divisions 'of fighting quality', although, apart from one armoured formation, they would all be Territorials. Eleven divisions were thought to be fully equipped but inexperienced. It was also believed that they could only move on foot or by rail, presumably because German infantry divisions did not have troop-carrying units of trucks. The Germans also expected to meet the remnants of fourteen divisions returned from France but anticipated finding them devoid of artillery and anti-tank guns.

In practice the British Army, though woefully deficient in many items, was gaining in strength faster than the Germans allowed, the United States having released vast quantities of arms that had been in store since 1918. Included in the windfall were 875 75mm field guns each with 1,000 rounds of ammunition. Though not the equivalent of the new 25-pounder, the 75mm was a good reliable gun and the number that arrived was sufficient to equip ten divisions. The drawback was that the pieces had no limbers and their old-fashioned iron-shod wheels would collapse if towed at more than 6 mph. In I Corps a gunner commanding officer devised a trailer on which the gun could be towed behind a truck and had specimens made by a local firm at £80 each. This the War Office refused to pay, nor would they permit the gunner to meet the cost out of his own pocket. At this stage the Corps Commander, Alexander, intervened, saw a demonstration and, being satisfied, insisted that every artillery unit in the corps should devise its own trailer.

Also from the United States came 55,000 Thompson sub-machine guns, a weapon of which the army had only forty, and 800,000 Ross rifles, made to a British design of 1912 but using .300 calibre ammunition rather than the .303 of the standard rifle. These acquisitions were swiftly issued to the Home Guard (as the LDV had been retitled from 14 July) so that their Lee Enfields could be returned to the regulars, who were still short of rifles. Preparing the Ross rifles for service was a stern test for the part-time soldiers. As John Brophie wrote:

> Every rifle was coated inside and out with protective yellow grease, denser and stiffer than vaseline, and the first job after unpacking was to remove this grease and substitute a thin coating of oil. Everywhere there were volunteers eager for the dirty job, and throughout the country men in overalls or old clothes were busily at work from morning till night – for by night the invasion might have begun. The clean rifles were tacked, after barrels and bolt actions had been examined. The sealed metal ammunition boxes were prised open with tin-openers, when they emitted a sweetish smell resembling pear-drops; for the first time the Home Guard saw the possibility not merely of going into action but of continuing the fight for more than a few desperate minutes.

Not all shortages were cured so quickly. The 6th Battalion of the Gordon Highlanders, which had returned from France with 22 officers and 326 other ranks, was ordered in July to raise a 'tank-hunting platoon mounted on bicycles'. They were armed with rifles.

The increasing strength and mobility of the Army led to controversy about the deployment of reserves. Ironside, commanding Home Forces, insisted that the time had not come to reduce the strong beach defences he had stipulated at the end of May. As he saw it early in June:

> I think that if the Germans decide to attempt an invasion they will
> do so on a very broad front in order to reduce their vulnerability
> to air and sea attack, and to find the 'soft spots' in our defences.
> South of the Humber and along the South Coast they will use
> a great many small craft for this purpose and will endeavour
> to land a large number of troops over a wide area; they will
> also endeavour to capture a certain number of ports for the
> disembarkation of tanks and stores.

This view was disputed by many of the younger commanders, notable among them Lt. Gen. Sir Alan Brooke, commanding II Corps.

> To my mind our defence should be of a far more mobile and
> offensive nature. I visualised a light line of defence along the
> beaches, to hamper and delay landings to the maximum, and
> in the rear highly mobile forces trained to immediate aggressive
> action intended to concentrate and attack any landings before
> they had time to become too well established.

To this Ironside was able to reply that his 'highly mobile forces' consisted effectively of two armoured divisions neither of which had more than half their establishment of tanks and that the tanks they did have were obsolete.

The Intelligence agencies could come to no agreement as to where the invaders might land. On 10 July Naval Intelligence, while believing that a surprise landing in small craft on a large scale would be 'a most hazardous undertaking', conceded that in favourable conditions the enemy might succeed in putting 12,000 men ashore between the Wash and Dover and 5,000 more between Dover and Land's End. They added that in thick weather about fifty transports, sailing from German ports, might land 50,000 men between Rosyth and Southwold. A week later the Joint Intelligence Committee put forward the view that two landings would be attempted to encircle London. These would come ashore between the Wash and Newhaven. They calculated that five divisions could be transported by sea and a further 12,000 men by air.

Churchill had his own opinion:

> I find it very difficult to visualise the kind of invasion all along
> the coast by troops carried in small craft. . . . Except in very
> narrow waters it would be a most hazardous and even suicidal
> operation to commit a large army to the accidents of the sea in
> the teeth of our very numerous armed patrolling forces. . . . I
> find it difficult to believe that the south coast is in serious danger
> at the present time. . . . The main danger is from the Dutch and
> German harbours which bear principally upon the coast from
> Dover to the Wash.

The evident devastation of the Channel ports strengthened the general belief that the east coast was the most likely landing area and this belief was not shaken when, late in July, a *Luftwaffe* order was intercepted forbidding the bombing of south coast harbours.

Civilians in Britain continued to take an optimistic view of the chances of beating off invasion though they were convinced that invasion would come. In the Commons Mr Seymour Cocks (Labour, Broxtowe) asked the Home Secretary to consider issuing revolvers or other weapons to Members so that, if the time should come, they could 'sell their lives dearly'. In Notting Hill a social worker wrote in her diary:

> It is no use being prophetic about anything until a few more
> months have passed. If we were one hundred per cent British
> we should be all right. It is the Fifth Column we fear.

Although most enemy aliens were behind barbed wire, they had their defenders. One letter in the *Manchester Guardian* proposed that anti-Nazi aliens should be formed into a Foreign Legion trained in sabotage, espionage and demolition – 'All that is needed is another Lawrence of Arabia to lick this material into shape and train it for its allotted task.' Another correspondent protested against the harsh treatment of aliens, pointing out that Germany had not interned Czechs, Poles and Jews, 'nor excluded them from every kind of work'.

The Italian Ambassador, reporting on his return to Rome, was right in saying that 'the morale of the British is very high and they have no doubts about victory, even though it may come after a long time.' Naturally there were sources of irritation. The flying of kites and balloons was banned on 5 July and at Dover the Council agreed that the Ladies' Sea Baths should close since in the past four weeks only twenty-seven people had used them. It was considered that 'ladies should in future use the large baths as mixed baths which would save a certain amount of fuel.' At Tunbridge Wells a telephone operator was fined £25 for spreading a rumour that twenty parachutists had landed near Hawkhurst.

Intent on raising aircraft production, Lord Beaverbrook made a call to housewives:

> We will turn your pots and pans into Spitfires and Hurricanes,
> Blenheims and Wellingtons. Everyone who has pots and pans,
> kettles and vacuum cleaners, hat pegs, coat hangers, shoe trees,
> bathroom fittings and household ornaments, cigarette boxes,
> or any other articles made wholly or in part of aluminium
> should hand them over to the local headquarters of the Womens'
> Voluntary Services. . . . The need is instant. The call is urgent.
> Our expectations are high.

The response was overwhelming despite spoilsports who pointed out that there was plenty of scrap aluminium in the country and that little would be obtained from pots and pans. Equally well subscribed was an appeal for iron railings to be melted down, the little village of Ditton, near Maidstone, contributing eleven tons in a single weekend. In the *Daily Express* William Hickey agitated to have the great railings outside the British Museum torn down. The Ministry of Food announced that branded margarine was to disappear, the choice being reduced to Standard at 5d (2p) a pound or Special at 9d (4p).

The continued absence of air raids produced a wave of gaiety in London. Some precautions were nevertheless thought wise. Marshall and Snelgrove advertised a steel-lined hat for two guineas – 'Nobody knows you are wearing a Stelmet – it is concealed in the felt' – Barkers were offering 'anti-shatter window varnish' and from an enterprising manufacturer came 'Anti-concussion bandeaux. Made of sponge rubber. May be worn under a gasmask'. Early in July one American correspondent reported that 'London in the past few days has seemed more cheerful than it has for some time past'.

Part of this new cheerfulness came from a feeling that the country's defences were likely to hold but more came from evidence, largely illusory, that Britain was hitting back. On 26 June a communiqué had been published:

> In co-operation with the Royal Air Force, naval and military
> units yesterday carried out successful reconnaissances of the enemy
> coastline. Landings were effected at a number of points and
> contact made with German troops.

> Casualties were inflicted and some enemy dead fell into our hands.
> Much useful information was obtained.
> Our forces suffered no casualties.

This announced the first of all Commando raids. A hundred and twenty men, hastily assembled and transported in unsuitable craft, were landed between Boulogne and Le Touquet. They killed two Germans but the only information they obtained was that there were German troops in the Pas de Calais, a point no one had doubted. It was, however, a beginning and, as *The Times* said in a leading article, 'The point is that this incident is exactly what the public wants.'

On almost every night since 15/16 May RAF Bomber Command had been sending up to a hundred Whitleys, Hampdens and Wellingtons against industrial targets in western Germany, mostly in the Ruhr. The results were very small since the aircrew did not have the navigational skills or the navigational aids required to find their targets. After nine days of concentrating on ten specified aircraft factories, AOC Bomber Command wrote:

> Only three of these ten can be found with any certainty by average
> crews. Expert crews may be expected to find the remainder
> on clear nights with a full moon, and the average crews will
> sometimes find them after a good deal of time has been spent
> on searching.

The effect of all this activity was assessed from the reports of aircrew, who tended to be over-optimistic, and from some tendentious reports from SIS, but they were interpreted by Bomber Command in the light of their ingrained belief in the efficacy of bombing, a belief best summed up later in the summer by a senior adviser to the Command who wrote:

> However little damage appears in a photograph, an objective
> must have suffered damage in proportion to the weight of bombs
> dropped over it.

By August Air Intelligence was confidently claiming that industrial output in the Ruhr and elsewhere had fallen off by 30%, but this loss was not apparent to the Germans. The greatest benefit of the 1940 bombing campaign in Germany was the comfort it brought to the people of Britain who believed that the enemy was being hurt, but an exception must be made of one raid, made on the night of 12–13 August on an aqueduct on the Dortmund-Ems canal. Five Whitley bombers attacked at 150 feet and, although two were shot down, the one commanded by Flight Lieutenant R.A.B. Learoyd breached the aqueduct, halting the movement of invasion barges for ten days. Learoyd was awarded the Victoria Cross.

On 30 June Goering issued a General Order for the *Luftwaffe*'s own offensive against Britain. It was to start with probing attacks which, it was hoped, would induce the RAF to reveal their defensive plans and commit their main strength.

> By means of reconnaissances and the engagement of small units, enemy units will be drawn up and the strength and grouping of the defences ascertained.

In the second phase the main assault would be launched with two objectives:

> a) To make possible a successful offensive against the enemy's armament industries and lines of supply by defeating his air force, destroying his ground organisation and his aircraft industry. Simultaneously Germany and the territories she occupies will be protected.
> b) To dislocate Britain's supplies by attacking ports and harbour installations, ships bringing supplies into the country and the warships escorting them.

The final paragraph stressed that the overriding aim was to smash the British air defences, especially Fighter Command:

> While the enemy air force remains in being, the principles of air warfare insist that it must be attacked at every opportunity, by day and by night, in the air and on the ground, irrespective of any other task.

This was essentially Raeder's strategy of reducing Britain by siege but with a much shorter scenario. There was no mention of invasion and when, two days later, Hitler issued his warning order, Goering was forced to do some re-thinking. He did it reluctantly and in-adequately.

Two *Luftflotten* (air fleets) were deployed in France and the Low Countries, II under Kesselring and III under Sperrle. Between them they comprised some 850 serviceable level-flight bombers, 250 Stukas, 660 single-engined and 170 twin-engined fighters. There was also

Luftflotte V (Stumpf) based in Scandinavia which included 100 serviceable bombers and thirty twin-engined fighters with sufficient range to be used against Britain.

Goering boasted that it would take the main assault four days to destroy Fighter Command and four weeks to finish off the whole RAF. In this estimate he was misled not only by his own arrogance but by bad information. In mid-July *Luftwaffe* Intelligence produced a comparison of the two air forces which considerably underrated the British service. Their estimate (which was later revised upwards) of the strength of Fighter Command was near the truth, giving them 675 first-line aircraft, of which three-fifths were Hurricanes and the balance Spitfires. In fact the Command could field, including two squadrons of Defiants, some 660 planes. The capabilities of the aircraft were understated:

> Judging from their combat performance and the fact that they are not yet equipped with cannon, both [Spitfires and Hurricanes] are inferior to the Me109, particularly to the Me109F, while the Me110 is inferior to a skilfully handled Spitfire.

Admitting that only a few prototypes in the RAF yet had cannon, the Spitfire was, in almost all conditions, the equal to the Me109E, and the Me109F was not in squadron service until the battle to destroy Fighter Command had been lost. As for the Me110 it was inferior to both Spitfire and Hurricane and was shortly to require its own escort of 109s.

The German estimate of the British reinforcement rate was very misleading, putting output at 'about 180–300 first line fighters a month' and adding:

> In view of problems such as shortage of raw materials, reduction in production due to air attacks and a reorganisation in progress in the aircraft industry, there are grounds for believing that, in the immediate future, output will decrease rather than increase.

The reality was that, thanks to the expansion in production due to Lord Beaverbrook and his predecessor and prodigious work in the factories, the output was much larger than the *Luftwaffe* estimated – July 496, August 476, September 476.

There were two other serious errors in the German document. There was no mention of British radar and the fighter command system was described as 'inflexible', whereas the system Dowding had devised was superbly adaptable to the kind of test to which it was to be subjected.

The conclusion drawn was that Germany was in a position to finish the war by daylight operations 'since the air defences of the island are inadequate'.

> The *Luftwaffe* has clear advantages in strength, equipment, training, command and in the location of its airfields. . . .
> A decisive result can be obtained this year provided the main operation is launched in time to take advantage of the summer months – July to early October.

The British date the start of the Battle of Britain on 10 July, although the Germans reckon that the 'Contact Phase' began on the day France surrendered. Whichever date is accepted, the engagement started slowly with attacks on British shipping interspersed with small-scale night raids ranging as far as Merseyside. On the south and east coasts the *Luftwaffe* tried and failed to draw Fighter Command into large-scale action over the convoys. Dowding was prepared to give a measure of cover to the coastal traffic – his command averaged 530 sorties a day in their defence – but he refused to let this commitment jeopardize the defence of Britain. Between 10 July and 12 August 30,000 tons of shipping (out of a million tons a week) was sunk at a cost to the Germans of 286 aircraft, of which 105 were fighters. Fighter Command lost 150 fighters, of which two were Blenheims lost on night operations. This *Kanalkampf*, as the *Luftwaffe* called the fight over the Channel, was a limited victory for the Germans. Not only did they lose fewer fighters, they seriously impeded the coastal trade and forced the Royal Navy, after two sinkings, to withdraw the destroyers from Dover. The British public was unaware of this setback as this was the beginning of what John Terraine has called the Numbers Game. Each evening the Air Ministry announced the number of British fighters lost, a figure that was invariably accurate to within two or three, and the number of German aircraft claimed by the RAF. These claims were made in all good faith, but they were based on insufficient evidence and could not be checked for accuracy, with a result that they were frequently greatly exaggerated. These daily figures were unhesitatingly accepted not only by the British but by the far more sceptical American correspondents. Acceptance was made easier by the falsification consistently practised by the Germans. Not only were their claims for British aircraft shot down, a figure that could be checked in England, even more inflated than British claims, but they were far from honest about their own losses. For the period 10 July to 7 August they lost 192 aircraft from all causes but admitted to only sixty-three.

Both sides learned valuable lessons from this dress rehearsal for the main battle that was to come. Fighter Command learned that the tactics evolved in peace, based on a V formation of three aircraft, were ineffective and dangerous and switched to the technique, devised by the Germans in the Spanish Civil War, of operating with two mutually supporting pairs of planes. They also found that their latest fighter, the Boulton Paul Defiant, was not battleworthy. The Defiant was a two-seater, single-engined machine with its armament of four machine guns in a turret behind the crew space. Over Dunkirk they had achieved a notable success when Messerschmitts took them for Hurricanes which were unusually negligent about guarding their rear. On 19 July nine Defiants were attacked over Dover by Me109s coming from ahead. Six Defiants were lost and the remainder saved only by the timely intervention of some Hurricanes. The Defiant squadrons had to be withdrawn from the front line.

On the other side the *Luftwaffe* were very disappointed by the performance of the twin-engined Me110 and found that their bomber crews were becoming clamorous for fighter escort. This meant that the small superiority they had in single-engined fighters had to be whittled away by providing protection for slower aircraft, a function for which the admirable Me109 was not suited. They also found that the long-distance drop tanks designed for the single-engine fighters were so ill-constructed as to be unserviceable. This restricted the range of the Me109 to the extent that it could scarcely reach the north-west suburbs of London.

As the *Kanalkampf* was beginning Hitler was coming round to the idea of invading Britain. When Count Ciano arrived in Berlin on 7 July he found the Führer 'rather inclined to continue the struggle and unleash a storm of wrath and steel upon the British, but the final decision had not been reached.' Three days later the *Kriegsmarine* was instructed to start building coastal batteries near Calais which, since even a slow-moving coaster is an almost impossible target for a superheavy gun, were almost certainly intended to support landing operations.

At OKW Jodl was at work on an outline invasion plan codenamed *Lion*. He completed it on 12 July and four days later, renamed *Sealion*, it appeared as Hitler's Directive No.16, *Preparations for the Invasion of England*. It opened with, for Hitler, uncharacteristic diffidence:

> As England, despite the hopelessness of her military position, has shown herself unwilling to make a compromise, I have decided to begin to prepare for, and if necessary to carry out, an invasion of England. This operation is dictated by the necessity of eliminating Great Britain as a base from which war against Germany can be fought and, if necessary, the island will be occupied.

It is clear that Hitler still hoped that Britain could be brought to the conference table either before *Sealion* was launched or as soon as the landing had been accomplished so that the occupation of the island would not be necessary. He laid down a number of preconditions for the operations. The RAF must be defeated 'to such an extent that it will be incapable of putting up any substantial opposition'. The sea routes must be cleared of British mines and German mine barriers must be laid across the Straits of Dover and across the English Channel 'on a line from Alderney to Portland'. For this Raeder was authorized to obtain mines from French stocks. He was also instructed to establish coastal batteries to 'dominate the entire coastal area'. He was not told where he could obtain guns with sufficient range to carry from Cherbourg to the Isle of Wight.

> The largest possible number of heavy guns must be installed as soon as possible to safeguard the crossing and to cover both flanks against interference from the sea. For this purpose, anti-aircraft guns mounted on railway bogies (supplemented by all available captured guns) with railway turntables will be used.

The *Kriegsmarine* was also to provide the sea transport required and to draw away the attention of the British Home Fleet. It was allowed that the Mediterranean Fleet could be left to the Italians.

The *Luftwaffe* was to prevent all British air attacks, destroy all coastal defences covering landing-places, 'break the initial resistance of the enemy land forces, and annihilate reserves behind the front'. They were also to attack roads behind the front and to prevent British ships from interfering with the embarkation, the crossing and the landing.

By contrast to the vast tasks put upon the sea and air forces, the *Wehrmacht* was told merely to draft a plan for the crossing and 'the operations of the first wave of the invading force'. Nothing was said about succeeding waves. There was to be co-operation between the *Wehrmacht* and the *Kriegsmarine* about the allocation of landing-craft and 'the points at which the embarkation and landing will take place'.

The main executive paragraph was a curious amalgam of a consultative document and the orders for an unopposed attack:

> The landing operation must be a surprise crossing on a broad front extending approximately from Ramsgate to a point west of the Isle of Wight. Units of the *Luftwaffe* will do the work of artillery while the *Kriegsmarine* will do the work of engineers. I ask each of the fighting services to consider the advantages, from their own point of view, of preliminary operations such as the occupation of the Isle of Wight in advance of the full-scale invasion, and to inform me of their proposals. I shall be responsible for the final decision. Preparations for the full-scale invasion must be complete by the middle of August.

It is clear that a soldier was responsible for this outline plan and that he had not consulted the Navy. To propose a landing on a front of some 225 miles in face of an overwhelmingly superior navy with a transport fleet which had yet to be assembled, if it could be assembled, was to expect a miracle from the *Kriegsmarine*. To expect it to be done within four weeks was to ask the impossible.

One point would greatly have intrigued the British had they been able to secure one of the eight copies of the Directive that were issued:

> I invite suggestions concerning the use of airborne troops, and in particular whether it would be advisable to keep them in reserve for use only in case of emergency.

While much of the manhood of Britain was organizing itself to guard against attack from the air, Hitler and his advisers could not make up their minds how their airborne forces were to be employed or even whether they were to play any part in the main invasion plan.

It cannot be said that *Sealion*, as outlined in Directive No.16, had much contact with reality, descending as it does from the realms of high strategy to details like the provision of railway bogies for anti-aircraft guns. Quite apart from the unbearable load placed on the *Kriegsmarine*, there was no instruction to the *Luftwaffe* to deal in advance with the Royal Navy, clearly the most dangerous threat to seaborne invasion. If the *Luftwaffe* at full stretch could not prevent British warships extricating the BEF from Dunkirk, what chance had they of preventing those same ships from creating havoc among the slow-moving convoys of improvised craft which would have to carry the *Wehrmacht* across the Channel? Nevertheless Hitler had, for the time being, made up his mind. On the same day on which the Directive was issued, he sent 'a long letter to [Mussolini]. It announces the attack on England as something decided, but declines in a definite and courteous way the offer to send an Italian expeditionary force.'

8

'Appeal to Reason and Common Sense'

Having given orders for making ready the iron fist, Hitler publicly displayed the velvet glove. On 19 July the Reichstag met in the Kroll Opera House where, after making awards to various dignitaries, the Führer presented batons to twelve newly promoted field-marshals and advanced Goering to the unprecedented rank of *Reichsmarschall*. He then broadcast a long speech in what Ciano described as 'an unusually humane tone'. Embedded in it was a peace offer to Britain:

> In this hour, I feel it my duty before my own conscience, to
> appeal once more to reason and common sense in Great Britain
> as well as elsewhere. I consider myself in a position to make this
> appeal since I am not the vanquished begging favours, but the
> victor speaking in the name of reason. I can see no reason why
> this war must go on.

More in sorrow than in anger, he added a threat to destroy the British Empire, 'which it was never my intention to destroy or even to harm'.

In Germany, where the idea that the war was as good as over had been allowed to flourish, this seemed an offer which the British would be eager to embrace and when the BBC late-night bulletin 'heaped ridicule on Hitler's every utterance' the Germans were amazed. William Shirer, CBS correspondent in Berlin, wrote:

> Officers from the High Command and officials from various min-
> istries, sitting around the room [at German radio headquarters],
> could not believe their ears. One of them shouted at me: 'Can
> you make it out? Can you understand those British fools? To turn
> down peace now?' I merely grunted. 'They're crazy,' he said.

To the British it was far from clear that Hitler had actually made a peace offer – one reaction was 'Nothing tangible and nothing new'.

Neville Chamberlain wrote in his diary:

> I guess he made no specific offer of peace, only an appeal
> to 'common sense', because, if he had, it would have been
> refused.

The Times reported the speech under the headline 'Hitler's Threats
to Britain' and in a leader on Monday, 22 July wrote that it 'was
remarkable for its lack of content and purpose'. On 20 July the
Ministry of Information's Home Intelligence report commented:

> On the whole, people have treated it less seriously than the press
> has done. People laughed and jeered.

Two days later it reported that the peace offer 'seems to have disap-
peared from public conversation'.

The War Cabinet decided that no official reply was required, but,
in a broadcast on 21 July, Lord Halifax remarked, 'We shall not stop
fighting till freedom, for ourselves and others, is secure'. To Count
Ciano this seemed to be 'an inconsequential speech about Germany,
in which Hitler's proposals for peace are not taken into account'. In
an attempt to get his offer through to the British people, Hitler had
copies of the speech printed and dropped by aircraft over southern
England. The recipients remained apathetic and, angry and hurt,
Hitler returned to the contemplation of invasion.

Apart from the *Kanalkampf* and sporadic night raids, the opening
assault was verbal. Dr Goebbels was establishing a number of radio
stations which represented themselves as broadcasting clandestinely
from within Britain. This 'Concordia Network' had started in February, 1940, with two stations, the New British Broadcasting Station,
which favoured a Britain of 'peace and welfare', and the Voice of Peace,
which was Christian Pacifist in its message. Three more stations were
added in July – Plan S or 'Workers' Challenge', a revolutionary
socialist channel calling for strikes in favour of peace; Radio Caledonia,
advocating independence for Scotland using force if necessary; Plan
W which did the same for Wales, where it was largely inaudible.
In practice none of the five stations gave adequate reception and all
drew very small audiences. Since they were allegedly British, they
were instructed to 'begin every broadcast with attacks on National
Socialism' and, said Goebbels, 'since German propaganda must not
be apparent, they must conceal their real intentions in moral tales
and good advice'.

In the week following the Reichstag speech, Goebbels gave orders that:

> The secret transmitters . . . should make it clear what lies ahead for Britain once the offensive starts. The Workers' station should call for action committees against Churchill. As a catchy slogan every transmission should be prefaced by 'The Empire is ruled by a fool. Churchill is a fool'.

On 25 July the New British Broadcasting Service told its few listeners that, 'At any moment the invasion of this country may begin with all its horror, bloodshed and destruction.' On Goebbels' orders this was to be followed by a bogus evacuation plan designed to block the roads with refugees when the landing took place. A Frenchman was to tell of the horrors which overcame France when Hitler's offer of peace was spurned and the Voice of Peace was to transmit a special rogation service for an end to the war. The effects of bombing were to be described by eye-witnesses from Warsaw and Rotterdam and the stations were to give instructions in Air Raid Precautions 'of which the details must be described so accurately that the civilian population will be seized with panic from the start'.

Hopes of peace without further fighting were not wholly dead in Berlin. On 22 July the War Diary of Naval Operations Division recorded a story, said to emanate from the Swiss Minister in London, of 'increasingly violent opposition to Churchill' and of 'a strong and influential group who would like to know what peace terms would be offered'. Another story told of Lloyd George having had an audience of King George and of a cable from the Duke of Windsor urging his brother to change his ministers. There was hope that the Duke might prove a help to the German cause. It was reported that, when he had fled to Spain to escape the occupation of France, he had said to an American diplomat that, 'The most important thing now is to end the war before thousands more are maimed to save the face of a few politicians'. Certainly his behaviour and that of his Duchess while in France, Spain and Portugal was indiscreet and embarrassing to the British Government who were glad to see him on board ship, bound for the Governorship of The Bahamas.

Another move towards peace was initiated by Dr Albert Plesman, founder and head of Royal Dutch Airlines (KLM), who approached Goering and was entertained by him at his country house, Karinhall. Plesman proposed that a KLM plane grounded in England should be

116

flown to Rotterdam by a Dutch crew and return with him on board carrying the German peace terms. Goering, who seems not to have heard that, after the rejection of his Reichstag offer, Hitler had said that he 'did not desire further attempts to build bridges with the British', spent 24 July thrashing out draft terms with the Dutchman. Apart from a proposal to return to gold as a medium of trade, they came up with four main points:

I. That the Royal Navy should be left intact.
II. That, apart from the return of the German colonies of 1914, there should be no territorial adjustments.
III. That German troops should be withdrawn from Norway, Denmark, the Netherlands, Belgium and France; that no military demands should be made on those countries which should be free to choose their own governments, provided that fruitful co-operation with Germany was assured.
IV. That Poland and Czechoslovakia should 'not be disturbed in their national development, appropriate regulation of those countries being left exclusively to Germany'.

A message on these lines was drafted for transmission to the exiled Dutch Government by way of Stockholm, but the Foreign Ministry refused to transmit it and, on the following day, Plesman took it in person to the Swedish capital where he persuaded the Dutch Legation to forward it. The Dutch Foreign Minister in London consulted Lord Halifax before replying:

I cannot attach great importance to [the proposals] considering . . . the withdrawal of permission on the part of the Germans to despatch the telegram on 25 July and the time that has elapsed since that date.

In the meantime the Swedes had made their own *démarche*. At the end of July the Swedish Government advised King Gustav to propose to the respective heads of state that he should use his good offices to arrange secret peace talks in Sweden. Hitler replied on 6 August that he saw no point in holding talks with the existing British Government. King George replied, after having consulted the Governments of the Dominions, that no such meeting could be held until Germany had given effective guarantees for the freedom of the countries she conquered and for the security of the British Empire. The Swedes were disappointed at these negative responses and hurt that King George, unlike Hitler, had not seen fit to thank King Gustav for his offer.

While Hitler was making his peace offer on 19 July, General Sir Alan Brooke was succeeding Ironside at the head of British Home Forces. The War Office explained the change on the grounds that it was 'essential to place the command of Home Forces in the hands of a Commander-in-Chief who had immediate experience of command in France and Belgium'. The real reason was that Churchill had lost confidence in his old friend and especially in his determination to fight the main battle on the beaches, falling back, if necessary, on his embryo defence lines.

Brooke agreed with Churchill:

> Much work and energy was being expended on an extensive system of rear defence, comprising an anti-tank ditch and pill-boxes, running roughly parallel to the coast and situated well inland. This static rear line did not fall in with my conception. . . . To start with we had not got sufficient forces to man this line, even if we had wanted to do so.

He favoured a light screen on the beaches to impose sufficient delay on the invaders for 'highly mobile forces trained to immediate aggressive action' to arrive and deal with those who had managed to get ashore. This controversy between the strength of the 'crust' and that of the mobile reserve is age-old and was to arise in acute form four years later when the Germans were defending Normandy. In July and August, 1940, it has to be admitted that Brooke's mobile reserves consisted of a small number of obsolete tanks grouped into two incomplete armoured divisions and one army tank brigade. Their supporting infantry would have to move to battle in requisitioned motor coaches driven by civilians.

One result of Brooke's new view of defensive techniques was that much work that had been done on static defences had to be dismantled. Since the Home Guard had been formed the country had been dotted with concrete pill-boxes many of which, as can be seen half a century later, were in unsuitable positions, while road blocks of increasingly solid appearance had been constructed in thousands of more or less likely places:

> Another form of defence which I found throughout the country and with which I was in total disagreement consisted of massive concrete road-blocks at the entry and exit of most towns and of many villages. I had suffered too much from these blocks in France

not to realise their crippling effect on mobility. Our security must depend on the mobility of our reserves and we were taking the very best steps to reduce this mobility. . . . I stopped any further construction, and instructed existing ones to be removed where possible.

It was ironic that on the day that Brooke assumed command a summary produced by *Kriegsmarine* Intelligence credited the British defence with exactly those features that its new chief was complaining that it lacked:

The English defence is based on mobility and the concentration of all available firepower. There is no fixed defence line with built-in defences. The task of the fleet and the RAF would be to render impossible the landing of armoured units or surprise troop landings. The RAF is so organised that strong units can speedily be concentrated at any point of danger while attacking the new German bases in Northern France and searching for such activities as the assembly of transports and barges.

Brooke would have been delighted if this had been true, since the only air supprt definitely allotted to him in case of invasion comprised two squadrons of Blenheim light bombers. Co-operation with the RAF was rudimentary, a state of affairs the Air Staff seemed anxious to preserve, since, following the Trenchard doctine, close support for land operations was considered 'a gross misuse of air forces'.

In making this assessment the *Kriegsmarine* had drawn widely on its imagination, but its purpose was clear. Raeder and his senior commanders were appalled at the prospect of invasion and were determined to scotch the project if they could. They were not foolhardy enough to tell the Führer that his orders were impossible to execute so they fell back on the policy of making all possible preparations with notable efficiency and alacrity while drawing attention to the risks and difficulties involved in the hope that wiser counsels would prevail. Passing the Intelligence assessment to Hitler, the Admiral drew attention to the magnitude of the tasks allotted to the under-strength navy and underlined once more the crucial importance of air supremacy and the threat posed by the Royal Navy:

So far the enemy has not needed to use his fleet fully, as a matter of life and death. The landing in England will find him resolved to throw in all his naval forces to achieve a decision. It cannot be assumed that the *Luftwaffe* alone will be able to keep the

119

enemy naval forces clear of our convoys since its operations are dependent on the weather.

On receiving Raeder's memorandum, Hitler called him to a meeting on 21 July which was also attended by the Commander-in-Chief of the army, von Brauchitsch and his Chief of Staff, Halder. Hitler began by speculating on the possibility of a new British Government under Lloyd George and then embarked on a *tour d'horizon*:

> The war has been decided but Britain will not admit that fact, probably because she sees some hope for the future from either Russia or America. The United States lost so much money in the last war that she will not fight this time. She lent ten billion dollars and got less than a billion and a half paid back. Nor will Russia go to war with Germany of her own accord. Stalin is flirting with Britain to keep her in the war so that Germany will be engaged while Russia takes what she wants in the east. Our situation is therefore favourable but we must work for a quick end to the fighting so as to make the most of the political and military advantages we have gained. *Sealion* seems to be the best way of ending the war in our favour. We should at the same time pursue diplomatic initiatives with Spain, Russia and Japan, though these will inevitably be long and difficult since the world seems to expect that England will be saved by a miracle.
>
> Invading Britain would be a very daring operation because, even though the sea crossing is short, there is more to it than a large-scale river crossing since the sea is dominated by the enemy. We cannot compare it with the invasion of Norway which required only a single sea-borne crossing.
>
> Tactical surprise was unattainable. The enemy is utterly determined, defensively prepared and dominates the intervening sea. The *Wehrmacht* will require forty divisions and their supply will be extremely difficult since we must assume that no supplies will be available for them in England.
>
> The prerequisites are absolute control of the air, the use of heavy artillery in the Straits of Dover and effective protection from mine barriers on the flanks. The main landing must be carried out by 15 September and, if all the preparations are not complete by the beginning of that month, other plans would have to be discussed.

After this extended monologue the Führer questioned Raeder about the availability of transport, the state of the new coastal batteries and the Navy's ability to protect the crossing. The Admiral promised definite answers within four days.

Raeder must have been gratified by Hitler's apparent appreciation of the difficulties involved in mounting *Sealion* and he needed all the understanding he could get, since, just before the meeting, he had received the Army's first outline plan for the landing which confirmed his worst fears. The proposal was to launch six armoured, four motorised and thirty infantry divisions on a front which stretched from the mouth of the Thames to Lyme Bay, a span of about two hundred and thirty miles. The first assault was to be carried out by thirteen infantry divisions, each of which would land with two regimental (brigade) groups, complete with armoured detachment, in the assault wave. This would entail transporting 100,000 men and their equipment from ports reaching from Dunkirk to Cherbourg. With total incomprehension of the difficulties involved OKH added:

> Further waves must follow in the quickest succession so that
> the local bridgeheads established can rapidly be expanded and
> followed by mobile warfare in the interior. This requires a
> rapid turn-round of transports after the disembarkation of the
> first wave.

The *Kriegsmarine* estimated that this first wave would require 155 merchant ships, 1,722 barges, 471 tugs and 1,161 motor boats and such an array could only be assembled if the Baltic traffic, including the import of iron ore, was brought to a halt and the inland waterways, on which Germany largely depended for internal transport, were denuded of barges. Even on purely tactical considerations, the Army's plan seemed to the Navy to be a work of fantasy. Not only did it greatly extend the area in which even minimal protection could be given but it took no account of tides, currents, rough weather or the time that must be taken in unloading transports and barges over open beaches. Nevertheless the *Kriegsmarine* policy was to be seen to be co-operating up to the hilt and they set about recruiting 24,000 men, preferably with some maritime experience, to man the barges, converting such barges as were immediately available and, with the help of the Todt labour organization, putting in order the shattered harbours of northern France. On 25 July Raeder reported to Hitler that arrangements for collecting the transport fleet and the mines for the barrage were well in hand while the coastal batteries were approaching completion. The Führer took a keen and continuing interest in these great guns and, unasked, gave permission for them to open fire as soon as they were ready.

Before the next inter-service meeting on the last day of July, Hitler developed a new interest which was soon to override his always luke-warm enthusiasm for *Sealion*. On 23 July he had attended a special performance of *Götterdamerung* at Bayreuth and left the opera house with the conviction that he must attack Russia. For the moment this decision was not communicated to the three services but within OKW a study group was established to work on a plan. To the chosen staff officers Jodl explained that the defeat of Russia would dishearten Britain to such an extent that she would surrender. Hitler believed that the Soviets were becoming too friendly with the British, a phenomenon which was made clear by the fact that the new British Ambassador, Sir Stafford Cripps, was received by Stalin within two days of his arrival in Moscow. One result of the new decision was that the *Wehrmacht*, which was in the process of being reduced from 159 to 120 divisions, was to be expanded to 180 divisions.

Unaware of this diversion, the Navy sent the Army their estimate of what was possible in the way of landings. This, wrote Halder, 'upsets all previous calculations [since it] will take ten days to land the assault echelon. . . . If this is the case, a landing is not possible.' A senior staff officer was sent to OKM to clarify the position and he was told that the number of landing-craft (barges) available would not permit the embarkation of the second wave until forty-eight hours after the landing of the first wave and that the time needed to get the second wave across the Channel would be eight to ten days. OKH set about rethinking their scheme armed with a new naval memorandum.

This, from the Army's point of view, was a most depressing document:

> It is possible that the first wave might succeed in getting ashore in spite of all the obstacles we have already pointed out and others not yet mentioned. After that two enemies might come between the troops ashore and their bases – the weather and the British fleet. As far as we can tell the effect of air attack on warships is slight if the ships have room to manoeuvre and are alert. On this occasion the British will be very alert. They are awaiting invasion with confidence since they believe it will enable them to bring their most powerful weapon, their fleet, into play. They are convinced that their ships will inflict a severe defeat on the *Wehrmacht*, breaking its run of victories. Neither the *Luftwaffe* nor the *Kriegsmarine* are adequate to deal with an all-out onslaught by the British fleet. Air attack has a very limited effect on heavily armoured vessels and the use of aircraft is, in any case, wholly dependent on the weather.

The meeting called by Hitler on 31 July was attended by Keitel and Jodl on behalf of OKW, von Brauchitsch and Halder for the army and Raeder for the navy. No airman appears to have been present. Naval business was taken first and the Admiral reported that, although the mid-August date could not be met, all would be ready by mid-September and, since the Army insisted on landing at first light and the Navy would require at least half-moonlight for the passage, the earliest period for the landing would be 19–26 September, although records suggested that this was normally a time of poor weather.

So far this was Raeder running exactly true to form. Whatever his private doubts about the wisdom of invasion, the Navy could and would have everything ready by the first practicable date, even if he cast doubt on that date by his meteorological information. He was doing everything a loyal subordinate ought to do, including, as was his duty, drawing attention to the dangers. Then he went one step further. He suggested that, purely from a naval point of view, the wise course would be to postpone *Sealion* until the following year since by then *Bismarck* and *Tirpitz* would be in commission and, with *Scharnhorst* and *Gneisenau* repaired, the *Kriegsmarine* would be able to face the British Home Fleet on more equal terms. He recognized, however, that political and military considerations might have to overrule naval concerns and that it might be vital to finish the business in 1940. That being the case, the Navy would prefer it if the landing could be on a narrow front – say, ten regimental groups in the Folkestone area. The *Wehrmacht* must realize that if they insisted on the very wide front they had postulated it would be very difficult to protect the convoys during the unloading period which, he calculated, would take thirty-six hours. Losses at that stage, both in time and ships, would make the transport of the second wave very difficult.

Hitler would not agree to postponement until 1941, on the grounds that it would give Britain more time to prepare her defences, but he agreed that the dislocation of Baltic and inland shipping must be accepted. In addition, he said that he would give orders to the *Luftwaffe* to open their main offensive against Britain and the future of *Sealion* would depend on their success. Meanwhile all preparations were to be pressed forward.

Since the rest of the conference was to deal with army matters, Raeder then left and Hitler, alone with his generals, first, almost casually, approved their broad-front strategy for a landing and went

on to reveal his plan for an attack on Russia as a way of defeating
Britain:

> We must eliminate Britain's hopes, which are based on Russia
> and America. If her expectations of Russia fail, America too will
> fall out as the elimination of Russia increases Japan's threat to
> the United States in the east. . . . If Russia is smashed, Britain's
> last hope is gone. . . . The sooner we smash Russia the better.
> . . . Five months will see the end of it.

The Army chiefs were much taken aback by this extreme example
of the Strategy of the Indirect Approach. They saw, far better than
their master, the problems involved in conquering a country as vast
as Russia which could defend itself merely by retreating into its own
inner vastness. The prospect greatly increased their enthusiasm for
undertaking *Sealion*, since, if they were to be forced to drive deep into
Russia, they did not wish to have the British snapping at their rear.

Meanwhile the British were tightening their belts. On 23 July an
interim budget was introduced in the Commons. Income tax was
increased by one shilling (5p) to a rate of $42^1/_2\%$, with higher rates for
surtax. The price of twenty cigarettes went up by a penny to around 8p.
2p was added to the cost of a bottle of wine and 4p to port and sherry,
both of which were becoming more difficult to obtain. Purchase tax at
$33^1/_3\%$ was introduced on a wide range of goods.

9

'Wipe the British Air Force from the Sky'

On 1 August OKW circulated to the heads of services the conclusions of the conference on the previous day, although no mention was made of the invasion of Russia. Preparations for *Sealion* were to be completed by 15 September and, as a preliminary, the *Luftwaffe* was to begin the air offensive against England on the earliest possible day after 5 August.

> After eight or at the most fourteen days . . . the Führer will decide, in accordance with the results of the air attack, whether *Sealion* is to be undertaken this year.
>
> Should the decision be *against* undertaking *Sealion* in September, all preparations will be continued but in such a form as to avoid damage to the economy by the paralysis on inland water traffic. Planning is to continue, for the time being, for an attack on a broad front despite the Navy's belief that it can only protect the operation on a narrow front.

On the same day Directive No.17 appeared over Hitler's signature:

> In order to prepare for the final conquest of Britain, the air and naval war against the British homeland is to be intensified.
>
> For this purpose I issue the following orders:-
>
> I. The *Luftwaffe* is to use all means at its disposal to overcome the British air force in the shortest time possible. They will concentrate their attacks on the aircraft, their ground installations and supply organisations. In addition the aircraft industry, including factories for anti-aircraft material, is to be attacked.
>
> II. Once temporary or local air superiority has been achieved, attacks will be directed against ports, especially those used for importing food, and against food supply installations in the interior of the country. Only small-scale attacks will be made on harbours in the south in view of our projected operations.
>
> III. Attacks on warships and merchant shipping should be

undertaken only if highly advantageous targets present themselves.

IV. In undertaking these operations the *Luftwaffe* must remain ready to support the *Kriegsmarine* in adequate strength against advantageous targets. It must also retain sufficient strength to support *Sealion*.

V. I reserve the right to order retaliatory terror raids.

These two documents of 1 August show a highly ambivalent attitude towards invasion. Though Hitler himself had recognized that total domination of the air was a prerequisite, the *Luftwaffe* was told that only 'temporary or local air supremacy' was needed. Lip service is paid to *Sealion* by forbidding the heavy bombing of south coast ports – though Dover seems to have been an exception – but the *Luftwaffe* is discouraged from attacking British warships, which were the force most likely to make landing impossible. Similarly the *Kriesgmarine*'s arguments against a broad-front landing are noted but disregarded. It is hard not to feel sorry for Grand Admiral Raeder whose understrength navy was required to do the impossible with no help from the other services.

While Hitler was postponing *Sealion* until mid-September, Britain was expecting the onslaught to begin at any moment. In Churchill's private office John Colville heard on 31 July that the Secret Service had

> received news of imminent invasion from over 260 sources. The main attack will be against the South, with diversions against Hull, Scotland and Ireland, which will be exploited if successful. Parachutists will be used only in the South. It is clear that all preparations have been made; whether they will be used depends on Hitler's caprice.

Two weeks later, Commander-in-Chief Home Forces wrote in his diary that the War Office

> called up early to inform me that the Admiralty had received accurate information that the Germans in Norway had embarked on the night of the 11th [August] and that they expected invasion in the north.

On the same day, Vice Admiral Ramsay, commanding at Dover, wrote:

> Shortly after 0600 hours a signal from Admiralty indicated that the threatened invasion might be under way; this was

quickly followed by another ordering all available vessels to raise steam. Very soon afterwards the RDF [Radar] plots showed a very large number of aircraft assembling in the vicinity of Calais. Information was received from Fighter Command of an impending air battle on a very large scale, with a request that every rescue craft might be at immediate notice. At 0715, the barrage balloons were attacked and four shot down. This was not surprising as these particular balloons were being flown above a thick layer of cloud which prevented the attackers from being seen, so that no fire was opened on them.

At 0740 a trawler was sunk by dive bombers. . . .

At 1003 ships were reverted to normal notice.

In Berlin Dr Goebbels was devising ways of putting the British into a fright and on 5 August his instructions were:

Propaganda against Britain must be stepped up over the next few days even more than in the past, and the secret transmitters must try to achieve the maximum effect. In this connection the Minister praises the Air Raid Precaution transmissions [see p 116] and suggests that gas defence programmes should now be broadcast, and fear promoted of accidents in connection with Air Raid Precaution classes.

Three days later he instructed the Director of Overseas Broadcasting:

to keep handy for the secret transmitters a British report that 100,000 British uniforms fell into our hands at Dunkirk. At the right moment the transmitters should broadcast the story that parachutists have been dropped over Britain in these uniforms.

The right moment was judged to have come on the night of 13 August when a large number of unmanned parachutes were released over Derbyshire, Yorkshire and Scotland. On 15 August the *Daily Telegraph* reported that seventeen parachutes had been found near a small market town in the Midlands but no parachutists or crashed aircraft had been found in the vicinity.

In the early morning members of the Home Guard saw a parachute with no occupant land in a field. Church bells were rung in the district. The parachutes were said to be capable of bearing a weight of 400 lbs. They were complete with harness and haversack.

This was not the first news available of the occurrence, as, on 14 August, before the news became known even to the authorities, the supposedly clandestine New British Broadcasting Service announced that parachutists 'in civilian clothes or British uniforms' had landed near Birmingham, Manchester and Glasgow and were being sheltered by Fifth Columnists. They ran the story for about a week, adding the detail that in the surrounding confusion three policemen had been accidentally shot.

This incident aroused little reaction in Britain and on 16 August the *Telegraph* told its readers that seventy or eighty parachutes had been dropped, adding,

> It is evident that the whole incident was organised by the Germans partly for the purpose of spreading alarm . . . and partly as an aid to their defeatist propaganda.

This explanation failed to satisfy one of their readers who wrote:

> The principal aim of the dropping of the parachutes by the enemy in the Midlands and North was to ascertain the time lag between dropping and discovery as a test for possible operations. This information we have obligingly given them over the air.

The disinclination of the British to panic at this stage must have been a sad disappointment to Dr Goebbels but his analysts may have found some consolation in advertisements for 'Bob Martin's Fit and Hysteria Powders in special ARP cartons to calm dogs and cats in air raids', and for 'The Belling Bomb Snuffer for Incendiary Bombs. Only 12/6d [62^1/$_2$p].' The fact was that, as the veteran Alexander Kerensky told reporters when he reached New York on 13 August, 'The British morale is wonderful and in strong contrast to the French.'

Quite why this was so is scarcely explicable in rational terms. On the face of it, Britain's situation was as perilous as ever, but the people had regained their confidence. No rain of bombs had yet fallen and they were genuinely uplifted by Churchill's speeches and, over-optimistically, they felt that they were striking back at the enemy. According to an American correspondent:

> The success of the RAF raids on Germany continues to do excellent things to the British morale. . . . It also seems certain that the British fliers' night navigation is better than the Germans and it is easier to find their objectives on the continent, where roads are long and straight and where the rivers and big towns are unmistakable landmarks, than in England, where the crooked and

ambling roads, the straggling towns and the jumble of absolutely identical fields and hedgerows are a navigator's nightmare.

Although they felt obliged to forbid 'any person without authority [to send] a message by homing pigeon', the British Government were regaining their nerve and began to release Category C aliens from internment. One of them, on her way back from the Isle of Man, told the *Telegraph*, 'We had a lovely time'. On 2 August Colonel William J. Donovan, over on a fact-finding mission for President Roosevelt, was laying 'odds of 60–40 that the British will beat off the German attack'. The US Military Attaché thought the chances 'a little better, say 2 to 1, barring some magical secret weapon'. The War Cabinet was sufficiently confident to release a regiment each of cruiser, infantry and light tanks for the Middle East, together with sufficient 25-pounders to equip a field regiment and twenty light anti-aircraft guns. This meant parting with one third of the heaviest tanks in Britain and may well mark the moment at which Churchill stopped believing in the possibility of invasion.

On 8 August Bletchley Park deciphered an Enigma signal from Reichsmarschall Goering to all units in *Luftflotten* II, III and V:

> Operation *Adler*. Within a short time you will wipe the British Air Force from the sky. *Heil Hitler*.

Adler Tag, the day of the Eagle, was originally scheduled as 10 August but both on that day and the next the weather was too bad for anything but the routine skirmishing of the *Kanalkampf*. The forecasters promised better weather to come and *Adler Tag* was rescheduled for 13 August. This left 12 August for a small-scale rehearsal with a substantial raid on Portsmouth and attacks on the forward fighter stations. Manston, Hawkinge and Lympne, the last a small emergency landing ground, were all put out of action for up to twenty-four hours and the radar station at Ventnor on the Isle of Wight was disabled. The *Luftwaffe* claimed to have shot down forty-six Spitfires, twenty-three Hurricanes and one Morane 406. The actual loss was twenty-one fighters and there were no Morane 406 in the United Kingdom. That day cost the *Luftwaffe* thirty-one aircraft of all types.

For his attempt to 'wipe the British air force from the sky' Goering could deploy (figures for 10 August) 875 level-flight bombers, 316 dive bombers, 702 single-engine and 227 twin-engine fighters apart from 45 long-range reconnaissance machines, one of whose key tasks was taking meteorological readings to the west of the British Isles where the Germans could not maintain weather-ships. All these aircraft belonged to *Luftflotten* II and III in France and the Low Countries. *Luftflotte* V in Scandinavia could send to Britain 123 level-flight bombers and thirty-four twin-engined fighters. Against this array Fighter Command could put in the air about 700 planes, almost all of them Spitfires and Hurricanes.

On the revised Eagle Day the first waves of attackers were already airborne when early morning mist persuaded Goering to recall them. This produced confusion as some formations heard the signal and others did not. In the heaviest raid of the morning seventy-four Dornier 17s attacked Eastchurch unescorted, their fighters having heard the signals. As it happened, the defenders misread the bombers' intention and several were able to reach their objective where they did much damage and destroyed five Blenheims on the ground. From the *Luftwaffe*'s point of view it was unfortunate that Eastchurch was a Coastal Command station and thus irrelevant to their overriding aim of destroying Fighter Command. In another potentially heavy raid the reverse situation occurred. Bombers headed for Portland heard their recall but their escort of Me110s flew on to be ambushed by two fighter squadrons. Also during the morning the defence beat off attacks on the airfields at Odiham and Farnborough. There was a series of better coordinated attacks in the afternoon, but, apart from a heavy raid on Southampton docks, serious damage was only done at Detling and Andover, neither of them fighter stations.

The long-awaited air offensive had opened in anti-climax. Although the Germans flew, including some small night raids, 1,485 sorties, they had signally failed to harm Fighter Command though they claimed to have shot down seventy single-engine fighters and destroyed eighteen Blenheims on the ground at Eastchurch. The actual British loss was thirteen fighters and five Coastal Command Blenheim light bombers. The British claimed to have disposed of seventy-eight German aircraft and, although the actual loss was only forty-five, the Stuka dive bomber was shown to be very vulnerable. On the following day cloud over the Channel cut down the scale of attack, only 489 German sorties being flown. Hangars were destroyed at Manston and damage was done at Middle Wallop in Hampshire, which the Germans believed to be

Netheravon, twenty miles away. The day cost the *Luftwaffe* nineteen aircraft and Fighter Command eight.

The forecast of a gloriously fine day over southern England gave the Germans the chance to put the full *Adler Tag* programme into operation on 15 August and all three *Luftflotten* were sent into the attack in the hope of splitting up the opposition. 1,786 sorties were flown in the twenty-four hours, the daylight targets being spread from Newcastle to Portland. A significant point was that only 520 of the raiders were bombers since it was already recognized that two fighters were needed as escort for each bomber. From Scandinavia *Luftflotte V* made its first intervention in the battle and was very severely handled. Expecting to find that the bulk of the single-engined fighters had been drawn away south, they sent over 123 bombers and thirty-four twin-engined fighters only to find themselves opposed by Spitfires and Hurricanes backed by Defiants and Blenheims. At a cost of 12% of their bombers and 20% of their fighters they damaged a bomber field north of Hull and blew up an ammunition dump near Bridlington but did not destroy a single fighter. *Luftflotte V* took no further part in the daylight battle.

Luftflotten II and *III* had more success in the south. They put the landing ground at Lympne out of action for two days, did some damage at Hawkinge and destroyed two Spitfires on the ground at Manston, and heavily attacked Martlesham where they failed to stop operations. They also caused some disruption at the bomber factory at Rochester and made ineffective attacks on four radar stations. There were besides attacks on Middle Wallop (which this time the Germans took to be Andover), West Malling (mistaken for Biggin Hill), Croydon (not yet operational) and the Fleet Air Arm station at Worthy Down, near Winchester. That day Fighter Command claimed 182 German aircraft but the actual loss was seventy-five. The Germans claimed 101 aircraft of which eighty-seven were fighters, but in fact destroyed only thirty-four fighters.

During the day Goering held a conference for the *Luftflotten* commanders engaged and urged them to concentrate attacks 'exclusively on the enemy air force, including the aircraft industry'. He proposed that attacks on radar stations should be discontinued since 'none of those attacked has been put out of action'. In view of the mounting losses, he decreed that no air crew should contain more than one officer and, since he believed that 'the enemy is concentrating his fighters against our Stuka operations', he ruled that every *Gruppe* (wing) of dive bombers should be escorted by three *Gruppen* of fighters.

16 August was another fine day and the *Luftwaffe* sent over 1,715 sorties and achieved somewhat better results than on the previous day, damaging fourteen aircraft, including seven Hurricanes, on the ground at Tangmere and putting West Malling out of action for four days. At Ventnor the radar station was again damaged but the gap in the chain was plugged by the introduction of a mobile apparatus. There were also attacks, more or less severe, on a number of stations belonging to other commands – Gosport, Lee-on-Solent, Harwell, Farnborough and Brize Norton, at the last of which forty-six training aircraft were destroyed. This was the day on which Fighter Command won the first, and surprisingly the last, Victoria Cross during the Battle of Britain. Flight Lieutenant J.B. Nicholson, on his first day in combat, had his Hurricane hit and set on fire over the Solent when he saw an Me110 in his sights. Although the skin on his hands was already blistering from the heat, he shot the enemy down before taking to his parachute. On landing he was wounded by an over-enthusiastic Home Guard.

Having lost forty-five planes that day, the *Luftwaffe* claimed to have shot down ninety-two British machines, although Fighter Command had actually lost only twenty-one, apart from the seven Hurricanes damaged at Tangmere. Both sides implicitly believed their own claims for enemy losses but this was less important for the British since they had started with a considerable over-estimate of the *Luftwaffe*'s strength. The Germans not only believed their own claims but added an optimistic gloss to them. On 17 August *Luftwaffe* Intelligence issued an estimate of the remaining strength of their adversary:

> In the period 1 July to 15 August, the enemy loss in fighters, in the air and on the ground has been confirmed as:
>
> | | |
> |---|---|
> | Spitfires | 373 |
> | Hurricanes | 180 |
> | Curtis Hawks | 9 |
> | Defiants | 12 |
>
> To this total of 574 fighters destroyed should be added at least 196 machines damaged beyond repair in accidents. Thus the enemy has lost 770 fighters. 270–300 fighters were built during this period so that the overall reduction in strength can be estimated at about 470. On 1 July there were 900 modern fighters in the squadrons, thus there would be 430 available on 16 August. Only 70% of

these will be serviceable so that there will now be some 300 aircraft available for operations.

Unconfirmed but previously reliable reports indicate that these aircraft are disposed as follows:

South of the line Wash–Bristol Channel	200
Midlands	70
Northern England and Scotland	30

This essay in wishful thinking was wrong in almost every particular, starting with an over-estimate of Fighter Command's strength on 1 July, which was 791 rather than 900. Since then the combined loss of Spitfires, Hurricanes and Defiants was only 318 rather than 574 claimed and apart from the ninety-two claimed on 16 August. Further to confuse the issue, the estimate of the production of new fighters was less than half the truth, 720 having been passed for service, rather than the 270–300 postulated. On 17 August the serviceable strength of Fighter Command was not 300 but 672, of which 570 were Spitfires and Hurricanes. Behind these were 289 planes ready for immediate issue and eighty-four more were in Operational Training Units.

Although Fighter Command's situation was far better than the *Luftwaffe* imagined, it was far from satisfactory. The publicly announced and wholly honest figures for Spitfires and Hurricanes lost in battle took no account of machines damaged in combat or lost in accidents and, despite heroic work by the repair services, the margin between supply and consumption was, at best, narrow. Even more serious was the supply of pilots. Pre-war economies and the high standard demanded combined to ensure that there was no large reserve of trained men to take the places of those killed or taken out of the fight by wounds for longer or shorter periods. On 8 August Fighter Command had been 160 pilots below establishment and in the following eleven days ninety-four had been killed and sixty wounded. Since the training units could not produce more than fifty pilots a week, a serious shortage was inevitable. The Fleet Air Arm, apart from putting two squadrons of Fulmars under command of Fighter Command, seconded fifty-eight pilots to fly Spitfires and Hurricanes, while the squadrons of Coastal Command and Army Co-operation also made contributions. Rather reluctantly Bomber Command permitted twenty volunteers from the Battle squadrons which had been decimated in France to transfer to fighters. These could only be palliative moves and it was clear that if the fighting went on at the level that had followed

Adler Tag there would be insufficient pilots to man the planes available. To make matters worse, fatigue was becoming a serious problem among the survivors, some of whom were flying three or four sorties a day.

Fortunately fatigue and shortages were also affecting the *Luftwaffe* and the number of attacks diminished. Between 13 and 16 August Fighter Command averaged 736 sorties daily but in the following seven days the average fell to 492, far from a rest period but at least a slight relaxation of pressure on the pilots and their controllers. In that week only thirty-eight British fighters and 106 German aircraft were lost. The heaviest fighting of the week was on Sunday 18 August when the *Luftwaffe* tried a new technique of low-flying attacks on airfields and achieved a measure of success against the Fighter Command stations at Kenley, Biggin Hill and the newly operational Croydon, in addition to Coastal Command's Thorney Island and the Fleet Air Arm bases at Ford and Gosport. Twenty-seven British fighters were lost that day, the German losses being claimed as 153. In fact the *Luftwaffe* lost only seventy-one but that was sufficiently serious to convince Goering that new tactics must be tried. The Stukas were withdrawn from the battle and relegated to their next role as artillery for *Sealion*.

Two days later Winston Churchill paid his famous tribute to 'the British airmen who, undaunted by odds, unwearied in their constant challenge and mortal danger, are turning the tide of war by their prowess and by their devotion. . . . Never in the field of human conflict was so much owed by so many to so few.' In the same speech he said:

> The enemy is, of course, far more numerous than we are. But our new production already . . . exceeds his, and the American production is only just beginning to flow in. Our bomber and fighter strength now, after all this fighting, are larger than they have ever been. We believe we shall be able to continue the air struggle indefinitely and as long as the enemy pleases.

On the same day *Luftwaffe* Intelligence produced another dose of self-deception, giving an estimate that, between 12 and 19 August, they had destroyed 644 British aircraft and that in the first five of those days they had rendered eleven British airfields permanently unusable, had severely damaged twelve more and done lesser damage to twenty-one. The fact was that only two airfields had had to be closed for any substantial period, and of the eleven fields they believed they had destroyed only five were actually fighter stations.

134

By this time the people of Britain were regarding the duel between Fighter Command and the *Luftwaffe* as some spectacular sporting event, avidly following the reports of the number of planes shot down each day as if they were the close of play scores in a timeless test match. Belief in the totals announced by the Air Ministry was as complete as was the scorn poured on the counter-claims from Berlin. There was one justification for this since the Germans doctored their claims in a way that the British did not. After the heavy fighting on 15 August, as has been seen, the RAF claimed 180 German planes against a true figure of seventy-six but Berlin admitted only twenty-nine losses. While the British claims were inadvertently exaggerated, those of the Germans seem to have been deliberately inflated. In the period 10 July to 31 October British claims were 55% above the truth, those of the Germans 234%.

It was something quite new for thousands of people, living in comparative security, to be able to watch the rival champions fighting and dying above their heads, to be able to see war in progress. At a time when vapour trails were something of a novelty, the *Daily Telegraph* informed its readers on 20 August;

> By making smoke rings and trails over towns in Britain, German pilots are aiding navigation for bombers.

Four days earlier the *Dover Express* had reported another by-product of air warfare:

> The Ministry of Transport has made an order prohibiting, as from 26 August, the use on the highway by any unauthorised person of any vehicle so painted or otherwise treated as to resemble a camouflaged vehicle. . . . The Ministry advises the use of any neutral colour other than greys and khaki adopted by the Services. Glossy and bright colours should be avoided.
> A method advocated by the British Industrial Design Group is that one half of the car, divided longitudinally, should be painted to harmonise with the country, and the other half with the town. If there is an air attack in the country the car is driven up against a hedge or bushes so that the colouring for town is screened. If in town, it is drawn up close to a building or a wall so that the half intended to harmonise with the country is screened.

The Battle of Britain was not the only activity over the island at this time. Since June German bombers had ranged over the country, partly on reconnaissance and partly on what Goering described as 'dislocation raids, made so that the enemy defences and population shall be allowed no respite'. The Thames estuary and Merseyside were favourite targets but small numbers of bombs were dropped as far afield as Plymouth, South Wales and Aberdeen. The *Luftwaffe* were insistent that they were attacking only military targets, but, as with the RAF over the Rühr, more bombs fell in open fields than on buildings and few hit their intended targets. London was deliberately avoided, although a few bombs fell on outlying suburbs. It is arguable that the Germans had even less excuse than the RAF for dropping their bombs in the wrong place for, unlike Bomber Command which had resolutely declined to experiment with electronic aids to navigation, the *Luftwaffe* had the assistance of the *Knickebein* beams which were capable of guiding them to their objective. These beams had been identified in June by Dr R.V. Jones and from mid-August they could be bent and confused by counter-measures.

While Goering was trying to make good his boast to 'wipe the British air force from the sky', the other German services were pressing on with their preparations for *Sealion*. The *Wehrmacht*, which had been lukewarm in support of a Channel crossing, swung over to being enthusiastic supporters. The Operations Division of the *Kriegsmarine* noted with something approaching horror:

> It appears that OKH, which a short time ago was strongly
> opposed to such an operation, has put aside its doubts and
> regards the landing as perfectly practicable although ignorant
> of the difficulties which the shipping will face and the problems
> of protecting it. Nor does it realise the great dangers facing the
> troops taking part. On our part, the *Kriegsmarine* is in no doubt
> that, should the enemy act correctly, the success of the landing
> will be very doubtful.

The assault wave of troops was being moved to the coast and the soldiers were busy practising embarkation and landing from such transports and barges as were available. Some were being given rifle practice on swinging frames which would, it was hoped, reproduce the swaying movements of a barge on the waves of the Channel. The Army Command, though constantly irritated when its careful plans were disrupted by naval objections based on such abtruse factors as tides, currents and the time it would take to unload transports into small boats, were becoming optimistic about the chances of success. They did have their disappointments. Their plan for a huge tank which would crawl across the Channel on the seabed was shown to be impractical and up to 15 August they had not succeeded in disembarking a single tank from a barge. They were hopeful that things would improve and were beginning to have success with a snorkel tank that could operate twenty-five feet under water.

The *Kriegsmarine* were doing all and more than could be expected of them. They had not managed to lay their hands on all the sea transport for which they had hoped, but they had got enough to land a substantial force. It amounted to 155 cargo ships totalling 700,000 tons, 1,277 barges and lighters with 471 tugs or steam trawlers to tow them. There were also 1,161 small motor-driven craft. The barges were being fitted with concrete floors, ramps and drawbridges to enable them to carry vehicles, including armoured cars, and fifty self-propelled barges were being adapted so that each could carry two medium tanks which, it was hoped, could be disembarked over ramps on the side. Cargo ships and barges had been specially fitted to accommodate the large number of horses that would be required. A bare minimum of this great fleet was brought forward to the Channel ports so that the Army could practise amphibious operations but, for the most part, it was held in German ports or, in the case of barges, in the canal system in greater safety from British bombing. It would not be brought forward to the embarkation harbours until it was required.

Another naval responsibility was the coastal guns, Hitler's favourite weapon. A battery of four 11″ guns was installed near Cap Gris Nez early in August and fired some ranging shots on 12 August. Soon afterwards three 12″ guns were in position near Boulogne and from 22 August both batteries opened a fairly constant fire, weather permitting, mostly on the coastal convoys. Spotting, except in the clearest weather, was difficult and, since the delay between firing and the fall of shot was thirty-two seconds, even a convoy at five or six knots made a difficult target*. The guns, which were added to in September, could reach Dover, Folkestone and Deal.

Planning was still bedevilled by the controversy between the Army and the Navy on the width of the front of attack. After Raeder had

* Between 1940 and 1944 German coastal guns in the Strait of Dover only damaged seven merchant ships (totalling 8,000 tons) and sank none.

proposed a narrow-front landing near Beachy Head, the two Chiefs of Staff tried to resolve the dispute on 7 August but no progress was made. For the Army, General Halder declared, 'I utterly reject the naval proposal which I regard as suicidal from the military point of view. I might just as well put the assault wave straight through a sausage machine.' His naval counterpart, Admiral Schniewind, retorted that, in view of British naval superiority, 'It would be equally suicidal to land on a wide front.' In an attempt to break the deadlock, Raeder went to see Hitler and advised him that:

> Since both the naval strength and the available shipping are inadequate it would be advisable to launch *Sealion* only as a last resort if Britain cannot be forced to make peace by other means.

According to the naval record of the meeting, Hitler agreed, remarking that Britain would gain great prestige if the landing was beaten back. He would not, however, give any decision, saying that he would make up his mind when the effects of the air offensive were clear. In the meanwhile he would have more talks with von Brauchitsch.

The result of these talks was not very satisfactory to the Navy. The Army agreed to abandon the most westerly landing area, that in Lyme Bay, but still called for beachheads stretching from Folkestone to Selsey Bill, an extent far beyond the *Kriegsmarine*'s capabilities. This was embodied in an OKW order on 15 August which, once again, called for proposals for 'the possible employment of parachute and airborne troops'. Even now it could not be used as a firm basis for planning as one paragraph read:

> Dispositions should be made so as to leave open the possibility of attacking on a narrow front, should this be decided on at the last moment. There could also be a single landing in the Brighton area.

Such vagueness at a time when the launching date for the operation was only a month ahead was satisfactory to no one and matters were not improved when, a few days later, OKW came up with another suggestion – that there should be a concentrated landing on a narrow front near Folkestone and, simultaneously, an assault by four or five thousand men in motorboats in the Deal-Ramsgate area supported by the same number of airborne troops.

This sent von Brauchitsch back to Hitler after which there appeared a supposedly final plan dated 27 August which called for four landing areas:

Folkestone   –   Dungeness
Dungeness   –   Cliff End
Bexhill   –   Beachy Head
Brighton   –   Selsey Bill

As if this scheme did. not sufficiently overstrain the Navy's meagre resources, they were called upon to undertake two diversionary manoeuvres. The pocket battleship *Admiral Scheer* was to break out into the Atlantic on a commerce raid to divert heavy ships of the Home Fleet and, with the same end in view, the remaining cruisers were, two days after the landings in the south, to escort four large liners to the area east of Scotland and then retreat hastily to the Kattegat. This must have been the low point in Raeder's summer since, at about the same time, he was learning that the *Kriegsmarine's* greatest single asset had been lost. Since the outbreak of war they had been able to read the Royal Navy's operational codes. This fact had at last become clear to the Admiralty and they were changed on 20 August.

The *Luftwaffe* took no part in the Army-Navy arguments about the beachhead. Goering was preoccupied with his assault on the RAF which, he believed, would make *Sealion* superfluous. Kesselring, whose *Luftflotte II* would have to bear the main burden of supporting the landing, complained:

> I was left in the dark about the relation of the current air raids on
> England and the invasion plan; no orders were issued to the chiefs
> of *Luftflotten*. I received no definite instructions about what my
> command could look forward to in the way of tactical assignments
> or how we were to co-operate with the Army and Navy.

Up to the end of August the only instructions given to the *Luftwaffe* about *Sealion* were that, on the day before the landings, they were to make a mass attack on London so as to force the population to flee the city and choke the surrounding roads.

That Berlin believed such a mass panic possible is demonstrated by the orders given to his staff by Goebbels on 17 August:

> The important thing now is to intensify the mood of panic which
> is undoubtedly gaining ground in Britain. The secret transmitters
> . . . have the task of depicting the magnitude and volume of
> our attacks for that part of the population which has not yet

experienced the frightful effect of our air raids. . . . We must continue to emphasize that even the present attacks are only a foretaste of what is to come. . . . Reports from the London correspondents of [American] papers are already reflecting an incipient change in the mood of Britain.

There is little doubt that Goebbels believed that his broadcasts were having the effect he intended, since on 21 August he directed that Lord Haw Haw should be given 'a few cases of good cigars as a token of the minister's recognition [for his work] because it is based so entirely on the British point of view and uses British arguments.'

Meanwhile the British, who were showing few signs of panic or any other emotion except pride in their fighter pilots, were muddling along as best they could. Churchill inadvertently caused some confusion when he directed that the threatened invasion should be referred to as Operation *Smith*, since the German codeword had not yet been gleaned from the Enigma traffic. It so happened that a minor administrative branch of the War Office had been evacuated to Gloucestershire under the codeword *Smith* and all information reaching the War Office main building with that prefix was promptly forwarded to a bewildered officer near Tetbury who, recognizing its secret nature, conscientiously locked it in his safe and kept it there.

False alarms continued to proliferate. On 18 August the Press Association put out a report, cleared by the censor, that,

Five divisions of enemy troops reported to be massed on French beaches opposite south east coast, ready to be embarked for an attempted invasion, were bombed on Saturday [17th] and again today.

Hardly had this item reached the newspapers when the PA announced that no confirmation of this story could be obtained from official sources and an hour later the Air Ministry declared that the report of bombing was untrue. On 23 August the Combined Intelligence Committee, charged with giving warning of invasion, reported soothingly:

No serious threat of invasion yet exists from the Netherlands, France or the south-west Norwegian ports. This is evidenced by the lack of shipping concentrations on these coasts.

Despite this reassurance the naval War Diary for Dover recorded on 25 August:

During the night considerable disturbance was caused at Dover and at other places as a result of a report from a Portsmouth patrol to the effect that off Beachy Head he had encountered an unusual bank of fog with a smoky smell. As a result the Admiralty ordered all vessels from Harwich to Falmouth to raise steam, and the Army stood to all round the coast.

Things reverted to normal a few hours later but not before the cruisers *Galatea* and *Cardiff* had been despatched to the Humber from Scapa Flow and three motor torpedo boats had made an abortive sweep to the mouth of the Scheldt. On the following night church bells were rung in County Durham and both regulars and Home Guard went on full alert as the police were convinced that parachutists had landed.

24 August saw one of those mistakes, so common in war, which change the course of campaigns. About a hundred German bombers were despatched on disruptive raids which ranged from Tyneside to Cardiff, from Portland to Rochester. A dozen of them were ordered to attack aircraft factories at Rochester and Kingston-on-Thames and oil storage tanks at Thameshaven, but a group of them, due to faulty navigation, unloaded their bombs over London. In Bethnal Green a hundred people were made homeless and damage was done to civilian property in Islington, Tottenham, Millwall, Finsbury, Stepney, East Ham, Leyton, Coulsdon and in the City of London where the church of St Giles, Cripplegate, was set on fire. Far heavier damage to civilians was done that night at South Shields but the attack on the heart of London, the first since 1918, roused the country to anger. It could not be known that the bombing was not only inadvertent but directly contrary to Hitler's personal order.

No time was lost in responding. On the following night eighty Hampdens and Wellingtons from Bomber Command set out for Berlin. Few of them reached the city and those that did achieved little or nothing and it was not until a similar raid on the following night that the first casualty was caused. The effect was, nevertheless, considerable. William Shirer, who was in Berlin, wrote of the stunned astonishment of the inhabitants who had believed Goering's assurance that no enemy bomber could reach the city:

The invariable headline about last night's raid is COWARDLY BRITISH ATTACK. And the little *Doktor* makes the papers drum into the people that German planes attack only military objectives in Britain whereas the 'British pirates' attack 'on the personal orders of Churchill' only non-military objectives.

The fact was that, even with the best of intentions, the bombers of the two sides were quite incapable of hitting their targets at night. The other side of Goebbels' rhetoric can be found in the words of a correspondent in London:

> Naturally there has been a good deal of hopeful talk this week about retaliatory raids on Berlin, but it is realised that such reprisals, though satisfactory, would do less good than the present devastating RAF raids on German centres of war production. A campaign of destruction of factories, power plants and airdromes is more useful than the German policy of hitting and running where no possible military objective can exist.

10

'A Highly Dangerous Organisation'

A comparative lull, imposed by fatigue and poor weather, followed the heavy air fighting on 18 August. Goering held a further conference of his commanders and urged them to inflict 'the maximum damage on the enemy's fighter forces'.

> The enemy is to be forced to commit his fighters by constant attacks. In addition the aircraft industry and the ground installations of the air force are to be attacked by individual aircraft, by night and day, when the weather forbids the use of large formations.

It remained the *Luftwaffe's* aim to settle the battle by inducing Fighter Command to a series of mass combats between fighters, a series the Germans were likely to win since they had more single-engine fighters and the Me109 was superior to the Hurricane. They had only to inflict casualties equal to their own to clear the skies for their bombers.

This danger was seen clearly by Air Vice Marshal Keith Park whose 11 Group covered south-east England from, roughly, Lowestoft to Bournemouth. With the support of Dowding at Fighter Command, he determined that his aircraft must be committed sparingly and selectively. As he laid down on 19 August,

> Our main object is to engage enemy bombers.

This was becoming more difficult to achieve, since, when the battle was resumed at full intensity on 24 August, the Germans had greatly increased the ratio of fighters to bombers and had evolved a technique whereby large numbers of aircraft patrolled the French coast so as to confuse the radar plot and make it difficult to forecast the heavy thrusts which Park's Group would have to counter. Nor were the difficulties lessened by intrigues within Fighter Command. On

Park's left flank was 12 Group whose commander, Air Vice Marshal Leigh-Mallory, abetted by his brilliant but irresponsible subordinate, Squadron Leader Douglas Bader, disapproved of Park's tactics of committing only minimal forces against German thrusts. They pressed for large fighter formations, preferably from 12 Group to be sent to fight it out with the Messerschmitts. They failed to realize that this was precisely what Goering wished them to do and that, whatever success they might have in the 'Numbers Game', the result would be the irretrievable erosion of Fighter Command to a point where it would not be able to function effectively.

The new German offensive was mounted without the assistance of the Stukas and with a much reduced role for the twin-engined Me110, facts which in themselves greatly reduced the number of kills which the RAF was able to make or even to claim. On the other hand, the single-engine Messerschmitt was much in evidence, the Germans making fighter sweeps in large formations in the hope of drawing 11 Group up to challenge them, a temptation which was largely resisted. Nevertheless the two weeks which followed 24 August were the most perilous of the year and the balance of advantage swung to the *Luftwaffe*. On 1 September more British fighters (15) were lost than German aircraft of all types and on most days fewer German fighters were lost than British. In that period Fighter Command lost 286 aircraft destroyed and 171 seriously damaged, while only 169 new planes were forthcoming. At the end of August the fighter squadrons could on average muster only sixteen pilots against an establishment of twenty-six. To make matters worse the Germans were beginning to understand the British ground control system and were launching attacks on the all-important sector stations from which the defence was directed. If the *Luftwaffe* should maintain the same rate of attrition it must soon be doubtful whether the Spitfires and Hurricanes would be able to keep up their forward positions between London and the enemy.

Since the Germans were employing fewer bombers by day behind their heavy fighter escort, they had more bombers available for night raids and between 24 August and 6 September they flew 2,250 night sorties. They had occasional successes – on 1 September they destroyed four 10,000 gallon oil tanks in South Wales – but generally achieved little against significant targets, but between 28 and 31 August they launched a four-night offensive against Merseyside. An average of 157

10. Invasion barge with ramp near Calais.

11. Boulogne harbour with invasion barges.

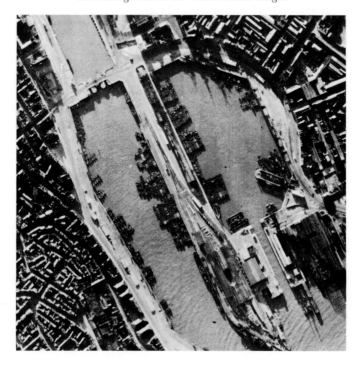

12. Dornier 217s flying up the Thames on 7 September
for the first onslaught on London.

13. General view of Mers-el-Kebir shortly before 3 July.

bombers were despatched each night and, of a total of 629 aircraft, 448 claimed to have found their target, dropping there 455 tons of high explosive and 1,029 canisters of incendiaries. This minor *blitzkrieg* was a failure and it was not until the fourth night that the British realized that Merseyside was the principal objective. On the first night there was no more than sporadic bombing in the suburbs of Liverpool and on the second, when the pilots claimed to have dropped 130 tons of high explosive, barely fifty tons fell in the Mersey area and those mostly in outlying districts. On the final night the commercial district of Liverpool was heavily hit, 160 fires being started, but the docks, the main objective, were almost unscathed. The Germans, relying on pilot reports, believed they had seriously disrupted the vital port.

Two days before the Merseyside blitz started, German bombers had dropped eight bombs in County Wexford in the south-east corner of neutral Ireland, at least sixty miles from the nearest British territory, and it was quite clear, to everyone except senior airmen, that, unless fires could be started in daylight to give a precise aiming mark, accurate bombing by night was an impossibility. Equally demonstrated was the impotence of the defence at night. Only seven of more than 600 planes flown against Merseyside were lost and there was no evidence that any of them fell to British action. British night fighters were, like their German counterparts, incapable of intercepting in darkness and while anti-aircraft guns and balloons could keep the raiders flying high the result was only to make the bombing more haphazard than it would otherwise have been.

On 30 August the *Wehrmacht* produced a 'final' plan (to which many modifications were subsequently made) for *Sealion*. The aim was stated as:

> The Army's landing force will first establish local bridgeheads with the specially equipped spearheads of the first-wave divisions. These bridgeheads will then be extended into a connected zone which will cover the landing of the follow-up echelons and secure command of the English shore. When sufficient troops are ashore an attack will be delivered towards the first operational objective, the line Thames estuary – heights south of London – Portsmouth. . . . Once this objective is secured, the Army will defeat the enemy forces still holding out in southern England, occupy London and establish itself on the line Maldon [Essex] – Severn Estuary.

Nine divisions, apart from airborne troops, were to comprise the first wave and, apart from those on the left flank, each was to land with two regimental groups, each including tank detachments and eight mountain guns, forward. These assault groups which would number about 3,300 men apiece who were to receive two weeks' amphibious training on the French coast should suitable craft be available.

The right-hand part of the front, stretching from Hythe to Cliff End (east of Hastings), was entrusted to General Ernst Busch's Sixteenth Army which was to have under command three battalions of U-Tanks, Mark III panzers equipped with snorkels. On the extreme right was XIII Corps which would put 17 Division ashore between Hythe and Dymchurch and 35 Division between Dymchurch and Dungeness. On their left VII Corps would land 7 Division on Camber Sands, near Rye, while 1 Mountain Division would storm ashore at Cliff End. The assault wave would embark at Antwerp and Calais with their supports coming from Rotterdam and the Hook of Holland.

The westerly assault was in the hands of Ninth Army (General Adolf Strauss) whose XXXVIII Corps (34 and 26 Divisions) were to land at Bexhill and Pevensey. They, like 6 Mountain Division, which was to land at Cuckmere Haven, and parts of 8 Division, detailed to seize Newhaven, would embark at Boulogne and Étaples. On the extreme left a detachment from 28 Division was to sail from Le Havre and attempt to make its way ashore at Rottingdean. Once ashore the boundary between Sixteenth and Ninth Armies was to run through Hastings and Reigate.

A second wave of nine divisions, including four armoured and the equivalent of three motorised divisions, was stationed near and to the east of Paris 'so deployed that from 15 September onwards they can be assembled within three days' to embark at Rotterdam, Antwerp or Boulogne. There were also six infantry divisions for the third wave. 'Where and when it will be possible to embark them will not be known in the early stages. They must therefore be so deployed that their leading units can reach the most suitable ports within three marches.'

Both Sixteenth and Ninth Armies were under the command of Field-Marshall Gerd von Rundstedt's Army Group A but, further to the west, another crossing had been pencilled in:

> If the naval situation develops favourably, Army Group C,
> starting from Cherbourg, may be employed later to force an
> air and sea landing in Lyme Bay and to occupy Weymouth and

the high ground twenty kilometres north of Lyme Regis [i.e. the area Crewkerne – Chard]. Further advance in the direction of Bristol would be made on orders from OKH. At a later stage elements of the Army Group may be instructed to occupy Devon and Cornwall.

No shipping could be allocated to Army Group C but their troops were ordered to be at five days' readiness to embark.

Knowing that naval support would be very limited, OKH was understandably concerned about fire support on the crossing, at the landing and once ashore:

> It is the responsibility of the troops to arm barges and tugs with weapons of all kinds to the extent that the naval authorities have not been able to do. . . . The curtain of fire from the sea to support the troops as they land will be supplemented by the guns of the naval ships (minesweepers etc).

It was intended to get eight batteries of medium guns across as soon as possible but, as with all the transport arrangements for supporting troops, the timings could not be fixed in advance. Everything must depend on the speed at which the barges of the first wave could be refloated and returned and, indeed, on how many would be in a state to return.

The assault troops were warned to expect 'bitter fighting and heavy counter-attacks' and the orders stressed that small detachments, even if isolated, must hold their ground until reinforcements arrived:

> Men and weapons must be ferried across as rapidly as possible and in as large numbers as possible even at the price of losing organic cohesion. Battle groups suitable for the tasks called for must be formed. . . . Each unit in the assault wave must be organised so that, once landed, it can operate independently whatever its size. Commanders of all units will accompany their first line troops.

The first wave of Sixteenth Army would consist of 40,000 men and their first task would be to occupy a line from 'the high ground between Folkestone and Canterbury' [the area around the villages of Barham and Waltham], through Ashford to the hills around Hawkhurst. From there the line would be continued by Ninth Army who would take up their positions through Uckfield and Lewes. In the orders of 30 August the left flank would be placed 'ten kilometres north of Worthing', in the area of Steyning and Washington, but this was quickly seen to

147

be impracticable and modified so that the flank guard would be on Newmarket Hill, between Rottingdean and Fulmer.

There are some strange silences in these orders. While the position of the left flank is pinpointed, nothing is said about securing the right flank or about capturing the vital port of Dover through which all the heavy equipment, in particular the main bodies of the panzer divisions, would have to come. The naval circumstances made it inevitable that 'the loading of the shipping for the second and subsequent journeys cannot be rigidly determined in advance', but, with only three weeks to go to the landing of the first wave, it might have been supposed that the timing of the landing might have been decided.

> Separate orders will follow regarding the *time* of the landing. The intention is to land at first light. Weather and tides may, however, necessitate a landing in daylight. Should that be the case, smoke from aircraft, ships and artillery will be used on a large scale.

This indecision arose from the long-running controversy between the Army and the Navy, with the Army insisting on debarkation at first light so as to have darkness for the approach, and the Navy concerned about navigation. As Raeder pointed out:

> Large numbers of slow and unwieldy transport units concentrated in a small space, mixed with motor-boats of the most varied types, and escorted by light units of the navy and auxiliary vessels, make it necessary to have a certain amount of light for navigational reasons.

No decision had been reached about the employment of airborne troops, which came under *Luftwaffe* control. It was thought that five parachute battalions would be available with a lift of transport planes sufficient to drop 4,000 men. The Army's plan was to employ most of these in the hills north of Dover to assist in the capture of that port but they also hoped that some could be spared for the seizure of Brighton and, if possible, for a landing near Beachy Head in support of the Cuckmere Haven landing. The *Luftwaffe*, however, insisted that 7 *Flieger Division* should be used as an entity and that it should be dropped close to the seaborne landings in case it should be overwhelmed in isolation. It was then proposed, probably by General Busch, that it should land close to the right wing of Sixteenth Army. Busch must have seen that, once his troops were ashore, their main difficulty would be the Royal Military Canal, sixty feet wide and unfordable, which ran in a great semi-circle from Hythe to Cliff

148

End, being, for much of its course, dominated by high ground on the far bank. Landing 7 *Flieger* in the Sandling – Etchinghill area, north of Hythe, would give a bridgehead across the canal and assist in seizing the battered airstrip at Lympne. General Richard Putzier, who commanded the airborne forces while Student recovered from his wounds, was not happy about this plan and no decision about it was reached until late in September. Equally Putzier's study of air photographs convinced him that the obstacles dug or constructed on every open space would make the landing of gliders, to say nothing of transport planes, unduly hazardous and it was decided to retain the air-portable division in OKH reserve.

The sea transport fleet could not be described as agile. The basic unit was a tug or steam trawler towing two barges each capable of carrying 300 men, the unit being known as a *Schleppzug* (tug-train). The assault wave for VII Corps alone amounted to 100 *Schleppzugen*, 100 tugs and 200 barges. With them went a large miscellany of small naval craft – mine-sweepers, patrol boats, launches with small vessels adapted to carry artillery. The plan was that each corps convoy should proceed in column with the naval vessels and artillery craft in the right-hand files and the *Schleppzugen* on the left. On reaching a point ten miles off the landing beach, every vessel was to make a ninety degree turn and advance in line towards the coast. This immensely complicated manoeuvre would be controlled by radio, by green light signals and by loud hailers.

According to Sixteenth Army orders each regimental group would move towards the shore with a front rank of naval vessels carrying stormboats, the small assault craft powered by outboard motors which engineers used for river crossings. These would be launched to send the first flight of 250 men ashore. In the second rank, interspersed with naval vessels, would be converted coasters each mounting one 75mm and one 37mm gun. The remaining ranks of vessels would consist of *Schleppzugen*, the tugs slipping their tows as close inshore as they safely could and leaving the barges to make the best of their way to the beach. Since less than half the barges were self-propelled, most would depend on being pushed ashore by motor-boats. As soon as the stormboats had put the assault flight ashore they would begin to operate a shuttle service from the larger vessels lying off. Two hours behind the first wave (*Staffel*) would come the second, that of VII Corps consisting of sixty-five steamers with 130 barges in tow. According to Sixteenth

149

Army calculations the first two *Staffeln* would consist of 110,000 men and 24,500 horses.

Ninth Army's transport arrangements from Boulogne and Étaples were broadly similar, but 28 Division on the extreme left were to make the 85-mile trip from Le Havre to Rottingdean in 300 motor-boats. These would advance in a huge column, twenty boats wide and fifteen deep, at a speed of seven knots, at least twice the speed to be expected from the *Schleppzugen*. Their supports, in steamers, would sail in part from Le Havre and in part from Boulogne.

With their few heavy ships committed to diversions in the North Sea and Atlantic, the *Kriegsmarine* could afford little protection to the convoys. With three ships in dockyards, the strength available was seven destroyers and some twenty torpedo boats*. All these were to be stationed on the west flank, based on Le Havre and Cherbourg. The protection of the northern flank, where the Straits of Dover made mining a less enormous operation, was entrusted to S Boats (known to the British as E Boats). In addition three groups of five submarines were stationed off Plymouth and in the Western Approaches. Six U-Boats were allocated to the North Sea. Four mine barrages were to be laid, starting eight days before S (*Sealion*) Day. One of these was off the Goodwin Sands, two covered the flanks of 28 Division's route from Le Havre to Rottingdean, while the fourth was to run south from Start Point.

The heavy work for *Sealion* had to be undertaken by about 200 small ships, some of them, mine-layers and patrol craft, built for the Navy but mostly requisitioned vessels adapted for war work. On them fell the duties of laying the mine barriers, sweeping and keeping swept the corridors needed for the troop convoys, escorting the unwieldy convoys, not only for the assault landings but for weeks to follow as reinforcements and supplies had to be fed into the beachheads, and to provide the covering fire for the troops as they landed, adding smoke-screens should they prove necessary.

The *Luftwaffe*, on the other hand, were scarcely included in the *Sealion* plan apart from routine references to the need for inter-service liaison. All in all the makeshift, complicated and incomplete plans for the operation underline the truth of Raeder's opinion, given on 29 July,

* The German destroyers were armed with five 12.7cm (5″) guns. The torpedo boats were in two classes of which the larger had three 10.5cm (4.1″) guns and the smaller a single gun of the same calibre.

that 'it seems possible that the first wave might succeed in getting ashore [but that it seemed] certain that the [British] Fleet will inflict a severe defeat on the *Wehrmacht*.'

The Royal Navy was indeed the greatest obstacle to *Sealion*. Even supposing that the major units of the Home Fleet were led away by the German diversions, there was an impressive array of naval strength either within the invasion area or within easy steaming of it. In the Nore Command, based on Sheerness and Harwich, were three light cruisers and thirty destroyers, and three more cruisers were moved to the Humber on 4 September. Although the destroyers had been withdrawn from Dover, up to forty light armed vessels – sloops, gun-boats, minelayers, anti-submarine trawlers and drifters – were based there. At Portsmouth was a light cruiser and a dozen destroyers, while at Plymouth there were not only a cruiser and four destroyers but the battleship *Revenge* with her 15″ guns. By German estimates there were two capital ships at Plymouth, since their aerial reconnaissance had spotted the old target ship *Centurion*, built in 1911 as a dreadnought, and identified her as an active battleship. For the *Kriegsmarine* the prospect could scarcely have been more daunting.

There was no hope of achieving surprise although the OKH orders of 30 August had done their best with the problem.

> The preparations cannot be concealed. In consequence it is most important to use every means to keep the time of the landing and the [location of] the crossing secret.

This was wishful thinking. Since it was conservatively estimated that it would take eight hours to get the convoys out of their harbours and a further ten hours to make the crossing, it was impossible in summer to carry through the whole programme under cover of darkness. Fog or artificial smoke, possibilities which sometimes alarmed the British, would have made navigation through the narrow seas even more chaotic than the *Kriegsmarine* clearly expected it to be even under good conditions.

If, through astonishing good luck or unimaginable British misman-agement, a fair proportion of the first *Staffel* approached the beaches, their prospects would not be very bright. Alan Brooke's 'light line of defenders' on the coast may have been light, but there was a limited number of places at which an invader could hope to land. Between North Foreland and Brighton there were two Territorial divisions, both inexperienced*, and a brigade of regulars hastily brought back from India, with the New Zealanders in immediate reserve. Within less than twenty-four hours' call, stationed south of London, was the southern corps of GHQ Reserve, 1 Armoured Division, 1 Canadian Division and 1 Army Tank Brigade.

It would be hard to put much confidence in the success of an opposed landing at Rottingdean, a mere cleft in the cliffs, and easy to see why OKH proposed a parachute landing on the high ground near Cuckmere Haven where the shape of the ground, a natural amphitheatre, puts troops landing from the sea in an ideal killing ground. At Newhaven it seems possible that a determined assault might get a foothold on the eastern, Seaford, side of the River Ouse, but against any kind of resistance it would have been very difficult to get across the river and storm the fortified heights beyond. The crux of the whole plan must have lain on Romney Marsh. If the Navy could deliver the two divisions of XIII Corps in reasonable order on the featureless seafront between Hythe and Dymchurch they could probably have established a beachhead, but breaking out across the water-intersected marsh and the Royal Military Canal would not have been easy unless the parachutists had successfully landed north of Hythe. General Herbert Loch, commanding 17 Division on the extreme right, seems not to have expected airborne support at this stage since his orders to the two leading regimental groups called for them:

> To break through the enemy's coastal defences between Hythe and Dymchurch . . . and gain the heights just beyond the Military Canal . . . to gain the high ground Postling – Etchinghill [where it had been proposed that 7 *Flieger Division* should land] and to attack Paddlesworth. At the same time to move via Saltwood and seize the fortified sector Sandgate – Folkestone from the west.

Thereafter, with the help of armoured units and parachutists, the division was to move on both Ashford and Dover, but it is interesting that, although all the objectives he gives are north and east of his right flank, his orders for the battalion of U-Tanks allocated to him called for them to land at the extreme western end of his divisional sector, near Dymchurch Redoubt.

---

* One brigade (168th, Queens) had, as 35th Brigade, fought a short and disastrous action near Abbeville on 20 May as a result of which two of the three battalions had had to be reconstructed.

The weakest point of the scheme appears to have been the rather secondary importance allocated to the capture of Dover, the best and most convenient harbour within reach. Without it it would be extremely difficult to land the armoured divisions, to say nothing of the supplies, which could make possible mobile warfare. Without them the campaign could easily degenerate into a war of attrition between infantry-dominated forces, a type of fighting in which the defenders always have an advantage. Even if they could be seized, the other ports on the projected invasion front would be no substitute for Dover. Newhaven was very difficult to enter, Rye was even more difficult to approach and far too small. Folkestone had been obstructed by a blockship as early as 29 July. Until Dover was in German hands and the inevitable demolitions rectified, the build-up on the beachheads would depend on a shuttle service run by the small Stormboats and the laborious grounding and, at the will of the tide, refloating of the cumbrous barges.

On 31 August, the day after the OKH order was issued, Lt. Gen. Sir Alan Brooke, Commander-in-Chief Home Forces, gave it as his opinion that 'the Army can now beat off an attack'. There were still worrying shortages, particularly in his mobile reserve. 1 Army Tank Brigade was almost up to strength in Mark II Matildas, which, if slow, could fight any German tank on at least equal terms but 1 Armoured Division still had only one-third of its complement of cruiser tanks, the balance being made up by the unbattleworthy Vickers Light tank which was useful only against infantry. His most urgent worry was over the command structure:

> There was no form of Combined Command over the three
> services. . . . There were far too many commanders. The Navy
> had the C-in-C Home Fleet, C-in-C Nore, C-in-C Portsmouth,
> C-in-C Plymouth, C-in-C Western Approaches. The Army had
> the C-in-C Home Forces; and the Air Force had AOC-in-C
> Fighter Command, the AOC-in-C Bomber Command, and the
> AOC-in-C Coastal Command. There was no co-ordinating head
> to this mass of commanders beyond the Chiefs of Staff Committee
> and the Admiralty, Air Ministry and War Office.
>   It was a highly dangerous organisation. Had an invasion
> developed, I fear that Churchill would have attempted as Defence
> Minister to co-ordinate the action of these various Commands.
> This would have been wrong and highly perilous, with his
> impulsive nature and tendency to arrive at decisions through
> a process of intuition as opposed to 'logical' approach.

11

'He's Coming! He's Coming!'

The first week of September, 1940, the week that saw the first anniversary of Britain's declaration of war, was the turning point of that exciting summer. On 31 August reconnaissance aircraft reported large numbers of enemy craft moving west off the Texel. Destroyers were sent out to investigate but found no invasion fleet although they stumbled on a newly laid minefield on which HMS *Esk* and *Ivanhoe* were sunk and *Express* was severely damaged. Three cruisers were sent south to reinforce Harwich but after a busy night of reconnaissances it was decided that invasion was not yet on the move.

The alarm was not unjustified. Two days earlier the Combined Intelligence Committee (previously known as the Invasion Warning Sub-Committee of JIC) had reported the presence of forty or fifty merchant ships at Kiel and of 350 large motor-launches at Emden. CIC, however, was growing cautious in its forecasts and remarked that these concentrations, while 'a new and unusual feature', might be due to 'suspected mining or other possible temporary restrictions'. At this stage CIC seems to have been determined not to be impressed by evidence of invasion. On 28 August photographic reconnaissance reported no barges at Ostend; on the following day there were eighteen and by 7 September the number was 270 and more were moving to all the invasion ports, about a hundred reaching Flushing in the first four days of September. CIC were prepared to admit that this might betoken invasion but that it might equally be due to the clearance of some blockage in the canal system. Hearing on 5 September that leave in the German services had been stopped, they commented that 'Army leave is stopped from time to time without special incident'. Next day their view was, 'If there is an intention to invade, the expedition is [probably] being held in readiness in the Baltic or Hamburg.'

If CIC, which had raised a number of false alarms in the past, was now prepared to take an anodyne view, Joint Intelligence Committee (which had spawned CIC in May) was more certain that the danger was imminent. Their reason was a rash of spies. The crash programme for the training and deployment in the British Isles of agents which had been initiated by Admiral Canaris in June (see p 65) had borne little fruit. In August two *volkdeucher* Danes had been dropped over Salisbury Plain where one broke his ankle on landing. His companion abandoned him and got in touch with a contact the *Abwehr* thought they had in the Welsh Nationalist movement but who was actually a retired inspector of police working for the Intelligence services.

At about 4 a.m. on 3 September two Dutchmen landed from a rowing boat on Romney Marsh near Hythe, having been brought close to the coast in a fishing boat, escorted by two mine sweepers. One of them, Jan Kieboom, had been a cashier in the YMCA, a position he had used to indulge in currency smuggling. The Germans knew this and used the fact to blackmail him into undertaking a mission to England. He spoke some English, with a strong foreign accent, but, considered as an agent, he suffered from the fact that his mother had been Japanese so that he had a 'markedly oriental' appearance. With him was a friend and fellow-dealer in currency, Sjoerd Pons, who spoke almost no English and seems to have come on the operation with the fixed intention of surrendering at the earliest possible moment.

An hour after they landed Kieboom was seen by Private Tollervey of the Somerset Light Infantry. On being challenged he replied, 'I do not know your codeword.' He was asked to identify himself and said, 'I do not understand what you say. I have come across the water. I am a Dutch refugee and, if I can see one of your officers, I can explain the position.' He was in civilian clothes with white shoes, but hanging round his neck was a pair of binoculars and another pair of shoes. A search revealed a loaded revolver and in the vicinity were found a suitcase and a sack containing tinned meat, chocolate and cigarettes, all of German origin. Further investigation produced a radio set. Pons gave himself up with alacrity.

While this was going on two more men, who had travelled in the same fishing boat, landed near Dungeness. One of these, José Rudolph Waldberg, had a German father and a French mother and, while he spoke both his parental tongues fluently, he had no English. With him

155

was a member of the Dutch Nazi party called Meier whose training in espionage techniques had only started in mid-August. He spoke fluent if accented English. As the pair rowed ashore they imagined they saw a patrol boat approaching and promptly dropped their pistols, codebooks and maps overboard. Having reached the beach, they hid their wireless set near a roadsign and put their other belongings under an upturned boat where they were stolen by a passing workman. They had a short sleep and woke with a raging thirst so it was agreed that Meier, the English speaker, should go to find something to drink. He knocked up a pub on the outskirts of Lydd and asked for bottles of cider. Pointing out that it was illegal to sell liquor at that hour in the morning, the landlady advised him to go and look at the church and return at ten when the pub would be open. On his return an Army officer was waiting for him. He claimed to be a refugee but did not reveal the presence of his companion.

Waldberg remained at liberty until the following day when he was challenged by a sergeant to whom he replied in French. Search of the area produced not only his radio but the log of messages he had sent. These were far from explicit:

> Arrived safely. Document destroyed. English patrol two hundred metres from coast. Beach with brown nets and railway sleepers at a distance of fifty metres. No mines, few soldiers. Unfinished blockhouse. New road.
> Waldberg.
> Meier prisoner. English police searching for me. Am cornered. Situation difficult. I can resist thirst until Saturday. If I am to resist, send aeroplanes Wednesday evening eleven o'clock. Am three kilometres north of point of arrival. Long Live Germany.
> Waldberg.
> This is [my] exact position. Yesterday evening three Messerschmitts fired machine guns in my direction south west reservoir painted red.
> Meier prisoner.*

All these inefficient agents, with the exception of Pons, were executed as spies, but their interrogation disclosed that their orders were to be ready in the following fortnight to report on the movement of British reserves in the area Oxford – Ipswich – London – Reading.

Waldberg's rambling messages probably never reached Germany

---

* Punctuation has been added.

since most of the wireless sets issued to German agents at this stage of the war had to be repaired by British technicians before they could be used to transmit misleading information back to the *Abwehr*. It may have been one of these British-controlled sets which, on 2 September, sent one of the few reports which actually reached Berlin:

> The area Tunbridge Wells to Beachy Head, especially the
> small town of Rye (where there are large sand-hills) and also
> St Leonards, is distinguished by a special labyrinth of defences.
> These defences, however, are so well camouflaged that a super-
> ficial observer on the sand-hills, bathing spots and fields, would
> not discover anything extraordinary. The area is extremely well
> guarded, so that it is impossible to reach there without a special
> pass.
> In Hastings, on the other hand, most of the defences can be
> recognised quite plainly. In the town are troops of every kind. The
> presence of numerous light and heavy tanks is most striking.
> Numerous armoured cars were also seen in St Leonards and in
> a small locality where there is a famous golf-course, probably St
> Joseph.

This striking piece of disinformation – most of the facts given were untrue, there were no tanks, light or heavy, within twenty miles of Hastings – was painstakingly analysed by the *Abwehr*, without much positive result:

> The agent was not able to give a clearer account of the number
> of armoured cars in the different localities, or the regiments he
> saw there. From the position of Beachy Head (west of Hastings)
> and Rye (east of Hastings), it can be deduced that the place
> in question near St Leonards was the western villa-suburb of
> Hastings. Tunbridge, which lies on the railway line from Hastings
> to London, must, according to the sense of the report, also lie on
> the coast, but, as in the case of St Joseph, this cannot be confirmed
> from the maps in our possession.*

The fact that the German authorities were prepared to spend so much effort on what was patently a useless message suggests that they had few if any more informative reports on which to assess the strength of the British defences.

---

* Peter Fleming (*Invasion 1940* p189) points out that in 1940 the Post Office in the village of Camber on Sea, 10 miles east of Hastings, was run by a Mr Tunbridge and that, after all place names were removed (see p 40), the signboard would have read TUNBRIDGE. POST OFFICE & VILLAGE STORES, followed by the painted-out name of the village.

The first week of September was the most difficult of the war for Fighter Command. German direction-finding equipment had succeeded in identifying the sector stations, the source of detailed direction to the British fighters, and raids were concentrated on them, fewer being wasted on airfields used by Bomber, Coastal and Training Commands. Moreover, bomber formations were being more and more heavily escorted by single-engine fighters making it correspondingly difficult for the Spitfires and Hurricanes to reach their real targets, the Dorniers and the Heinkels. A spell of gloriously fine weather meant that there were no comparatively restful days of rain and poor visibility when the hard-pressed defenders could find a short respite. 1 September was a particularly bad day with Fighter Command losing fifteen aircraft in the air while the *Luftwaffe* lost only fourteen. The sector station at Biggin Hill, which had suffered five raids on the last two days of August, was attacked three times, the runways being put out of commission. Four Spitfires were destroyed on the ground and the sector operations room was demolished and had to be transferred to improvised accommodation in a nearby shop. There were lesser raids on Eastchurch, Detling, Hawkinge and the much battered Lympne.

Biggin Hill was hit again on the following day, as were Eastchurch, North Weald, Kenley, Hornchurch, Debden and Detling, where thirty aircraft were wrecked on the ground. The loss that day was thirty-one fighters (and fifteen pilots killed or seriously wounded) against a German loss of thirty-five while on 3 September, on which day both sides lost sixteen aircraft, there was a damaging raid in the sector station at North Weald, although most of the other German attacks were beaten off. 4 September saw damaging attacks on Eastchurch and Lympne as well as heavy raids on bomber factories at Rochester and Brooklands, there being almost 700 casualties at the latter. That day seventeen fighters and twenty-three German aircraft were shot down, but on 5 September twenty fighters (and eleven pilots) were lost against twenty-three German losses, while heavy damage was done to Biggin Hill and Detling. 6 September was a somewhat better day, particularly since a heavy attack on the Hawker works at Brooklands, source of half the Hurricane output, was broken up. Fighter Command lost twenty-three planes and the Luftwaffe thirty-five, of which sixteen were Me109s.

The defenders were approaching the point of exhaustion.

Experienced pilots were nearing the limit of their endurance and fresh pilots and squadrons, brought in to relieve the strain and replace casualties, were suffering unacceptable losses. In No.11 Group six of the seven sector stations had been damaged more or less seriously. As Air Vice Marshal Park wrote:

> Had the enemy continued his heavy attacks against Biggin Hill and the adjacent sectors and knocked out their operations rooms or telephone communications, the air defences of London would have been in a parlous state.

At night there were scattered raids all over the country which did little damage but, thanks largely to the overwide distribution of air-raid warnings, disturbed the sleep of many workers who were far from the track of the bombers and even further from their targets. There was, of course, a small proportion of defeatists. Lloyd George 'satisfied himself that the damage to aerodromes in the south-east and the loss of working time in factories generally was much greater than the public realised.' Liddell Hart 'stressed the crippling effect of the "sleep offensive" on production and in fraying the tempers of the civilian population.' An antidote to this gloom can be found in the diary of the US Military Attaché for 5 September:

> The results of [Hitler's] month of intensive air attack, which opened on 8 August, are remarkably slender. All the railroads are running, road circulation is normal, telephone and telegraph services in order, industrial production undamaged, food plentiful, London practically untouched, ports of the west country still operating, convoys coming and going. The unity and spirit of the whole country are quite amazing.

As to a German landing, he believed 'the betting on Britain's beating off an invasion this fall is now about 3 to 1, with the odds lengthening every week.'

Relief for the hard-pressed Fighter Command came from an unlikely source, the *Luftwaffe*. On 3 September Goering held a conference at The Hague with Kesselring and Sperrle, commanders of *Luftflotten II* and *III*. They heard a report from Luftwaffe Intelligence which claimed that 1,115 British fighters had been destroyed since 8 August, an estimate hard to reconcile with the calculation of 16 August that the RAF had only 430 fighters and a maximum production rate of

300 in six weeks. Sperrle refused to believe this estimate, asserting that Dowding still had 1,000 fighters, but Kesselring, whose planes had done most of the fighting, was ready to believe that Fighter Command was on its last legs. The Reichsmarschall agreed with him. The question of how to induce the RAF to commit its remaining fighters to a decisive final battle remained. The answer seemed to lie in a mass assault on London which the British must defend if they were to avoid the crushing bombardment which had broken Warsaw and Rotterdam*. This course could only be undertaken with the consent of the Führer who had specifically forbidden the bombing of London without his consent. Goering therefore applied for this consent and, probably influenced by the ineffective but humiliating RAF attacks on Berlin, it was forthcoming on 5 September. As a token of the new policy there was a daylight raid on Thameshaven on 5 September and small attacks on London docks on that and the following day.

While Goering was deciding his change of policy on 3 September, Goebbels was musing to his heads of departments:

> Views differ on whether the war in the air alone can achieve the final result, and reports on the effect achieved so far are contradictory. There is no doubt that these effects are considerably greater than the British have so far disclosed. Certainly a nation really determined to defend its freedom can only be brought down by hand-to-hand fighting. Whether Britain has this determination is another question. After all she is waging this war to dispose of her tiresome German competitor rather than to show a shining example of her love of freedom. We can expect that moderate influences will intervene soon. For a really clear picture of the situation we shall have to see what happens in the next few weeks.

Next day Hitler finally came into the open about *Sealion*. Since the idea of invading Russia had crystallized in his mind he had become lukewarm about the dangerous business of crossing the Channel and on 27 August had given orders for ten infantry and two panzer divisions, with one of the parachute battalions, to be transferred from France to Poland so as to be in a position to protect the Romanian oil fields, presumably against the Russians. However, on 4 September

---

* It seems not to have occurred to the *Luftwaffe* that Warsaw, with a population of $1\frac{1}{4}$ million, was less than a sixth of the size of London and consequently more easy to terrorize, or that Rotterdam was doing its best to surrender when the terror attack was delivered.

his attention had been jerked back to the west by the news that, in exchange for naval bases in the western hemisphere, the United States was to make fifty elderly destroyers available to Britain, a move which, according to Ciano, aroused 'a great deal of excitement and indignation' in Berlin. That evening he made an unscheduled speech to an audience consisting largely of women attending a rally in aid of the *Winterhilfe* (winter relief) project. So secret were the preparations that the Propaganda Ministry had to rush the foreign correspondents to the *Sportspalast* straight from the afternoon press conference so that they could hear the speech.

> Hitler was in his most rabble-rousing form.
> I waited three months without answering the British night bombing in the hope that they would stop this mischief.
> But Herr Churchill saw in this a sign of weakness. You will understand that we are now answering night for night. And when the British air force drops two, three or four thousand kilograms of bombs, then we will in one night drop 150, 250, 300 or 400,000 kilograms.
> When they declare that they will increase their attacks on our cities, then we will *raze* their cities to the ground.
> We will stop the handiwork of these air pirates*, so help us God! The hour will come when one of us will break and it will not be National Socialist Germany.
> In England they are filled with curiosity and keep asking 'Why does he not come?' Be calm! He's coming! He's coming! I now prefer to fight until a clear decision is reached.

It may be that this last paragraph was not what the Führer intended to say. He may have been carried away by his own oratory to an all-but hysterical audience. The fact remains that in it he committed himself publicly to invading Britain and thereby gave Churchill his greatest victory of 1940. Until that day no public statement of Germany's intention to attempt a landing had been made and, if no landing took place, it was always open to Hitler to maintain that he never had any intention of attempting invasion. After 4 September he was faced with a choice of undertaking a major amphibious operation which his senior naval adviser believed would end in 'a severe defeat for the *Wehrmacht*' or of losing face by appearing to be unwilling to face the risks involved after he had advertised his intention to undertake it.

* Fifteen days later Goebbels forbade the phrase 'air pirates' in the German media.

On the previous day OKW had issued to the usual restricted list of eight senior commanders a revised timetable for *Sealion*:

> The following dates for completing preparations for *Sealion* have been decided.
> i) The earliest date for the sailing of the invasion fleet has been fixed as 20 September, and that for the landing as 21 September.
> ii) Orders for the launching of the operation will be given on S-10, presumably therefore on 11 September.
> iii) Final orders will be given not later than midday on S-3.
> iv) All preparations are liable to cancellation until 24 hours before S-Hour.

It is clear that this instruction was more concerned with cancelling rather than with launching the invasion, for, despite his pledge at the *Sportspalast*, Hitler was far from happy about invasion. On 6 September he had a meeting with Raeder, just back from a tour of the invasion ports, who told him that the 20 September deadline could be met provided 'success in the air continues'. He did not conceal his opinion that the cross-channel voyage would be a dangerous affair, but said, 'The execution of *Sealion* appears possible provided command of the air is established and the weather is favourable.' As usual he was demonstrating that the Navy had the whole matter in hand while privately counting on being able to blame someone else, the *Luftwaffe* for choice, if things went wrong. He even went so far as to suggest keeping up a semblance of invasion preparations while actually going ahead with the seizure of Gibraltar and Suez before the United States could intervene. Hitler was happy to discuss such a plan and Raeder left the meeting reasonably content, noting in the Naval War Diary:

> The Führer has by no means decided to invade England as he is convinced she can be defeated without a landing. Nevertheless he views a landing as the way in which an immediate and definite end can be secured although he is determined not to attempt it if the risk is unacceptable. There must be no possibility of failure as that would give England a decisive gain in prestige.

On the morning of 7 September *The Times* published a letter from a reader who claimed to have seen a great crested grebe in an air-raid shelter near Euston station. While this was being read over British breakfast tables *Reichsmarschall* Goering, with ample provisions and a glittering staff, was establishing himself near Cap Gris Nez to watch his *Luftflotten* set out to deliver the decisive blow to London which would draw the mass of Fighter Command into the air for a mass battle which would leave the sky clear for German bombers. On the right Kesselring's *Luftflotte II* could deploy 458 serviceable bombers and 533 single-engine and 107 twin-engine fighters. On the left *Luftflotte III* added 314 bombers and 112 fighters.

The British were not unprepared for this onslaught, since, two days earlier, Bletchley Park had deciphered a *Luftwaffe* Enigma signal calling for an attack on London docks by more than 300 bombers with a huge fighter escort. This had enabled a suitable redeployment of fire and ARP resources to east London but, although Fighter Command had received a copy of the Enigma message, it does not seem to have made sufficient impact at No.11 Group. Three days earlier Keith Park had given priority to the defence of fighter airfields and aircraft factories and this seemed to have been justified on the morning of 7 September when his command beat off four heavy attacks on Hawkinge. He had been called away to a conference when, early in the afternoon, large numbers of enemy aircraft were found to be building up over Calais. This was usual German practice, but on this occasion the mass did not disperse but, joined by its fighter escort, approached London from the east. With 11 Group deployed to protect their airfields, only four squadrons were available to oppose 320 bombers and upwards of 600 fighters moving on London docks between 5 and 6 p.m., the bombers at between 16,000 and 20,000 feet with their escorts disposed on their flanks or behind them stepped up to 25,000 feet.

The bombs were dropped almost undisturbed, severely damaging Woolwich Arsenal, West Ham power station and Beckton gas works. They devastated much of the riverside and created 'a serious fire situation' in the docks. Silvertown, south of the East India Dock Road, was so ringed with fire that the inhabitants had to be evacuated by water while, on the south bank of the Thames, an area of more than an acre was wholly destroyed. The targets – docks, power stations, the arsenal, the gas works – were all legitimate military objectives but most of them were surrounded by small, tight-packed, jerry-built houses which must have been damaged or destroyed even if the standard of bombing accuracy had been far higher than it was. Before darkness fell forty-one German aircraft had been lost, the Air Ministry claiming 103. Fighter Command had lost twenty-eight planes, Berlin putting the figure at ninety-three.

As evening fell, the damage was visible from the West End of London.

> There stood St Paul's with a semi-circular background of red. The flames looked perilously near the dome; while to the left the pall of smoke was black – a dark pillar which drifted uneasily upwards. It grew in intensity; and then, dropping behind the four-hundred-feet-high dome, flickered into a mere reflection in the sky. Still the heavy bank of cloud formed a background – but now it looked not unlike heavy clouds on which the sun was setting.

In the Straits of Dover it had been a day of outstanding visibility and from the ramparts of Dover Castle could be seen large numbers of craft – barges, tugs and E-Boats, moving towards Boulogne. MTBs were sent against them, but ineffectively, and destroyers summoned from westward failed to arrive in time to engage. Reports of this migration of small ships, added to the reports of the interrogation of the four spies, seemed to the Joint Intelligence Committee to indicate imminent action and they advised the Chiefs of Staff that, in their opinion, invasion might be on the way. The Chiefs decided that they must warn the civil authorities and alert parts of the Army. At seven minutes past eight that evening the codeword *Cromwell* was sent to Eastern and Southern Commands, other commands being informed that this had been done.

Cromwell transformed a state where units were ready to move at eight hours notice to one of instant readiness. The actual implication of the codeword was not widely understood, the more so since, it being a Saturday, many senior officers were away and units received it through an unfortunate, and usually ill-informed, duty subaltern. Over a wide area, by no means confined to Eastern and Southern Commands, it was assumed that invasion had actually started. The Home Guard was called out and the church bells were rung. A ten-year-old boy, evacuated to his grandmother's house in the Cotswolds, later recalled:

> When the church bells rang out in the night, we thought the invasion had begun at last. I remember seeing the wife of the chimney sweep sharpening her carving knife on the stone sill of her cottage.

164

In some places bridges were demolished and mines laid, causing some casualties. In Lincolnshire a company commander of the Grenadier Guards

> went round the billets, doubled the sentries, released the men in arrest and ordered the drummer to sound the alarm in the streets of Louth. I told the men the Germans might already have landed but where I had no idea. Our buses purred quietly in the field outside, their civilian drivers talking quietly to the Guardsmen, drinking cups of tea. Then, for there was nothing else to do, we returned to the billets, wrote our last letters and waited. When, the next morning, we learned that no invasion had taken place, we relaxed, feeling slightly ashamed of our heroics on the night before.

In Kent a future Lord Chancellor of England was commanding a light anti-aircraft troop, whose armament consisted of three Bofors guns, fifty rifles and one pistol, stationed at Manston airfield. The Station Commander sent for the gunner officer:

> He informed me that significant movements across the Channel of enemy troops, planes and barges had been reported, that weather conditions for an air and seaborne invasion were perfect and that my troop should be ready for action an hour before sunrise.
> 'How long can your guns fire?' he asked me.
> 'To the last round, sir.'
> 'And how long will that be?'
> 'Seventy-five seconds, sir.' I explained that I had only 150 rounds for each of my Bofors guns and that they fired 120 rounds a minute.
> 'Where do you get your reinforcements from?'
> 'Dover Castle.'
> 'Do you realise that the Nazi paratroops are going to drop between here and Dover?'
> 'I mentioned this to a brigadier, when he came round recently,' I explained; 'but he said it was none of my business.'

The flurry of military activity was fortuitously increased by a scare in the West Country. According to *The Times*:

> A false alarm caused military and civil forces to stand to arms just before midnight.
> It was about 11 o'clock at a coastal town that boats were seen coming inshore through the mist. There were air-raids in the neighbourhood [and] it was decided that invasion was at hand. Some of the boatmen rushed to the parish church, and soon the

bells were sounding the alarm. Neighbouring villages took up the warning signal and soon it was passed from Cornwall eastwards until it reached the outskirts of Bristol.

Later it was established that the intruders were only fishing boats making an unintentional landfall in poor visibility.

A few minutes after the *Cromwell* codeword had been sent out, German bombers returned to London docks, guided by the great fires started in daylight which made *Knickerbein* or any other navigational aid superfluous. During the night about 250 aircraft came over, dropping 335 tons of high explosive and 440 canisters of incendiaries. There was no effective defence. Of the two squadrons of Blenheim night-fighters available, one was unable to leave the ground at Hornchurch as smoke from riverside fires made the runways unusable. In the Inner London Zone there were only ninety-two heavy anti-aircraft guns and, including those on the outskirts, the total figure for guns defending London was 264, little more than half the number estimated as necessary. Such guns as there were combined with the barrage balloons to keep the enemy high, so as to preclude the infliction of decisive damage. Nine of the fires started were officially rated as conflagrations – 'major fires which were spreading' – fifty-nine were reckoned as 'major fires' and there were almost a thousand other incidents requiring the fire services.

Although the bomber pilots had been ordered to attack the docks alone and their target could scarcely have been indicated more clearly by the fires, many bombs fell far away, some as far west as Putney. Battersea power station was hit and the railways out of Victoria, London Bridge and Liverpool Street stations temporarily blocked. The greatest damage was done among the little huddled houses of the East End and it was there that most of the casualties occurred. There it was a dreadful night but, apart from causing untold misery and stimulating astonishing courage, it achieved very little. Civilians were killed and maimed, thousands were made homeless, stores and provisions were destroyed, but the Port of London was not put out of action and civilian morale was not destroyed. As an official statement put it at the time, the damage was 'severe, but judged against the background of the war . . . not serious.'

In 1937 the Air Ministry had asserted that 6,000 tons of bombs would cause 200,000 casualties of which one third would be fatal (see p 22) In the raids of 7 September and the rest of that night

166

the *Luftwaffe* dropped rather more than 600 tons on London which, according to Air Ministry theory, should have caused 20,000 casualties, but, in fact, they caused only about 2,000 (430 dead and 1,600 seriously wounded). This was a sufficiently hideous butcher's bill, but it was only one tenth of the result calculated by the exponents of air power as a war-winning weapon. If it took one ton of bombs to kill two-thirds of a civilian, it was going to take more than the strength of the *Luftwaffe* to clear the way for *Sealion*.

12

'The Weather may break
at any Time'

Dockland was still burning on the night of 8 September when the bombers came back. It had been a relatively quiet day but when darkness fell 171 aircraft flew over the capital in waves dropping 207 tons of high explosive and 327 canisters of incendiaries, about two-thirds of the load on the previous night. They killed 412 Londoners and seriously wounded another 747. The damage they did on the ground was serious but far from fatal, the most spectacular incident being in the eastern basin of St Katherine's Dock where incendiaries set fire to barges laden with copra which ignited a row of warehouses stacked with copra and paraffin wax. 'The burning fat and wax floated upon the water until the basin became a cauldron of flame.' There was nothing the firemen could do but let the warehouses burn themselves out.

It was a pattern that was to repeat itself on almost every night until mid-November*, but the weight of attack was insufficient to cripple a town as widespread as London which sprawled over eight hundred square miles and the insufficiency was made greater on 8 September when Goering, convinced that a day and two nights of bombing would have crippled the Port of London, ordered the attack to be extended to 'the west of London which contains the power supplies and provision installations'. Thereafter the bombs were spread over the whole extent of the Great Wen, doing grievous damage but achieving nothing to the German purpose.

On 9 September another huge daylight attack was launched on the capital but this time Fighter Command was ready. Few of the 200

---

* Between 7 September and 13 November it was only on 3 November that no bombs were dropped on London. On six other nights in that period less than fifty German aircraft flew over the capital.

bombers got through, although one dropped a bomb on Buckingham Palace, but it did not explode until the following day. Twenty-eight German aircraft were lost and nineteen British fighters. That night 195 bombers dropped 232 tons of high explosive on London killing 370 and seriously injuring more than 1,400. By this time the ARP services were getting into their stride and were adjusting their organization, built to cope with a knock-out blow, to deal with a prolonged war of attrition. They found that their elaborate anti-gas precautions were, at least for the time being, superfluous, as were their arrangements for mass burials. There were fewer dead than had been anticipated, but far more homeless, and while there were too many stretcher parties there were too few heavy rescue squads to find and extricate men, women and children trapped in the wreckage of their homes. Another surprise was the number of unexploded bombs, some of them with delayed-action fuses but more with defective mechanisms. About one in ten of all the bombs dropped failed to explode immediately, causing great dislocation since there was no way of knowing whether, after a delay, there would be a shattering blast or whether, if handled with care, the bomb would prove harmless.

On 10 September there were only 148 planes over London and, in the middle of the raid, Ed Murrow broadcast a vivid description of London's ordeal:

> When you hear that London has been bombed for ten or twelve hours during the night, you should remember that this is a huge sprawling city, that there is nothing like a continuous rain of bombs – at least there hasn't been so far. Often there is a period of ten or twenty minutes when no sound can be heard, no searchlight seen. Then a few bombs will come whistling down. Then silence again. A hundred planes over London doesn't mean that they were all here at the same time. They generally come singly or in pairs; circle round over the searchlights two or three times; and then you can hear them start their bombing runs, generally a shallow dive. Those bombs take a long time to fall . . .
>
> As you know, the damage has been considerable. But London has suffered no more than a serious flesh wound. The attacks will probably increase in intensity, but things will have to get much worse before anyone here is likely to consider it too much to bear.

That night there were also raids on Liverpool and South Wales and, as far as the British could see, the bombing was 'quite indiscriminate', a charge the German pilots would, in all good faith, have denied. Thereafter Bomber Command were told that their planes over Germany were 'not to return with their bombs if they failed to locate the targets which they were detailed to attack'.

11 September was a bad day for Fighter Command, though they beat off an attack on the Supermarine works near Southampton, the principal production centre for Spitfires. About a hundred bombers attacked London, concentrating on the City and the docks. In splitting up the attacking formations twenty-nine fighters were lost, seventeen pilots being killed and six wounded. The Luftwaffe lost only twenty-five machines. That evening Churchill, speaking on the radio, put the nation on the alert:

> This effort of the Germans to secure daylight mastery of the air over England is of course the crux of the whole war. So far it has failed conspicuously . . . For [Hitler] to try and invade this country without having secured mastery in the air would be a very hazardous undertaking. Nevertheless, all his preparations for invasion on a great scale are steadily going forward. Several hundreds of self-propelled barges are moving down the coasts of Europe, from the German and Dutch harbours to the ports of northern France, from Dunkirk to Brest, and beyond Brest to the French harbours in the Bay of Biscay. . . .
>
> We cannot tell when they will try to come; we cannot be sure that in fact they will try at all; but no one should blind himself to the fact that a heavy, full-scale invasion of this island is being prepared with all the usual German thoroughness and method, and that it may be launched now – upon England, Scotland, or upon Ireland, or upon all three.
>
> If this invasion is going to be tried at all, it does not seem that it can be long delayed. The weather may break at any time. Besides this, it is difficult for the enemy to keep these gatherings of ships waiting about indefinitely, while they are bombed every night by our bombers, and very often shelled by our warships which are waiting for them outside.

Although Churchill warned that invasion might be imminent, he must, in his inmost thoughts, have been very doubtful whether the Germans would dare make the attempt. The latest batch of Enigma messages that had been deciphered suggested that 'the training is not complete and there is no indication of any firm decision in any particular direction.' This was not as conclusive as it might seem since only the *Luftwaffe* Enigma traffic could be read and the *Luftwaffe* was always reluctant to take *Sealion* seriously. In this case the messages did not distort the picture. No decision had been taken in Berlin and Hitler could fairly be described as dithering. On 10 September he received from Raeder a memorandum which, while making clear that the Navy would manage to play its part, was as discouraging as it tactfully could be:

> The weather conditions, which for the time of year are com-
> pletely abnormal and unstable, greatly impair movements and
> mine-sweeping for *Sealion*. Although the *Luftwaffe* have achieved
> a noticeable weakening of the enemy fighter force, it cannot
> be taken for granted that they have achieved superiority over
> southern England and the Channel. The English bombers and
> mine-laying aircraft are, on the evidence of the last few days, still
> at full strength and they have had successes even if no decisive
> obstacles have been put in the way of the movement of German
> transports.

He added that the *Kriegsmarine* believed that it could meet its com-
mitments although he could wish that the *Luftwaffe* would pay more attention to Portsmouth, Dover and the enemy warships within the invasion area. It may be, however, that the Führer believed that 'the protracted bombardment of London would produce an attitude in the enemy that would make *Sealion* unnecessary'.

On the following day, 11 September, Hitler deferred the decision, due that day, for launching the invasion. As Jodl explained to his staff at OKW, 'the Führer . . . has decided not to use the earliest possible deadline, as the results of the intensified air attacks could not yet be fully assessed'. The decision was deferred to 14 September which would make S-Day 24 September, which the Navy said would give an ideal combination of tide and moon.

That night 217 tons of high explosive and 148 incendiary canisters were dropped on London, but they were more scattered than on pre-
vious nights as the anti-aircraft barrage had been greatly strengthened and a new technique had been adopted. The night fighters, which had so far achieved nothing, were grounded to allow the guns free range. On 10 September Lt. Gen. Sir Frederick Pile, GOC Anti-Aircraft Command, had called a meeting.

> The commanders of every gun position in London with their
> battery, brigade and divisional commanders met me in the signals
> drill hall in the Brompton Road, and I told them personally what

I wanted to do. Every gun was to fire every possible round. Fire was not to be withheld on any account. Guns were to go to the approximate bearing and elevation. Searchlights were not to expose. RAF fighters were not going to operate over London, and every unseen target must be engaged without waiting to identify the aircraft as hostile. The result [on the night of 11 September] was as astonishing to me as it appears to have been to the citizens of London – and apparently to the enemy as well. For although few of the bursts can have been anywhere near the target, the heights of the aircraft steadily increased as the night went on, and many of them turned away before entering the inner artillery zone . . . It bucked people up tremendously. . . Not that everybody was pleased. The Council of one suburb wrote to say that lavatory pans were being cracked in the council houses, and would we mind moving the barrage somewhere else.*

Fragments of this intense barrage certainly killed more Londoners on the ground than Germans in the air but its effect on British morale was enormous – at least they could hear that something was being done to discourage their tormentors – and the aiming of German bombs became even worse than before. The expenditure of anti-aircraft ammunition, fortunately in reasonable supply, rose sharply. In August AA Command had reckoned that it had taken 232 rounds to bring down a German plane; in September the number rose to 1,798 and, since the number of aircraft claimed probably exceeded the number destroyed by at least three to one, the number of rounds fired for each aircraft brought down was unlikely to be less than six thousand.

Meanwhile the light bombers of the RAF were hammering away at the Channel ports and were joined by the heavier bombers who pounded the coastline from Antwerp to Le Havre, having no trouble in finding their targets since every harbour was a mass of flames and looked like Blackpool front. Ships from the Nore Command joined in, shelling the harbours and intercepting the convoys of barges. On the night of 10/11 September the destroyers *Malcolm*, *Veteran* and *White Swan* made a sweep off Ostend and saw a small convoy hugging the coast. Although under fire from coastal guns, they sank an armed trawler, a self-propelled barge as long as the destroyers themselves,

---

* A reader of *Picture Post* wrote to suggest that, since the noise of the guns could be mistaken for the fall of bombs, 'Would it be possible to accompany each salvo with a more reassuring sound, such as the loud banging of a gong. An inexperienced man in each gun crew could be detailed to beat the gong, which would have to be large.'

and a smaller barge being towed by a trawler which was damaged by shell fire.

Meanwhile, the *Cromwell* state of alert was still in force, keeping the army on constant 'Stand-to' so that there was a widespread shortage of sleep. In one battalion 'owing to the official view that invasion was imminent, the men, for a period of sixteen days were only able to remove their boots for short periods daily.' Most of the Home Guards had been persuaded to resume their civilian occupations, a fact that severely embarrassed one Essex unit near Epping Forest:

> We received a police message that fifty enemy parachutists had landed at High Beech at a time when all our men were at their jobs in the City of London and we had only half a dozen men (after half an hour) to deal with the situation. Later the police informed us that their message was incorrect and that the puffs from AA shells had been mistaken for parachutists.

The imminence of invasion seemed to be further indicated when, on the evening of 9 September, the big guns on Cap Gris Nez opened a bombardment of Dover. It was not a conspicuous success for, although two hundred rounds were fired in five hours, the report of damage read, 'Casualties and material damage remarkably light; five persons, including one soldier, were killed, two houses and a garage demolished and about twenty other buildings damaged.'

Bad weather kept aerial activity to a minimum on 12 September, Fighter Command losing no planes and the *Luftwaffe* only four, including some in night operations when only forty-three planes visited London dropping fifty-four tons of explosive. This was a welcome break to Londoners who were still not wholly acclimatized to the nightly onslaughts. As the US Military Attaché wrote in his diary:

> People are beginning to look a little fatigued, owing to lack of sleep. Some stay awake from curiosity, some from excitement, others from fear.

Readers of the *New Yorker* were told:

> For Londoners, there are no longer such things as good nights; there are only bad nights, worse nights and better nights. Hardly anyone has slept.

Although Goering was still making confident noises, the Germans were starting to doubt whether the heavy attack on London would bring about a British collapse.

The *Kriegsmarine* were disgruntled with the effect being produced.

> One cannot discern any effort on the part of the *Luftwaffe* to engage the units of the British fleet, which is now able to operate in the Channel almost unmolested and this would prove disastrous to a sea crossing. . . . Up to now the intensified air war has not contributed towards the landing operation; hence, for operational and military reasons, execution of the landing cannot be considered.

Even Goebbels had doubts, saying on 12 September:

> We should refrain from reports which might convey that London would be finished in the next few days. It is also in our military interest to represent the British people as being, for the moment, undaunted.

Above all, he was insistent that:

> Great care must be taken to maintain our assertion that our attacks are aimed solely at military installations. If civilian targets are hit as well, this is due to the fact that many military installations are situated in the built-up areas of London.

This contention was sorely tried when, on 13 September, a bomber, diving under low cloud, flew straight up the Mall and dropped a stick of six bombs across Buckingham Palace. Two fell in the forecourt, two in the quadrangle, missing the King and Queen by only thirty yards, one on the chapel and one in the garden. As one of the police on guard remarked to the Queen, 'A magnificent piece of bombing, Ma'am, if you'll pardon my saying so.' The King wrote, 'There is no doubt that it was a direct attack on Buckingham Palace,' and, given the isolation and size of the palace, it is difficult to believe that the bombing was a mistake. On the other hand it is most unlikely that the German High Command or even OKL would have authorized it and it was probably the personal act of some fanatical pilot. In the ordinary way the exact location of the fall of bombs was not revealed to avoid giving target information to the enemy. The attack on the Palace was publicized and added to the anger of the British against Germany. Goebbels was quick to realize that a serious error had been made and gave orders that:

> Major Woodarg [*Luftwaffe* liaison officer with the Propaganda Ministry] is to ascertain whether there are any military targets in the vicinity of Buckingham Palace. If not, it is to be asserted,

should foreign agitation increase, that secret military stores are concealed in its immediate neighbourhood.

At about the time that the Palace was being bombed, Hitler was host at a luncheon for twenty newly-promoted *Generalobersten* to whom he said that, since the air offensive was going so well, 'he had no thought of accepting so great a risk as that represented by a landing in England'. Jodl told his staff that the Führer appeared to have abandoned *Sealion* and the Navy was quietly confident that the decision, due for the following day, would be to abandon the operation. Hitler, however, was still dithering, probably as a result of a report from the Military Attaché in Washington, General Friedrich von Bötticher, a soldier with an optimistic view of the effect achieved by the *Luftwaffe* on London. According to the War Diary of OKW on 14 September:

> It appears from a series of reports on the morale of the population of London from the Military Attaché in Washington that the will to fight of that population is considerably affected by lack of sleep. This physical weakness is regarded as having the greatest effect on morale. He reports the damage done to include twenty-four docks being totally burned out and four gasometers destroyed. The railway stations Sherrycross and Waterloo and several underground stations are damaged. Of ten good airfields around London, seven are almost completely unusable.

This view of the situation seems to have been based on an analysis of the New York newspapers whose sub-editors, for the titillation of their readers, tended to make the most of the reports of their London correspondents. The *New York Times*, far from the most sensational of these papers, had produced a series of striking headlines, such as –

NAZIS POUND LONDON IN ALL-DAY RAIDS. BOMB
   NORTH WEST CITY FOR SIX HOURS (1 September)
NAZIS RAID BRITAIN IN WAVES (3 September)
GERMAN PLANES RAID LONDON ALL DAY
   (7 September)
MIGHTY NAZI AIR FLEET AGAIN BOMB LONDON –
   DOCKS AND PLANT HIT.
FIRES RAGE, 400 DEAD (9 September)
CENTER OF LONDON BATTERED BY HEAVY BOMBS
(10 September)

As the US Military Attaché in London remarked, 'If the *New York Times* prints such stuff, what may be appearing in the cheap press? . . . One would almost imagine we were groping from one corner to another with shells and bombs falling like rain.' Nor was the German Embassy the only place in Washington where the effect of the German bombardment was being exaggerated. According to Harold Ickes, Cordell Hull, the Assistant Secretary of State, reported to the American Cabinet on 6 September, the day before the attack on London began:

> England was undergoing a terrific attack. As a matter of fact it has been getting worse and worse over there . . . It was actually claimed in some quarters that England would be suing for peace before last week came to an end.

Hitler seems to have been affected by von Bötticher's reports from Washington, since on 14 September he appeared to go back on the cancellation of *Sealion* which he had foreshadowed at lunch on the previous day. According to Halder, he told a meeting of the heads of the services:

> A long war is undesirable. We have achieved the political and economic bases which we need. A landing in England would be the quickest way of ending the war. . . . The chances of subduing Britain are good. The effect of the air action so far has been terrific but the final effort, which is dependent on four or five days of good weather, has not been achieved, although the enemy is badly hurt.

He paid tribute to the preparations made by the *Kriegsmarine* and said that the work of the *Luftwaffe* was 'highly satisfactory' even if the complete elimination of the British fighter force had yet to be achieved. There was a chance that, even without this, 'mass hysteria' might break out in England.

Speaking next, Raeder said that he had always regarded *Sealion* as a last resort and that the risks of undertaking it were very great. He suggested that as 'the air position is not yet good enough to reduce the risks to a minimum' and since the air situation could hardly be expected to change greatly in a few days, the operation should be postponed until 8 or 24 October. For the Army, Brauchitsch strongly disagreed and recommended that *Sealion* should be launched as early as possible, preferably with S-Day on 24 September.

For the *Luftwaffe* Jeschonnek, the Chief of Staff who was representing Goering, said, 'While the material damage to London was beyond expectation, no mass panic of the populace had occurred because residential quarters had not been attacked and destroyed.' He asked for

14. The bombardment of Mers-el-Kebir begins 1700 hours.

15. 'Well camouflaged Home Guards meet enemy paratroops half way'.
(W. Heath Robinson)

permission to attack residential districts and was supported by Raeder. Hitler, however, declined to sanction this, saying that 'working up panic must be a last resort'. He deferred a decision once more and added that even if *Sealion* had eventually to be cancelled, that decision must be kept a close secret as 'British morale would be raised and the air attacks would be easier for the enemy to bear'.

The results of the meeting were summed up in a minute from Keitel dated 14 September and restricted to the usual eight addressees:

> 1. a) The start of Operation *Sealion* is again postponed. A new order will follow on 17 September. All preparations are to be completed.
> b) As soon as preparations are complete, the *Luftwaffe* will carry out attacks on the English long-range batteries.
> c) The measures for the evacuation of the coastal areas [of France and Belgium] are to be executed. Counter-espionage and deception measures are to be intensified.
> 2. The air attacks on London are to be continued and the target area is to be extended to include military and other vital installations, such as railway stations.
>
> Terror attacks against purely residential areas are to be held back as a means of applying final pressure, and are not to be employed at present.

Although Goering had been absent from the conference on 14 September, he had spoken to Hitler on the previous day and had assured him that air supremacy was within reach. The ever-sanguine *Luftwaffe* Intelligence was steadily exaggerating the damage done to London and pointed out, not without truth, that they had had a success against Fighter Command on 11 September when the RAF had lost more planes than the *Luftwaffe*. Even the pilots, who had a higher opinion than OKL of Fighter Command's ability to survive, thought they detected signs of weakening in the opposition. On 12 and 13 September there was thick cloud which prevented heavy attacks, but on the following day a not particularly successful attack on London resulted in equal losses, fourteen planes, on each side. Once again there was a feeling that the defence was weakening and, with a heavy attack planned for 15 September, only thirty-eight planes were sent to London that night, dropping fifty-five tons of bombs.

Sunday, 15 September, subsequently commemorated as Battle of Britain Day, was sunny with cloud patches which cleared late in the day. Aiming to repeat their success of 7 September, the *Luftwaffe* detailed 200 bombers with an escort of 700 fighters to attack London, while other forces, chiefly Me110s in their role as light bombers, made diversionary but ineffective raids on Portland and Southampton. Apart from these two subsidiary operations the attack was delivered with none of the elaborate massing of aircraft over France that had misled the previous attack. The defence was given plenty of warning as the bombers massed over the French coast and moved straight off towards their target. 11 Group were able to meet them in their preferred two-squadron formation and even 12 Group had time to contribute a 'Big Wing' of five squadrons, three of Hurricanes, two of Spitfires. Thus the raiders arrived over English airspace to find themselves confronted with twenty-two squadrons already airborne. Many of the bombers jettisoned their bombs before they reached the capital and the few that broke through hit mostly residential property in the southern suburbs, although a few bombs fell in Kensington and Westminster. Once again, although this time clearly in error, a bomb fell on Buckingham Palace, damaging the Queen's private apartments, and a Dornier crashed in the forecourt of Victoria Station, its crew, descending by parachute, landing on the Oval cricket ground. Their plane had been rammed by a Hurricane piloted by Sgt. Pilot R. Holmes who had used up all his ammunition shooting down another bomber. His parachute landed him safely in a Chelsea dustbin.

After the morning raiders had been shepherded away there was a pause of about two hours, giving the fighters plenty of time to refuel and rearm, so that, when the second wave crossed the coast soon after 1.30 p.m., the defence was again ready for them. Although some bombers turned back, the fighting was heavier than in the morning. More bombs were dropped on London than earlier, but there was little aiming, although, possibly by design, a gas-holder was hit at East Ham. There was no question of this second massed daylight attack making London uninhabitable and the *Luftwaffe* paid heavily for attempting to make it so. All Britain was overjoyed to hear that evening that the fighters and anti-aircraft guns had brought down 186 German planes for the loss of twenty-six fighters and thirteen pilots. It was a resounding victory, even if the actual loss of German aircraft was only sixty. It taught the *Luftwaffe* that there was no future in massed daylight raids on heavily defended targets in Britain. If London was to be brought to a halt, the task must be carried out by night bombing with all its inevitable inaccuracy. That night 181 bombers dropped

178

224 tons of explosive and 279 incendiary canisters, doing grievous but inessential damage. Apart from those who suffered directly from that bombing, it was a night of rejoicing all over the country. No one doubted that the Germans had suffered a severe beating and if, as it turned out, it was not quite the beating the Air Ministry believed, it was a good enough to ensure that there was no future for *Sealion*.

13

'Revert to Normal'

On the day that the *Luftwaffe* failed to win the battle that was to make *Sealion* possible or superfluous, the commanders of the armies and corps which had been detailed for the assault on the English beaches were reading a document issued on the previous day, 14 September, by von Rundstedt's Army Group A entitled *Forecast of Early Fighting on English Soil*. It said nothing about the losses and confusions that must result on the sea crossing but did not minimize the difficulties which would be met with once ashore:

> The leading assault troops and the advanced echelons of the first *Staffel* will land at dawn* in the face of more or less severe opposition. As it becomes light the troops ashore will call for artificial smoke as it seems necessary. On the day before S-Day known coastal batteries and fortifications will be neutralized or at least reduced in effectiveness by the *Luftwaffe*.
>
> Once local bridgeheads have been won, junior commanders will set about co-ordinating small units in their vicinity and use them to seize significant features on their front. Weak but continuous fronts will gradually be formed. These will be extended and deepened by a continuous flow of reinforcements.
>
> Heavy counter-attacks by an enemy with artillery and heavy weapons must be expected at an early stage. By comparison our forces will be weak in numbers and equipment but, by courageous and determined leadership, junior commanders will keep their forces tightly under control and will not yield a metre of ground. . . . After daylight, but not before, the *Luftwaffe* will support the main effort of the assault troops, acting as artillery. Other air units will obstruct the movement of enemy reserves in southern England. Key railway lines in central and northern England will not be disrupted until a later stage.

* On the day this order was issued the Army finally yielded to the Navy's plea not to land at first light (see p 148)

> Small but complete panzer units will be included at an early
> stage in the first *Staffel* to support the infantry.

Almost one third of the matter in the *Forecast* is devoted to keeping
senior commanders and their staffs out of the beachhead. It was
pointed out that the function of Corps and Army staffs was to remain
'on the continent [and] do their utmost to supply reinforcements to
the troops who will be fighting hard under difficult conditions.'

> Senior commanders with *small* staffs will cross only when the
> strength of the assault troops has been adequately reinforced.
> They will leave behind either their chiefs of staff or their
> operations officers.
> Premature crossing by higher staff will be valueless during the
> initial, small-scale fighting on the beaches as it would interfere
> with the flow of reinforcements, such as artillery and complete
> tank units. It will be the duty of divisional, regimental and
> battalion commanders to control the early fighting. Senior officers
> will take over later. The restricted area of the bridgehead will
> not, in the early stages, be able to accommodate vehicles, supply
> columns and staffs of all kinds.

This is unexceptionable advice, but it might have been supposed that
the order in which various categories of personnel, equipment and
stores would be transported would have been laid down in advance in
loading tables agreed with the Navy rather than left to the last-minute
discretion of corps and army commanders.

Inevitably the *Forecast* is thin on co-operation with the *Luftwaffe* since
OKL was taking no interest in the invasion. All they had done was to
make available the surviving dive bombers, and the Stuka commander,
Freiherr Wolfram von Richthofen, a cousin of the First World War
hero, had given it as his opinion that he had insufficient planes to
support the landing of more than a single corps. Nor had any plan
yet been agreed for the employment of the parachutists, one battalion
of which had, as has been seen, been diverted to eastern Germany.

As laid down in the executive order of 30 August (as modified by
amendments) the bridgehead would be complete with the consolida-
tion of the line Barham – Ashford – Hawkhurst – Lewes and the
Forecast laid down that,

> When the connected bridgehead has been achieved, *days* will
> elapse before a consolidated attack can be launched against the
> first operational objective.

This first operational objective was laid down as the line Gravesend – Guildford – Portsmouth, an advance surely requiring tanks, but the *Forecast* was definite that,

> The landing of complete armoured divisions will take place only when a sufficient area of the island has been secured, since the employment of armour depends for its effect on the use of tanks *en masse*.

This left open the question of where the panzers were to be landed. As has been seen (p 148), Dover was the only port, with the possible exception of the much less convenient Newhaven, at which the landing could take place and at no stage was there any plan for the capture of Dover. The 'connected bridgehead' had its right flank at Barham where it would have been unable to give any significant protection to Dover, even supposing the port had been captured.

As to the amount of opposition to be encountered, the *Kriegsmarine* estimated with approximate accuracy that the Royal Navy would have available three battleships, two battlecruisers, two aircraft carriers, eight heavy and twenty light cruisers, seventy destroyers and some 500 lighter craft. Of these they believed that four of five light cruisers and about twenty destroyers would be in the immediate vicinity of the landing area.

The *Wehrmacht*, by contrast, overrated the number of British troops they were likely to encounter. The *Abwehr*'s estimate throughout the summer had varied slightly on either side of thirty-five divisions, of which between eighteen and twenty-two were fully operational, apart from shortages of up to half their artillery. Notwithstanding this, OKH issued on 20 September, in time for the latest considered S-Day, a map showing forty divisions and one independent brigade. Of these divisions, nineteen are shown as fully operational, sixteen as 'partially operational' and the remainder (apart from one which is not classified) as non-operational.

The actual strength of Home Forces at that time was twenty-eight divisions, the New Zealand contingent of two brigades and eleven independent brigades. The latter may have caused some confusion to the Germans since 37 Independent Brigade was stationed not far from the position indicated for 37 Division and both 29 and 36 Division Brigades were within fifty miles of the stations given for 29 and 26 Divisions. Similarly the supposed location of 23 Division was not all that far from the actual position of 23 Army Tank Brigade.

In Northern Ireland the Germans placed one unidentified division and some foreign troops, although it might have been supposed that Goertz's organization (see p 66) or the legation in Dublin might have discovered the identities of the two divisions there, which OKH placed in Norfolk and Surrey respectively. Two formations which were changing places in Iceland were both shown as being in Britain and the garrison of Scotland was inflated by 9 Division which had been broken up to recreate 51 (Highland) Division. Two non-existent divisions, 7 and 8, are shown as being 'fully operational', and 5 Division, which was north of Edinburgh, was believed to be in Caernarvonshire. 28 Division was identified as 38 and it must be assumed that 52 Division was represented as 62 Division, although it was wrongly placed.

On the intended operational front, the Germans expected to meet XI Corps with, in front line, 45 Division, from North Foreland to Lydd, 55 Division, between Lydd and Beachy Head, with 12 Division (which had been disbanded) to the west of it and 61 and 66 Divisions in reserve. In fact they would have met XII Corps with, from east to west, 1 London (later 56) Division, 45 Division and 29 Independent Brigade, with the New Zealanders in reserve near Maidstone. GHQ mobile reserve (southern portion) was believed to be between Aldershot and Salisbury, whereas it was actually stationed much nearer the danger point, being in the Guildford area.

On the British side of the Channel, despite the *Luftwaffe*'s onslaught on London which might herald an invasion, confidence was building up. On 15 September Ed Murrow told his American listeners:

> Much of the talk, as you would expect, is about invasion. On that score there is considerable confidence. Everyone is convinced that it will be beaten back if it comes. There are some who fear that it will not come.

One of those who was not looking forward to it was C-in-C Home Forces who wrote in his diary on the same day:

> Our exposed coastline is just twice the length of the front that we and the French were holding in France with about eighty divisions and the Maginot Line. Here we have twenty-two divisions, of which only about half can be looked upon as in any way fit for any form of mobile operations.

Looking back after the war, General Brooke felt that this exaggerated his pessimism and added:

> It should not be thought that I considered our position a hopeless one. . . . Far from it. We should certainly have had a desperate struggle and the future might well have hung in the balance, but I felt that, given a fair share of the fortune of war, we should certainly succeed in finally defending these shores.

The equipment position was far more healthy than in June. Instead of only fifty-four 2-pounder anti-tank guns there were 498 at the end of August and, to add to the field guns available after Dunkirk, there were not only the American 75mm guns (see p 102) but a further 425 field pieces, nearly half of them the new 25-pounder and the remainder the made-over 18/25-pounder. According to the Secretary of State for War (though the Official Historian gives lower figures) 'We had on 29 September 179 cruiser tanks in this country and 259 I[infantry] tanks', quite apart from more than 500 light tanks.

In reality everything turned on the ability of the Royal Navy and the RAF to break up any invasion attempt and the reputed score of 186 German aircraft shot down on 15 September certainly gave confidence in the latter's ability to do its part. On the naval side, a further flotilla of modern destroyers had been sent to Plymouth to counter the activities of the German destroyers which had moved to Cherbourg and in the Home Fleet an intelligence report, wholly false, that the Germans would be employing *Bismarck, Scharnhorst, Gniesenau* and the two antique (1906) battleships *Schleswig-Holstein* and *Schliessen* to support the invasion, led to a move of *Nelson* and *Rodney* with two cruisers and eight destroyers to Rosyth, where *Hood* was already stationed.

Tension was nevertheless rising, heightened by the *Cromwell* alert and the heavy attacks on London. Alan Brooke's diary gives something of the atmosphere:

> *8 September.* All reports still point to the probability of an invasion starting between the 8th and 10th of this month.
> *11 September.* Evidence of impending invasion has been accumulating all day . . . The next day or two are bound to be very critical.
> *13 September.* Everything looks like an invasion starting tomorrow from the Thames to Plymouth.
> *15 September.* This coming week must remain a critical one, and

it is hard to see how Hitler can now retrace his steps and stop this invasion.

16 September. Still no invasion. Rumour has it that tonight is to be the night.

17 September. Still no invasion, and today a mild hurricane which should be stirring up the Channel well.

It was not to be. The defeat of the *Luftwaffe* on 15 September had finally induced Hitler to make up his mind that invasion had no chance of success and on 17 September, the day on which 'a new decision' had been promised, a cryptic signal went out to the usual eight addresses:

> *Sealion.* Postponed until further notice.

As the War Diary of the *Kriegsmarine*'s Operations Division noted:

> The enemy air force is still far from defeated; on the contrary it shows increasing activity. The weather situation as a whole does not indicate a period of calm . . . The Führer therefores decides to postpone *Sealion* indefinitely.

In fact Hitler had not intended to postpone the operation indefinitely but merely to put back S-Day to 12 October. Moreover, he was insistent that preparations should be kept going at full pressure. The British Secret Service, a body for which he had an almost limitless admiration, would be certain to detect any slackening in the preparations. He had not allowed for the *Luftwaffe* habit of chattering away on Enigma.

Also on 17 September Churchill spoke to the Commons in secret session, telling them that in the recent bombing 2,000 civilians had been killed and 8,000 injured, four-fifths of them in London. He went on to speak of the possibility of a German landing, saying that the shipping assembled in the invasion ports was sufficient to carry half a million men.

> We should, of course, expect to drown a great many of them on the way over, and to destroy a large proportion of their vessels. But when you reflect upon the many points from which they could start and the fact that even the most likely sector of invasion, i.e. the sector in which enemy fighter support is available for their bombers and dive-bombers, extending from the Wash to the Isle of Wight, is nearly as long as the whole front in France from the Alps to the sea, and also upon the dangers of fog or artificial fog, one must expect many lodgments or attempted lodgments to be

185

made on our island simultaneously. These we shall have to deal with as they occur, and also to cut off the supply across the sea by which the enemy will seek to nourish his lodgments.

The difficulties of the invader are not ended when he sets foot on shore. A new chapter of perils opens upon him. I am confident that we shall succeed in defeating and largely destroying this most tremendous onslaught by which we are now threatened, and anyhow, whatever happens, we will all go down fighting to the end. I feel as sure as the sun will rise tomorrow that we shall be victorious.

As he was speaking, a *Luftwaffe* Enigma message was being deciphered at Bletchley Park. All it said was that the Führer had authorized the dismantling of air-loading equipment at Dutch airfields, but its significance was at once recognized and it was taken round to the Prime Minister by Group Captain F. W. Winterbottom, who acted as the liaison between Bletchley and SIS. Churchill was at a meeting of the Chiefs of Staff when Winterbottom arrived.

> [He] read the signal, his face beaming, then he asked the Chief of Air Staff, Sir Cyril Newall to explain its significance. Cyril Newall . . . gave it as his considered opinion that this marked the end of *Sealion** at least for this year. . . . The conference knew that the dismantling of the air-loading equipment meant the end of the threat and so it was accepted. There was a very broad smile on Churchill's face as he now lit up a massive cigar and suggested that we should all take a little fresh air. As we surfaced, the air raid was at its height.

Two days later the *Cromwell* alert was cancelled and replaced by a new state of readiness known as 'Stand To', but this was a coincidence, since it was imperative that Britain appeared still to be expecting invasion. Nothing could prejudice her chances for the future more than that the Germans should have any suspicion that she could read Enigma messages. Moreover, it was important that the British public should continue to expect invasion lest they sink back into the lethargy from which Churchill had roused them in May. The news that *Sealion* was no longer impending was kept within a very narrow circle which, if the evidence of his diary is to be accepted, did not include the Commander-in-Chief, Home Forces. On 18 September Brooke wrote:

* Group Captain Winterbottom's memory failed him on one detail. The British did not discover the codeword *Sealion* until 21 September, four days after this incident.

Every indication continues to look like an invasion being staged, ready to be launched at any time. I wish the weather would really break up.

A week later he felt it necessary to put a further brigade group between North Foreland and Dungeness.

It is that narrow neck of sea that constitutes a danger point now that he has all his shipping assembled on the French coast opposite to it. It is very hard to fathom what he really intends to do and whether he still contemplates invasion.

It was not until 13 October that he began cautiously to relax:

I am beginning to think that the Germans may, after all, not attempt it. And yet!

Even then he was writing four days later,

Evidence is amassing . . . of an impending invasion of some kind or other. Rotterdam is filling up with shipping.

A few days after the *Cromwell* alert was cancelled there was another major invasion scare. In the small hours of 22 September John Colville, on duty in Churchill's office, was telephoned by the Foreign Office

to dictate a telegram from Roosevelt who has heard from 'a most reliable source' in Berlin that the invasion is to be put in train at 3.00 a.m. today. . . . The report . . . came from Kirke, the American *Chargé d'Affaires* in Berlin, who was right about the invasion of Holland and Belgium – though a change in the weather made him twenty-four hours too soon on that occasion.

Churchill was 'slightly sceptical' but passed the news on to the Chiefs of Staff who implemented the new 'Stand To' procedure. At the American Embassy the Military Attaché arrived in his office to find a state of confusion.

The ambassador (Kennedy) had called from the country and told the Naval Watch Officer that he had news that there would be an invasion at 3 p.m. and what did they know about it? [The Watch Officer] called up the War Office who didn't know of any invasion but sent an officer boiling up to find out how the ambassador had heard of a message from Lord Lothian [British ambassador in Washington] to the Foreign Office at 2 a.m.

During the morning Churchill telephoned Eden, the Secretary for War, who was at his country cottage near Folkestone, saying that

President Roosevelt had telephoned saying 3 o'clock this afternoon was zero hour for the German invasion. If I thought I should come back he would give me dinner. I replied that it was wet and blowing and I felt quite safe. I went to the top of the hill which overlooks the Channel and afterwards sent a message, reporting it was so rough that any German who attempted to cross the Channel that day would be very sea-sick.

At Dover the Training Battalion, Irish Guards were in garrison.

> At midday Garrison HQ sent an urgent message 'President Roosevelt has just heard from a secret source in Berlin, which he considers most reliable, that the invasion of Britain is timed to start at 3 p.m. today.' Battalion HQ passed it on to companies with the addition 'No men will proceed out of barracks. The Battalion will stand to at 1330 hours. Posts will be warned to expect dive bombing attack.'

At 1.30 p.m. the battalion duly took up its defence positions and issued reserve ammunition. All those in a position to do so spent the next ninety minutes staring out over a windswept sea.

> Three o'clock duly came but no Germans. At twenty past a second message came from Garrison HQ. 'Re previous message. Correction. For "England" read "Indo-China." Revert to normal.'

That day Japanese troops occupied Saigon in French Indo-China.

On the other side of the Channel the Germans were busily keeping up a pretence of invasion and elaborate map exercises dealing with its problems were held in Sixteenth Army on 21 September and in Ninth Army three days later. It seems that even the Chief of Staff at OKH, General Halder, was not in the secret of the cancellation since on 28 September he was complaining of the 'chronic state of indecision' about *Sealion*. The Navy was much relieved at not having to undertake an operation in which they had no faith but they were still suffering casualties. By 20 September twenty-one merchant ships, 214 barges and five tugs had been sunk in the invasion ports and, despite the orders to keep up the preparations, Raeder quietly gave orders for the invasion fleet to disperse. Hitler confirmed the order a few days later. The attacks on the ports continued, reaching a climax when the battleship *Revenge* shelled Cherbourg on 11 October. An attempt to use the 1916 monitor *Erebus*, little more than a floating platform for two 15″ guns, to shell Calais was a conspicuous failure.

For the well-informed in Britain the relaxation in invasion preparations soon became clear. Air photography had identified 1,004 barges
between Flushing and Boulogne on 18 September. Only 691 could be
seen at the end of the month and the count was down to 448 before
October was out. Six destroyers seen at Cherbourg on 18 September
had left two days later. The fact that no invasion had eventuated gave
rise to a widespread rumour that it had been launched and had come
to a disastrous end. All over the country people were telling each
other that they had it on the best authority that, at one or other
stretch of coast, the sea was 'white with bodies'. In fact a total of
thirty-six German corpses were washed up at various places between
Yarmouth and Land's End. Almost all of these were reported at the
time in local newspapers, such as this paragraph in the *Dover Express*
of 25 October:

> A German soldier believed to be one of thousands who perished
> in Hitler's rehearsal attempt to invade Britain last month was
> washed ashore at Littlestone on the south-east coast on Monday.
> He was wearing the uniform of a German infantry regiment and
> was apparently a non-commissioned officer aged between 25 and
> 30. He had been in the sea for several weeks and death is believed
> to be by drowning.

Perhaps because no one had told them that *Sealion* had been cancelled, the *Abwehr* sent another three agents who landed on the coast
of Banffshire on 30 September from a rubber dinghy, having been
transported by seaplane. Two of them, a male German and a female
Scandinavian, were apprehended while still soaked in seawater, the
man being found to have about his person a torch stamped 'made in
Bohemia', £327 in notes, nineteen rounds of pistol ammunition and
a piece of German sausage. Nearby was found a suitcase containing
a pistol, a long-range radio transmitter, a code machine made of
cardboard and a list of RAF stations in East Anglia. Their companion
had a longer run. Although carrying two suitcases, both damp, and
having wet trousers and a strong foreign accent, which he claimed to
be Swiss, he caught a train and, after two changes, reached Edinburgh.
There he deposited his cases in the left luggage office with the assistance
of a porter and, while he waited for the evening train to London, had
his hair cut and went to a cinema. By this time the dinghy had been
found and his two companions arrested. Thanks to the assistance of
the porter, the police were waiting for the newly barbered spy when he

tried to reclaim his baggage. He had a loaded pistol in his pocket and his cases contained a radio set, £194 and some Norwegian coins. Both men were subsequently hanged but no charges were brought against the woman who, it may be supposed, became a double agent.

By the end of September the War Cabinet were sufficiently convinced that they did not have to reckon with invasion at least until the following spring that they agreed to release the Australian Brigade Group, the headquarters of 2 Armoured Division and its support group, together with two regiments of cruiser tanks and two of light for service in the Middle East. Since this represented more than half the cruiser strength in the country it is inconceivable that they would have left if any danger of invasion persisted.

The air attacks continued relentlessly until well into November, after which they tapered off apart from the occasional heavy strike. Many of the army formations were withdrawn for much-needed training, but the national vigilance against parachutists continued to such an extent that late in September the Air Ministry felt it necessary to put out a statement:

> While there is a continuing necessity for vigilance on the part of the public in regard to parachute landings, it is emphasised that only in the event of parachutists adopting a threatening attitude or attempting to commit hostile acts should force be used. Not only is there a chance of the parachutist being a British fighter pilot, but he may be one of our Polish, Czech, French or Belgian Allies, who is unable to speak English at all.

One who did not adopt a threatening attitude was a German pilot who, while being escorted to Chatham railway station, contributed a five mark note to the Spitfire Fund when someone thrust a collecting box at him.

It was not until 2 March, 1942, when the German armies were deep into Russia, that OKW formally cancelled *Sealion*, undertaking to give a year's notice should the project be revived. In November, 1944, with the allied armies poised on the German frontier, the body which had started life as the Invasion Warning Sub-Committee was disbanded. The Home Guard 'stood down' on the last day of that year.

14

'Why does he not come?'

In the fifty years that have passed since *Sealion* was conceived and aborted it has often been suggested that Hitler had no serious intention of invading Britain, that all the preparations were a gigantic bluff designed to frighten his one remaining enemy into submission. If this was the case it was a serious psychological error, since the threat had precisely the opposite effect and played directly into Churchill's hands by making vivid the need for the British to take a grip on themselves if they were not to end the war as permanent losers. The truth seems to be that, in the days immediately following the collapse of France, Hitler convinced himself that peace could be obtained without further fighting, by a mere 'appeal to reason'. There followed a period when, reluctantly, he saw invasion as essential if his previous triumphs were to be consolidated. Finally he was driven to the conclusion that the risks were too high and that he had no option but to ignore Britain and strike in other directions where success appeared to be more dependable. In each case he changed his mind slowly and parts of his thinking from earlier periods tended to resurface in subsequent phases. As late as April, 1941, orders were being prepared for Operation *Haifisch* (Shark), a revised version of *Sealion*.

It was not altogether stupid of Hitler to assume in June, 1940, that Britain would be ready to compromise. With his memories of the reoccupation of the Rhineland, of Mussolini's seizure of Ethiopia, of the *Anschluss* with Austria, of the Munich agreement and of the absorption of Czechoslovakia, he had good grounds for expecting the British to come to terms as best they could and he was prepared to offer what he considered to be very handsome terms. The point he overlooked was that all the earlier British capitulations had taken place in time of peace. Throughout the centuries Britain had been prepared to make enormous sacrifices to maintain peace, especially if the sacrifices fell on other people. Once war was declared the situation changed since the British had a less than justified belief that they did not lose wars. There was a national tradition of hanging on in the most unpromising positions and waiting for something to turn up. This was the way in which they had finally beaten Napoleon. The Russians had turned up then and, if Britain could sit tight for long enough, they might do so again. There was even a chance, remote in 1940, that the United States might feel that Hitler menaced their security and decide to do something about it. As for a compromise peace during Germany's pleasure, the most recent precedent, the Peace of Amiens in 1801, was not one to be looked back on with any satisfaction.

It was understandable that Hitler should fail to realize that the British would cling to peace up to, and beyond, the last possible moment but he might have understood that, once at war, they would go on to the end, whether bitter or victorious. He might have thought back to an October day in 1914 when the tenuous British line in front of Ypres was clearly broken wide open by an overwhelming German attack. Then three companies of the Worcestershire Regiment had put in a counterattack which, by all the rules of war, was bound to fail. They recaptured the chateau and village of Gheluvelt and plugged the gap, driving back, among other units, 16 Bavarian Reserve Regiment in which the future Führer was serving as *Meldeganger* (company runner). It is unlikely that he would have heard of the absurd British boast that they lost every battle but the last, an arrogant way of concealing the incompetence and unpreparedness with which they habitually start wars. All he could see in June, 1940, was a small nation which had been heavily defeated and which had only been saved from annihilation by a narrow strip of water. Obviously they would wish to make peace. What he did not realize was that once the British got round to declaring war their patience with Hitler was exhausted. Whatever he promised, whatever treaty he signed, they could not trust him to keep his word, so there was no point in making peace. They were faced with the alternatives of being defeated or going on to a victory, however improbable that might be on any logical premise. There may have been politicians – Hitler was probably right in identifying Lloyd George as his best bet – who would have formed a peace government but King George would never have offered him a commission to do so and he could never have achieved a majority in either of the Houses of Parliament. The country had realized that there was no middle way, that it was all or nothing.

The idea that Britain would make peace must have begun to fade quickly since on 2 July the first warning order for invasion was issued. It was a very indefinite document and made no bones about the fact:

> All preparatory work must take into account that no decision
> to invade England has been taken and all that is required is
> preparations for an eventuality which may not arise.

The Führer was still hoping that his public offer of peace, scheduled for 7 July, would induce the British public to override the bellicose stance of Churchill's Government. Such hopes were severely dented by the brutal strike against the French ships at Mers-el-Kebir, its unanimous approval in the British press and the overwhelming reception Churchill's statement about it brought in the Commons. The wrecking of the *Force de Raid* made Hitler realize that invasion was the only way in which Britain could be forced to make peace in any reasonably short period and, in less than two weeks, there appeared, over Hitler's signature, Directive No. 16 *Preparations for the Invasion of England*. On the same day, 16 July, he wrote to Mussolini describing 'the attack against England as something decided'.

Three days later he made his long-heralded public offer of peace but this was irrelevant. The Germans had been led to believe in the imminence of peace and there must be no possibility that they could think that peace did not come because the Führer had not offered it. The speech of 19 July was a muddle; even Ciano, Foreign Minister of Germany's main ally, thought the proposals 'vague', but in Germany it was seen as a peace offer because they had been told that that was what it was. In Britain it was not recognized; 'people laughed and jeered'. It sounded like a lot of foreign waffle. British rejection was not unexpected, but Hitler felt he had done his duty towards peace. He no longer expected his enemy to capitulate.

> The Führer does not desire further attempts to build bridges
> with the British. If they crave their own destruction, they shall
> have it.

Encompassing the destruction of Britain was one thing, achieving it was quite another and, four days after the 'peace offer', he made up his mind to invade Russia. It was not until eight days later that he communicated this decision to the heads of his army and air force and they might have expected that the first result of this new project would be an intensification of preparations for landing in England. After all he had told them on 23 November, 1939, that 'We can only oppose Russia when we are free in the west' and, many years earlier he had written much the same thing in *Mein Kampf.* Moreover, on the day he disclosed his plans for Russia he authorized a high degree of disorganization in the interior of Germany to be caused by the requisitioning of barges and almost stopped the import of iron ore from Sweden on which the armament industry depended.

On the other hand, he told the generals that 'If Russia is smashed, then Britain's last hope is extinguished', a phrase that implied that Britain would still be in the field after the five-month campaign which, he estimated, would put paid to the Soviet Union. If Britain was not to be invaded, there would be no point in dislocating the armament industry which, with the planned expansion of the army, would be required to produce even more weapons. The *Wehrmacht* may not have caught this implication since it was after they knew of the Russian project that they 'put aside . . . doubts and regard the landing as perfectly practicable'.

Hitler did not resolve this ambivalence until the middle of September when the shortage of time available made up his mind for him. On the one hand he knew that he must establish peace in the west, which could only be done by conquering Britain, before he could safely advance in the east. On the other hand he could not convince himself that Operation *Sealion* would succeed, a sentiment remorselessly encouraged by Grand Admiral Raeder who administered carefully calculated douches of cold water while simultaneously striving to make a landing possible with an assiduity that stopped short only of appearing ostentatious.

The indecision about whether *Sealion* should be launched was mirrored by the havering about how it should be executed. The disagreement between the *Wehrmacht* and the *Kriegsmarine* about the width of the beachhead was fundamental to the entire project and, since Hitler declined to permit any close co-operation between the heads of his armed services, only he could decide between the tactical imperative of the Army's wish for a wide lodgment and the logistic imperative of the Navy's knowledge that only a narrow invasion corridor could, at best, be protected and supported. Once again Hitler temporised. The Army had asked for a landing front stretching from North Foreland to Lyme Bay and he cut this down by excising the landing north of Folkestone, which would be outside the mine barrier secured on the Goodwin Sands, and the Lyme Bay beachhead which, it might have been supposed, even the most land-minded general could have realized to be far outside the area for which any naval protection could be offered. Nevertheless, he authorized a front stretching from Folkestone to Selsey Bill, almost a hundred miles and still unrealistically extended. Even this he qualified by considering last minute changes to narrow fronts either at Brighton, a thoroughly inconvenient destination, or Folkestone.

Those who believe that there was never any intention of invading Britain and that the preparations were an elaborate bluff tend to assert that the aim was to prevent Britain from intervening in some other sector. It is pertinent to ask what intervention was open to Britain in the summer of 1940? Given that German information about the British Army was inadequate, the *Abwehr* estimate in mid-September gave the British only nineteen 'fully operational divisions' many of them short of half their artillery. It was not a force with which even the most sanguine strategist could have engaged in an invasion of any part of occupied Europe, least of all France where there was a large and victorious army. It could have been that Hitler was anxious to stop Britain from reinforcing Egypt, although it was unlike the Führer voluntarily to assist an ally, but even there the disparity in strength of five to one in Italy's favour should have reassured him that there was little their enemy could achieve there. The widespread dislocation of German industry which he authorized in support of *Sealion* preparations would seem to be taking bluff too far, since he knew that, from May onwards, the British had convinced themselves that they were to be invaded. Preparations on a much smaller scale would have served the purpose just as well. Since the British were already suffering from the illusion he wished to create, the only people whom his bluff deceived were the senior commanders of his Army and Navy.

The most convincing piece of evidence against the bluff interpretation is Hitler's declaration at the *Sportspalast* on 4 September:

> In England they are filled with curiosity and keep asking 'Why does he not come?' Be calm! He's coming! He's coming!

He had always maintained that *Sealion* must not fail, since the British would gain great prestige if they beat back the invaders. This is indisputable, but the British would gain even more prestige if it could be seen that Hitler did not even dare to try invasion. By publicly proclaiming that invasion was coming, he associated himself with a humiliating failure not of arms but of nerve.

Once he had made this public declaration of intent the dithering that had marked his attitude towards invasion intensified until even Halder was complaining of 'a chronic state of indecision'. The Führer had landed himself with an insoluble dilemma. He knew that he must dispose of Britain to secure the future of the thousand-year Reich but he also knew that failing in the attempt to conquer her would cost him more than he could afford to hazard. He solved his problem by pretending it did not exist.

It cannot be said that Hitler was wrong in the end to reject the risk of invading Britain. In 1940 Germany had neither the doctrine nor the facilities to carry out an opposed landing on any sort of scale. The *Kriegsmarine* viewed the prospect with barely concealed horror. The *Luftwaffe* took no interest in the operation. Only the *Wehrmacht* came to view invasion with a confidence born of incomprehension. No machinery existed to allow the three services to work out the problem together. The nearest approach to a combined operations headquarters was OKW, Hitler's military office, headed by Keitel, who had never commanded anything and owed his position more to his enthusiasm for the Nazi party than to his military competence. He was despised by the commanders of all three services. OKW was essentially only another army headquarters, its senior naval representative no more than a *Fregattenkapitän*, a commander, the air force representative a major. At no time did a committee of senior officers sit down together to try to thrash out their differences. Apart from one meeting between the chiefs of staff of the Army and the Navy (which ended with both men having a different idea of what had been decided), two methods of inter-service liaison were used. In one each service would submit a paper to OKW where the Operations Staff, headed by the competent but over-ingenious Jodl, would fit the irreconcilable pieces into some sort of a pattern, here cutting off an awkward corner, there overlooking the fact that some pieces could never fit together. If the resulting jigsaw was totally unacceptable there was nothing for it but to adopt the other method, referring the difficulty to Hitler. On most occasions he saw the service heads separately and later gave his decision, if he made one, to Keitel and OKW to be passed on to the services. At interviews with Hitler discussion tended to range widely and be interspersed with soliloquies from the chief participant. It is not difficult to imagine the frustration of Admiral Raeder when anxious to obtain important decisions on the future of naval warfare to find himself having to listen to theorising about the settlement of the Jews in Madagascar. On the rare occasions that Hitler presided over a meeting of all three services, Goering usually left air force representation in the hands of *General der Flieger* Hans Jeschonnek, a very junior lieutenant-general but the *Reichsmarschall* regularly saw Hitler and usually managed to convince him of the virtues of whatever axe the *Luftwaffe* was grinding at the time.

Part of the problem was that there was no German tradition of combined operations and neither the Army nor the Navy had any significant experience of putting troops ashore on a hostile coast. Nor was inter-service co-operation helped by the fact that the Army was very much the senior service and tended to treat the Navy and the Air Force *de haut en bas*, while the Air Force, the most strongly Nazi of the services, had more influence with Hitler than the other two could achieve even if they combined. Nor was the apparatus of amphibious operations in existence. Apart from a handful of experimental models, there were no landing craft for men, tanks, vehicles or the indispensable horses. By prodigious efforts the *Kriegsmarine* managed to assemble sufficient craft to transport the first wave proposed by the Army and to make some of the modifications that were needed for their new purpose but no one, least of all Raeder, could pretend that they were anything but unsuitable for the difficult crossing, particularly in the hands of crews who, to a large extent, had been hastily recruited within eight weeks of the intended S-Day.

Some improvements which would have increased *Sealion*'s chances of success were made during the planning process but these occurred by erosion rather than logical thought. The best example is the length of the intended lodgment which, as has been seen, Hitler reduced the Army's original plan for a front of 225 miles to 100 miles between Folkestone and Selsey Bill. In the final plan (insofar as there was a final plan), Army and Navy had agreed to cut this down to some seventy miles from Hythe to Rottingdean. Closer co-operation about practical details would have produced a more practical plan than that which emerged in mid-September and it is interesting to speculate on the plan which might have emerged if the three chiefs of staff, Halder for the Army, Schniewind for the Navy and Jeschonnek for the Air Force, had been formed into a working party to devise an inter-service scheme.

One decision they might well have reached was the need for a supreme commander, giving orders to all three services. As things stood the only overall operational commander would have been Hitler himself, since every field commander had to report back to, or seek instructions from, his superior in his own service at least as far back as Army Group (or its equivalent) which was responsible, through OKW, to the Führer. Thus, in the early stages of the landing, *Generalleutnant* Loch, commanding 17 Division as it came ashore near Hythe, would be reporting to *General der Infanterie* Vietinghoff, of XIII Corps at Calais and through him to *Generaloberst* Busch, Sixteenth Army at Turcoing, who in turn was responsible to *Generalfeldmarschall* von Rundstedt whose Army Group A had headquarters at Fontainebleau outside Paris. If a higher authority was required the Field-Marshal would have to get in touch with Führer Headquarters at Ziegenberg, north of Frankfurt-am-Main, the headquarters of the three services having been instructed to establish themselves 'within 50 kilometres of my headquarters'. It was clear that if General Loch was in dispute with his naval opposite number on the beaches it would take a long time for the dispute to be adjudicated.

It has been argued that Hitler would not have agreed to placing so much power and potential prestige in the hand of anyone other than himself. The evidence points the other way. In his first directive, dated 1 March, 1940, for the Norwegian campaign, he nominated General von Falkenhorst to the direction (*Führung*) of the entire operation. He was dissuaded from this course by Goering's protests and on 4 March left each service to its own commander, responsible to Hitler himself, only sea transport being left on an inter-service basis.

However much a joint-service planning committee might have improved on the design for *Sealion*, it is improbable that they could have brought it to a point where it could have succeeded in 1940. The time for planning was too short. The latest date on which it was reasonable to count on adequate weather not only for the crossing but for the subsequent reinforcement and supply was 27 September. The first warning order was issued on 2 July, eighty-four days to S-Day, and the executive order followed two weeks later, leaving seventy-two days. Although any direct comparison must be misleading, the allied landing in Normandy in 1944, which had a smaller assault wave (five seaborne divisions rather than the Germans' intended nine) had been under intensive planning for more than two years and studies had begun nearly four years previously. Even in Normandy, an operation mounted with the full panoply of naval and air supremacy and a host of special equipment, the Anglo-American forces had no easy time establishing themselves ashore in the face of German divisions which might charitably be described as second-line. Moreover Operation *Neptune*, unlike *Sealion*, had the benefit of many rehearsals, not only 'dry runs through' against beaches in Britain, but actual operations against an active enemy ranging from the disaster at Dieppe to the difficult victories at Salerno and Anzio. The allied operation that most nearly matched *Sealion* in scale and speed of launching was *Husky*, the landing in Sicily (and the largest amphibious assault of the war), where seven divisions went ashore in the first wave. There the planning started late in January and the landing took place on 10 July, more than five months later. There was an adequate, if not generous, supply of purpose-built landing craft and overwhelming superiority in both the air and at sea, yet it is not too much to say that had the defenders of the Sicilian coastline not been third-rate Italian formations, reluctant to fight and convinced that their country had already lost the war, the invaders might well have failed to make good their landing.

The Germans had no possibility of a large-scale rehearsal for *Sealion* nor did they have a chance of achieving even local superiority at sea. A force of seven destroyers and twenty torpedo boats was grotesquely inadequate to challenge the world's most experienced and second largest navy in its home waters. The only practicable way of reducing the strength of the Royal Navy in advance of the landing was by bombing and this the *Luftwaffe* was strangely reluctant to attempt, nor did Hitler actively urge Goering to do so. As for the balance of power in the air, the crucial factor was the range of the Messerschmitt 109 which, from existing bases, did not extend beyond north-west London. Had the preliminary air fighting gone badly against the RAF Dowding would have been forced to withdraw the advanced fighter squadrons from their airfields in Kent, Sussex and Surrey and relocate them beyond London. There they would, even if with a reduced time for action, still have been able to operate over the beachheads and, although the suffering of London and the south-east would have been greatly increased, they would still have been able to strike effectively against the landings. The range of the Me109s would not have been increased by one inch until the Wehrmacht had captured airfields in England and it is noticeable that the intended 'connected bridgehead' included only one airfield, the battered and small Lympne. Nothing illustrates better the lack of liaison between the *Wehrmacht* and the *Luftwaffe* than the omission from the orders for XIII Corps of any mention of the urgent need to capture Hawkinge airfield, perched on the escarpment behind Folkestone and little more than a mile beyond 17 Division's intended right-flank guard at Paddlesworth.

The weakest part of the whole *Sealion* plan was sea transport. Given a flat calm and clear moonlight it is possible that the vast armada of unwieldy *Schleppzugen* might have chugged their way to their destination despite the inexperience of most of the crewmen and the notorious difficulties of navigating the Dover Strait, provided there was no opposition from the air or the sea. It was inconceivable that such an unopposed crossing could be made. The Royal Navy was close by and in great strength and, as Raeder had written on 29 July, 'are certain to inflict a severe defeat on the *Wehrmacht*'. From north and west several cruisers and at least two dozen destroyers, reinforced by scores of smaller armed vessels, were within easy striking distance and would descend on the slow-moving convoys like vultures. Some would probably fall victim to the mine barriers, some perhaps to the U-Boats, though a fast steaming destroyer is a difficult target for a torpedo. Once they got in among the barges with guns and depth-charges, the chaos would be unimaginable and made worse by the orders that the German soldiers were 'to arm the barges and tugs with weapons of all kinds'. Experienced sailors know well the dangers of firing into each other during a night action and there can be no doubt that, as soon as the British ships appeared and started firing, the soldiers, insecure because out of their element, would be loosing off at anything that moved. It seems possible that some of the small German naval craft which were to carry the detachments with storm boats might reach a point somewhere near their objectives but, if any of the tug trains followed them in, it would be a miracle if they carried the troops who were scheduled to land on the beach they actually reached. The defenders should have had little difficulty in mopping up such disorganized, and probably seasick, parties as managed to get ashore. *Sealion*, as planned in 1940, was bound to fail.

Peter Fleming put forward the theory that Hitler's wisest course would have been to leave Britain severely alone in the hope that she would have reverted to the boredom and apathy of the Phoney War. Germany could have gone on building up her U-Boat fleet which would, with the help of the *Luftwaffe*, have set about strangling Britain's lines of communication. The British people, who had been roused to unexampled defiance by largely imaginary perils in May and June, would soon have sunk back into inertia when they discovered that nothing threatened them except a distant prospect of starvation. As Margery Allingham wrote at the time:

> It is all very well to summon your courage one day, but to keep
> it swordbright for a week, or a month, or a year, if no sign of
> danger materialises is quite another matter.

In September, Churchill told the Commons:

> The process of waiting, keyed up to concert pitch day after day,
> is apt after a time to lose its charm of novelty.

He gave the country magnificent, inspiring leadership, but, sooner rather than later, the country would have lost sympathy with leadership which could not lead anywhere.

Instead the Germans had the worst of two worlds. The notion of a beleaguered Britain standing alone against an all-conquering Germany caught the admiration and sympathy of the world. The self-governing dominions renewed their determination to do all they could to help the mother country. The United States, informed by radio and press correspondents of outstanding ability, determined to give all help short of actual belligerency. The conquered countries began to hope that all was not irrevocably lost. Even Germany's allies, Italy and the Soviet Union, could not conceal a reluctant admiration, and Fascist Spain withdrew into a more resolute neutrality. When winter came and there had been no invasion the world began to revise its opinion about German invincibility. Germany had, in fact, been defeated. The vaunted *Luftwaffe* had been repulsed by Fighter Command and its bombing had failed to cow the civil population of Britain's great cities. The *Wehrmacht*, the most imposing and efficient army the world had ever seen, had appeared to baulk at the high fence that would have given them irreversible victory in Western Europe.

The victory was Churchill's, perhaps the greatest of all his achievements. Before the war he had been the only public figure to raise the spectre of invasion. Every other pundit had poured scorn on the idea and, as late as 1939, Liddell Hart, doyen of military thinkers, had written in *The Defence of Britain*:

> The development of air-power has greatly diminished the possibility of sea-borne invasion. A landing on a foreign coast has always been the most difficult operation of war. It has now become much more difficult, indeed almost impossible.

Liddell Hart may well have been right but Churchill continued to raise the possibility until events in Denmark, Norway, Holland and Belgium made airborne invasion seem not only possible but probable. It is now plain that most of these reports were wildly exaggerated but at the time they pointed to a real and imminent danger. On 14 May, only four days after Germany had struck at the Low Countries and before the BEF had seen significant action, men (and so far as they were permitted to do so, women) were flocking to join the Local Defence Volunteers, a body specifically raised to repel airborne attack.

Nothing could have suited Churchill better. His first and most important task was to arouse the spirit of the country and, almost without official prompting, the people had rallied to meet an apprehended danger. Britain had insisted on putting herself on a war footing and was standing to arms expecting parachutists to descend in large numbers on even the most unlikely parts of the island. The problem would have been to keep this new-found ardour alight but here events and the enemy conspired to assist. The catastrophic campaign in France, however much relieved by the 'Deliverance of Dunkirk', brought home to all the danger the country was facing and few of the 300,000 servicemen brought back to England did not have their horror stories of the ubiquitous panzers and the screaming, spine-chilling Stukas. Even as the last of the Dunkirk survivors was coming ashore on the south coast, Churchill was widening the possible danger. In his great speech on 4 June the phrase that remained, and remains, in most memories was 'We shall fight on the beaches'. Up to that point the fear had been of parachutists and soldiers transported in aircraft. Now seaborne invasion was added to the prospect.

The fall of France heightened the menace and heightened the

passionate patriotism and defiance that had infected Britain. Now she saw herself as the sole champion in arms of freedom, liberty, democracy and many other abstract conceptions that, in normal times, received very little consideration from the man in the British street. All those tricky foreigners, who were certainly incompetent and were probably cowardly as well, had let her down and left her to finish the job alone. If the prospect of the British army marching unaided into Berlin seemed somewhat remote, the chance of pushing those presumptuous Germans back into the sea seemed very promising, especially as the British army had the assistance of Australians, Canadians and New Zealanders, to say nothing of all those Poles in funny hats.

In keeping the fighting spirit of Britain alive, the Prime Minister found an unlikely ally in Dr Goebbels. As Churchill realized there is a limit to the amount of inspirational oratory that even the most emotional nation, least of all the phlegmatic English, could be expected to stomach, but the German attempt 'to intensify the mood of panic which is undoubtedly gaining ground in Britain' was so inept as to be counter-productive. The idea that Goebbels was intent on frightening her into surrender was so unflattering to Britain's new-found self-esteem that it was not even considered. Instead it was assumed that all the German threats must be the prelude to something decisive and the only thing that could be decisive for Britain was invasion. Hitler's hysterical cries of 'He's coming! He's coming!' merely confirmed from impeccable authority what they had long been expecting. From Churchill's point of view, it was a great help in keeping the pot boiling.

No one can say to what extent Churchill really believed in the possibility of a full-scale invasion being attempted. As he wrote on Trafalgar Day, 1939:

> I should be the last to raise those 'invasion scares', which I combatted so constantly during the early days of 1914–15.

As he became Prime Minister the greatest invasion scare since 1805 sprang spontaneously into being and he certainly did nothing to discourage it. Instead he nursed it and turned it to his advantage. His most memorable call to repulse the invader was delivered four weeks before Hitler had given so much as a warning order to prepare for a possible landing. It may even be that Churchill blackmailed Hitler into giving orders for *Sealion*, a venture he was most reluctant to undertake, but which, thanks to Churchill, the world, not excluding Germany, was expecting him to attempt and would look askance if he failed even to launch.

It may well be that in May and June, when the government and military authorities were scarcely better informed of the capabilities of airborne troops than were the newspaper-reading public, Churchill may have feared the kind of *coup de main* that Milch was advocating at the time (see p 48), but a man with his pride and confidence in the Royal Navy can scarcely have taken seriously the idea that Raeder's minuscule navy (even if overestimated by the Admiralty) could hope to escort across either the North Sea or the Channel convoys carrying a force large enough to subdue the United Kingdom. It would certainly seem that by the beginning of August, when three armoured regiments and forty-eight precious 25-pounder field guns were sent to the Middle East, he must have decided that a full-scale landing was very unlikely. If he had believed otherwise it would have been irresponsible to have sent these vital munitions out of the country. They might, and did, dispel the Italian threat to Egypt but if Britain had been overrun the fate of the Middle East would have been irrelevant. Whatever his private opinions, Churchill never allowed the public, or even his Cabinet colleagues, to believe that invasion was not likely to happen. He was ably seconded by German propaganda.

Appendix A

German Command Structure (simplified), September 1940

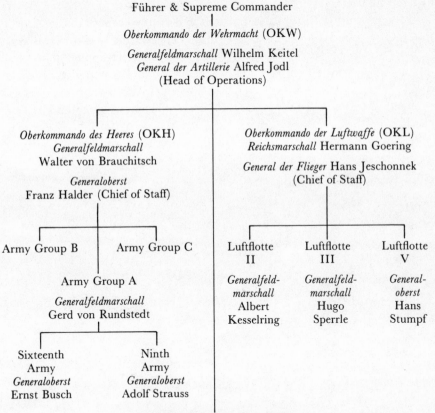

Adolf Hitler
Führer & Supreme Commander

Oberkommando der Wehrmacht (OKW)

Generalfeldmarschall Wilhelm Keitel
General der Artillerie Alfred Jodl
(Head of Operations)

Oberkommando des Heeres (OKH)
Generalfeldmarschall
Walter von Brauchitsch

Generaloberst
Franz Halder (Chief of Staff)

Oberkommando der Luftwaffe (OKL)
Reichsmarschall Hermann Goering

General der Flieger Hans Jeschonnek
(Chief of Staff)

Army Group B   Army Group C

Army Group A

Generalfeldmarschall
Gerd von Rundstedt

Luftflotte II	Luftflotte III	Luftflotte V
Generalfeld-marschall Albert Kesselring	*Generalfeld-marschall* Hugo Sperrle	*General-oberst* Hans Stumpf

Sixteenth Army
Generaloberst
Ernst Busch

Ninth Army
Generaloberst
Adolf Strauss

Oberkommando der Marine (OKM)
Grossadmiral Erich Raeder
Vizeadmiral Otto Schniewind
(Chief of Staff)

205

Appendix B

The Balance of Capital Ships in late June, 1940

Ship & Date of Launch	Displacement (tons)	Main Armament	Speed (knots)	
Britain				
Nelson (1925)	33,950	9 × 16″	23	Home Fleet
Rodney (1925)	33,900	9 × 16″	23	Home Fleet
Royal Sovereign (1915)	29,150	8 × 15″	22	Alexandria
Resolution (1916)	29,150	8 × 15″	21	Gibraltar
Ramillies (1916)	29,150	8 × 15″	21	Alexandria
Revenge (1915)	29,150	8 × 15″	21	Convoy Duty
Queen Elizabeth (1913)	30,600	8 × 15″	24	Home Fleet
Warspite (1913)	30,600	8 × 15″	24	Alexandria
Valiant (1914)	30,600	8 × 15″	24	Gibraltar
Barham (1914)	31,100	8 × 15″	24	Home Fleet
Malaya (1915)	31,100	8 × 15″	24	Alexandria
Hood (1918)	42,100	8 × 15″	31	Gibraltar
Renown (1916)	32,000	6 × 15″	29	Home Fleet
Repulse (1916)	32,000	6 × 15″	29	Home Fleet
Nearing completion				
King George V	35,000	10 × 14″	30+	In service December, 1940
Germany				
Scharnhorst (1936)	32,000	9 × 11″	27	
Gneisenau (1936)	32,000	9 × 11″	27	
Admiral Scheer (1936)	10,000	6 × 11″	26	
Lützow (1931) (ex *Deutschland*)	10,000	6 × 11″	26	
Nearing completion				
Bismarck (1939)	41,000	8 × 15″	30+	In service March, 1941

207

Ship & Date of Launch	Displacement (tons)	Main Armament	Speed (knots)	
		Italy		
Littorio (1937)	35,000	9 × 15″	30	
Conte de Cavour (1911)	23,622	10 × 12.6″	27	
Giulio Cesare (1911)	23,622	10 × 12.6″	27	
Caio Duilio (1913)	23,622	10 × 12.6″	27	
Andrea Doria (1913)	23,622	10 × 12.6″	27	
Nearing completion				
Vittorio Veneto (1937)	35,000	9 × 15″	30	In service August, 1940
		France		
Dunkerque (1935)	26,500	8 × 13″	29.5	
Strasbourg (1936)	26,500	8 × 13″	29.5	
Bretagne (1913)	22,189	10 × 13.4″	21.4	
Provence (1913)	22,189	10 × 13.4″	21.4	
Lorraine (1913)	22,189	8 × 13.4″	21.4	
Courbet (1911)	22,189	12 × 12″	16	
Paris (1912)	22,189	12 × 12″	16	
Nearing completion				
Richelieu (1939)	35,000	8 × 15″	?30	Due to complete summer, 1940
Jean Bart (1939)	35,000	8 × 15″	?30	Due to complete early, 1941

208

Appendix C

Sealion Ashore. A Speculation

Up to this point this book has been based on facts or what were believed to be facts at the time. What follows is an appreciation based on a study of the ground of what might have happened had Hitler given the order to launch *Sealion* in the period 24–27 September, a period when, as it happened, the weather would have been favourable for the sea crossing. For the purpose of this speculation it is assumed that a fair proportion of the first *Staffel* managed, for one reason or another, to evade the Royal Navy and that by using its level-flight bombers against London the *Luftwaffe* managed to achieve a temporary command of the air over the landing area. In the unlikely event of both these conditions being favourable, it is fair to assume that such good luck for the *Wehrmacht* would not last more than twelve hours.

On the right the two centre divisions of Sixteenth Army, 35 Division south of Dymchurch and 7 Infantry Division at Camber, would have had a very good chance of getting ashore as the long open coastline would be extremely difficult to guard in strength. It would, however, have taken quite outstanding efforts by the engineers to breach the very powerful sea wall without special equipment and there is no evidence that the need for this had been foreseen. Until a substantial breach had been contrived it would be impossible to get the surviving U-tanks off the beach. The story would have been different on the flanks. On the left 1 Mountain Division would have been very hard pressed to make good a landing at Cliff End where there is a bad rocky beach overlooked at short range by high ground and where the serious obstacle of the Royal Military Canal is only a few hundred yards beyond the sea wall. It is unlikely that even the legendary toughness of the German infantry would have enabled them to make a serious lodgment and any support they might expect from 7 Division would depend on the latter's ability quickly to make a crossing of the River Rother, dominated, as they would be, by the defenders ensconced in Rye. On the right the chances of 17 Division establishing itself between Hythe and Dymchurch cannot be rated highly. They would be under short-range artillery fire from the escarpment and, once again, the canal would be a serious obstacle, especially on the extreme right where the houses of Hythe would be a considerable help to the defenders. It should be added that the artillery support for the first wave would be very limited – a handful of mountain guns with the dubious assistance of 75mm and 37mm pieces on improvised mountings on board small ships. Against such guns the Napoleonic Martello Towers, to say nothing of Dymchurch Redoubt, with walls up to six feet thick, would still form formidable strongpoints which could only have been reduced by a lavish expenditure of ammunition, which, in the circumstances, would be very hard to replace.

Assuming that the two centre divisions and some remnants of the flanking formations established themselves ashore, their difficulties would only be beginning. The great semi-circle of Romney Marsh is flat, largely devoid of cover and intersected by watercourses which would have been impassable to wheeled vehicles and in many cases have required bridging for tanks, while forming tedious and difficult obstacles to men on foot. The roads leading to the inland perimeter are narrow and winding and the whole area is overlooked by high ground, giving perfect observation for artillery, so that movement by day would be impossible, while the ditches and dykes would have made a night advance a nightmare. Bounding the marsh is the Royal Military Canal, a very serious obstacle, sixty feet wide and at least seven feet deep, and everywhere within rifle range of the high ground on the far bank. At best there are few bridges and it is reasonable to suppose that they would have been demolished. The canal should have formed an impenetrable barrier unless the defenders could be terrorised by dive bombers and by the time the attackers had struggled across the marsh the British mobile reserve would have had ample time to reach the canal line where even the obsolete light tanks would have served a valuable purpose as armoured and mobile machine-gun posts firing downhill at short range.

The only hope for Sixteenth Army breaking out of Romney Marsh would lie with the four understrength parachute battalions, say 2,000 men, of 7 *Flieger* Division. Landing on the high ground three or four miles north of Hythe, beyond the place where the M20 now cuts through the downs near Sandling, they might have rescued the right flank of the seaborne invaders and secured a crossing over the canal. It seems more probable that, given average British competence and luck, the parachutists would have been mopped up before they could link up with the remnants of 17 Division.

On the left Ninth Army would have had an even less enviable task, XXXVIII Corps might have made good their landing between Bexhill and Pevensey, but inland lie the Pevensey Levels where movement would have been at least as difficult as on Romney Marsh. Further west, 6 Mountain Division must have suffered appalling losses as they tried to get ashore in the natural killing ground of Cuckmere Haven and it is easy to see why the *Wehrmacht* asked for a parachute landing at the western end of the Beachy Head massif so as to ensure that at least one flank of the seaborne assault would be secured. It is equally easy to see why the *Luftwaffe* refused to contemplate such an isolated drop. On the extreme left any attempt to land parts of 28 Division at Rottingdean must have led to a situation similar to that encountered by the Royal Regiment of Canada at Puys, east of Dieppe, on 12 August, 1942. A cleft in the cliffs, comparable to that at Rottingdean, was defended by no more than two German platoons, but the Canadians lost every man who landed.

8 Division's assault at Newhaven was the Ninth Army operation which could have led to the greatest advantages – a thrust up the Ouse Valley into the flatter ground beyond Lewes – if it could have succeeded. Its chances would have been very poor. The beach in Seaford Bay is wide enough only to land a single brigade and is commanded by the projecting cliff above Newhaven harbour and the substantial River Ouse. Built into this cliff is the extensive Newhaven Fort, constructed in the finest mid-nineteenth century style of fortifications with underground galleries and masonry gun positions, which could enfilade the whole length of the landing beach. Newhaven Fort would not withstand an all-out assault by the heavy weapons of 1940 but since the most formidable weapons that could be brought against it would be 75mm guns mounted on ships little serious damage could have been done to it. Given a staunch garrison there is every reason to believe that it could have stood up even to prolonged attack from Stukas since ample shelter was available. The best chance of capturing the work would be the kind of glider-borne assault which overcame Fort Eben-Emael (see p 28). It is most unlikely that the *Luftwaffe* would have contemplated such a dangerous operation.

It would seem therefore that, by S+3, the *Wehrmacht* would hold two isolated beachheads, one at roughly two-division strength on Romney Marsh and one, at roughly half that strength, penned in by the Pevensey Levels. Each of these forces would be opposed by British troops of at least equal strength and much better equipped with artillery and tanks. They would still be dependent on re-supply over open beaches and would have no immediate prospect of laying hands on even a small port. By that time the Royal Navy would have been able to saturate the area with armed craft ranging from light cruisers to armed motor boats and there would be little prospect of reinforcements or stores reaching the beachheads. Even the superb German infantry could not be expected to break out without ammunition and, although they would have fought as long as they could, they would have no alternative but to surrender. The best that the *Kriegsmarine* had ever been able to offer as a reasonable prospect was the landing of the assault wave and, in the places where this might have been achieved, this would not have been enough to overcome the defensive forces which had been assembled by mid-September.

Bibliography

Herbert Agar, *Britain Alone, June, 1940–June, 1941*, Bodley Head, 1972.
Margery Allingham, *The Oaken Heart*, Michael Joseph, 1941.
Christopher Andrew, *Secret Service*, Heinemann, 1985.
Walter Ansel, *Hitler Confronts England*, Duke University Press (Durham NC), 1960.
G. Archer Parfitt, *History of the Herefordshire Light Infantry*, privately printed, nd.
Earl of Avon, *The Eden Memoirs vol. ii The Reckoning*, Casell, 1965.
I. M. Bates, *The Thames on Fire*, Terence Dalton (Lavenham), 1985.
P. M. H. Bell, *A Certain Eventuality*, Saxon House, 1974.
J. W. Blake, *Northern Ireland in the Second World War*, HMSO, Belfast, 1956.
Willi A Bölke (ed), *The Secret Conferences of Dr Goebbels*, Weidenfeld and Nicolson, 1970.
Brian Bond (ed), *Chief of Staff. The Diaries of Lt-Gen Sir Henry Pownall, vol. i*, Leo Cooper, 1972.
Andrew Boyle, *Trenchard*, Collins, 1962.
Asa Briggs, *History of Broadcasting in the United Kingdom, vol iii*, OUP, 1970.
John Brophy, *Britain's Home Guard*, Harrap, 1945.
Arthur Bryant, *The Turn of the Tide*, Collins, 1957.
Alan Bullock, *Hitler: A Study in Tyranny*, Odham's Press, 1952.
J. R. M. Butler, *Grand Strategy, vol ii*, HMSO, 1957.
Angus Calder, *The Peoples' War*, Jonathan Cape, 1969.
W. M. Carlgren (Tr. Arthur Spencer), *Swedish Foreign Policy during the Second World War*, Ernest Benn, 1977.
Winston S. Churchill, *The Second World War*, vols i & ii, Cassell, 1948–49.
Dudley Clarke, *Seven Assignments*, Jonathan Cape, 1948.
J. A. Cole, *Lord Haw Haw – and William Joyce*, Faber & Faber, 1964.
Basil Collier, *Defence of the United Kingdom*, HMSO, 1957.
John Colville, *The Fringes of Power vol i*, Hodder & Stoughton, 1985.
Paul Einzig, *In the Centre of Things*, Hutchinson, 1960.
L. F. Ellis, *Welsh Guards at War*, Gale & Polden, 1946.
Lord Elwyn Jones, *In my Time*, Weidenfeld & Nicolson, 1983.
Keith Feiling, *Life of Neville Chamberlain*, Macmillan, 1970.

D. L. Fitzgerald, *History of the Irish Guards in the Second World War*, Gale & Polden, 1949.

Peter Fleming, *Invasion 1940*, Rupert Hart-Davis, 1957.

Patrick Forbes, *The Grenadier Guards in the War of 1939–45, vol i*, Gale & Polden, 1949.

Eleanor M. Gates, *The End of the Affair*, George Allen & Unwin, 1981.

Martin Gilbert, *Winston S. Churchill 1874–1965, vols v & vi*, Heinemann, 1976 & 1983.

Charles Graves, *The Home Guard of Britain*, Hutchinson, 1943.

Duncan Grinnel-Milne, *The Silent Victory, September, 1940*, Bodley Head, 1958.

Nigel Hamilton, *Monty. The Making of a General*, Hamish Hamilton, 1981.

Basil Liddell Hart, *The Other Side of the Hill*, Cassell, 1948.

F. H. Hinsley, *British Intelligence in the Second World War*, vol. i, HMSO, 1979.

Vera Hodgson, *Few Eggs and no Oranges*, Dennis Dobson, 1976.

Alistair Horne, *To Lose a Battle*, Macmillan, 1969.

Brian Horrocks, *A Full Life*, Leo Cooper, 1974.

Anthony Howard, *RAB. The Life of R. A. Butler*, Jonathan Cape, 1987.

H. Montgomery Hyde, *British Air Policy between the Wars*, Heinemann, 1976.

Harold L. Ickes, *Secret Diaries, vol iii*, Weidenfeld & Nicolson, 1967.

Ironside, Edmund, Lord (ed. Macleod & Kelly) *The Ironside Diaries*, Constable, 1962.

B. S. Johnson, *The Evacuees*, 1968.

R. V. Jones, *Most Secret War*, Hamish Hamilton, 1978.

Thomas Jones, *A Diary with Letters, 1931–50*, OUP, 1954.

Louis de Jong, *The German Fifth Column in the Second World War*, (Tr. G. M. Geyl) Routledge & Kegan Paul, 1956.

Earl Jowett, *Some were Spies*, Hodder & Stoughton, 1954.

Albert Kesselring. (Tr. Lynton Hudson), *Memoirs*, William Kimber, 1953.

James Leutze (ed), *The London Observer, Journal of General Raymond E. Lee, 1940–41*, Hutchinson, 1972.

Ronald Lewin, *Churchill as War Lord*, Batsford, 1973.

Donald Lindsay, *Forgotten General, A Life of Andrew Thorne*, Michael Russell (Wilton), 1987.

Francis L. Loewenheim (ed), *Roosevelt and Churchill: Their Second World War Correspondence*, Barrie & Jenkins, 1975.

Ian Mclaine, *Ministry of Morale*, George Allen & Unwin, 1979.

Kenneth Macksey, *Kesselring: The making of the Luftwaffe*, Batsford, 1978.

Erich von Manstein, (Tr. Anthony G. Powell), *Lost Victories*, Palit & Dutt, Dehra Dun, 1970.

Arthur J. Marder, *From the Dardenelles to Oran*, OUP, 1974.

Anthony Martiensson, *Hitler and his Admirals*, Secker & Warburg, 1948.

J. Masterman, *The Double Cross System*, Yale, 1972.

Patrick Mayhew (ed), *One Family's War*, Hutchinson, 1985.

Drew Middleton, *The Sky Suspended*, Secker & Warburg, 1960.

Wilfred Miles, *The Life of a Regiment: History of the Gordon Highlanders*, vol. v, Aberdeen University Press, 1961.

Leonard Mosley, *Backs to the Wall*, Weidenfeld & Nicolson, 1971.

Malcolm Muggeridge (ed), *Ciano's Diary 1939–43*, Heinemann, 1947.

Malcolm Munthe, *Hellens. A Herefordshire Manor*, Duckworth, 1957.

Edward R. Murrow, *This is London*, Cassell, 1941.

Nigel Nicolson, *Alex. The Life of Field-Marshal Earl Alexander of Tunis*, Weidenfeld & Nicolson, 1973.

—— (ed), *Diaries & Letters of Harold Nicolson, 1935–45*, Collins, 1967.

Terence O'Brien, *Civil Defence*, HMSO, 1955.

Mollie Panter-Downes, *London War Notes* (Ed. William Shawn), Longmans, 1972.

C. Northcote Parkinson, *Always a Fusilier*, Sampson Low, 1949.

Frederick Pile, *Ack-Ack*, Harrap, 1949.

Friedrich-Karl von Plehwe, *Operation Sealion 1940*, Journal of the RUSI, March, 1973.

Alfred Price, *The Hardest Day, 18 August, 1940*, Arms & Armour Press, 1988.

Erich Raeder, *Struggle for the Sea*, Wm. Kimber, 1959.

Winston G. Ramsey (ed), *The Blitz Then and Now, vol. i*, Battle of Britain Prints International, 1987.

Robert Rhodes James. *Victor Cazalet: A Portrait*, Hamish Hamilton, 1976.

S. W. Roskill, *The War at Sea, vol. i*, HMSO, 1954.

Friedrich Ruge (tr. M. G. Saunders), *Sea Warfare 1939–45*, Cassel, 1957.

William A. Shirer, *Berlin Diary*, Hamish Hamilton, 1941.

Malcolm Smith, *Sir Edgar Ludlow-Hewitt and the Expansion of Bomber Command 1939–40*, Journal of the RUSI, March, 1981.

Peter C. Smith, *Hold the Narrow Seas*, Moorhead Publishing, (Ashbourne), 1984.

A. J. Smithers, *Rude Mechanicals*, Leo Cooper, 1987.

J. W. Spaight, *Air Power in the Next War*, Geoffrey Bless, 1938.

C. P. Stacey, *Official History of the Canadian Army in the Second World War, vol. i. Six Years of War*, The Queen's Printer (Ottawa), 1957.

Telford Taylor, *The Breaking Wave*, Weidenfeld & Nicolson, 1967.

John Terraine, *The Right of the Line*, Hodder & Stoughton, 1985.

E. S. Turner, *The Phoney War on the Home Front*, Michael Joseph, 1961.

C. Webster & N. Frankland, *Strategic Air Offensive against Germany*, vol. i., HMSO, 1961.

Siegfried Westphal (ed), *The Fatal Decisions*, Michael Joseph, 1956.

Anthony Weymouth, *Journal of the War Years*, Littlebury (Worcester), 1948.

R. Wheatley, *Operation Sealion*, OUP, 1958.

John W. Wheeler-Bennett, *King George VI*, Macmillan, 1958.

D. Williams, *The Black Cats at War*, privately printed, 1955.

Chester Wilmot, *The Struggle for Europe*, Collins, 1952.

F. W. Winterbottom, *The Ultra Secret*, Weidenfeld & Nicolson, 1974.

Derek Wood & Derek Demster, *The Narrow Margin*, Hutchinson, 1961.

David Woodward, *Ramsay at War*, William Kimber, 1957.

J. Evelyn Wrench, *Geoffrey Dawson and Our Times*, Hutchinson, 1961.

Index

Bournemouth, 143
Boyes A/T rifle, 50, 74
Bracken, Brendan, 61
Brauchitsch, FM Manfred von, 64, 71, 73, 120, 123, 138, 176, 205
Brecon, 9
Bremen, 18, 38
Bren gun, 33, 58, 75
Brest, 9, 50, 87, 91, 170
Briare, 87
Bridlington, 131
Brighton, 52, 55, 76, 84, 138, 139, 148, 151, 195
Bristol, 8, 9, 40, 133, 147, 166
British Broadcasting Corporation (BBC), 17, 18, 19, 32, 33, 45, 54, 65, 114
British Expeditionary Force (BEF), 1, 26, 39, 74, 75, 79, 112, 202
British Fascists Ltd, 19
British Industrial Design Group, 135
British Legion, 32
British Museum, 33, 105
British Union of Fascists, 19, 44, 55
Brooke, Lt-Gen Sir Alan, 103, 118, 119, 151, 153, 184, 186-7
Brooklands, 158
Brophie, John, 102
Broxtowe, 104
Bruce, Stanley, 61
Brunswick, 79
Buckingham Palace, 169, 174, 175, 178
Buckinghamshire, 55
Budapest, 138
Bullitt, William C., 60, 93
Burnham-on-Crouch, 35
Burton, Sir Montague, 34
Busch, Gen Ernst, 146, 148, 198, 205
Butler, Richard Austen, 62, 63, 64

Cadiz, 7
Caernarvonshire, 32, 183
Calais, 38, 39, 74, 110, 127, 146, 163, 188, 198
Calais, Pas de, 37, 106
Camber, 146, 157(fn), 209
Cambridge, 14
Cambridgeshire, 33
Campbell, Sir Ronald, 15
Canada, 35
Canaris, Adm Wilhelm, 64, 65, 155
Canterbury, 147
Cape Verde Islands, 76
Cardiff, 141
Casablanca, 89, 92
Cavan, FM Frederick Rudolof Lambart, 10th Earl of, 32
Cawdor, Col John Campbell, 1st Baron, 9
Chamberlain, Neville, 2, 11, 20, 23, 38, 59, 60, 61, 99, 115
Chandler's Ford, 32

Channel Islands, 69(fn)
Channel Pilot, 84
Chard, 147
Chatham, 33, 190
Chelmsford, Bishop of, 27
Chelsea, 176
Cherbourg, 50, 87, 111, 121, 146, 150, 184, 188, 189
Chester, 8
Chester, Archdeacon of, 54
Chicago Daily News, 41
Churchill, Winston Spencer, 99, 116, 126, 140, 141, 161, 193
    Forms government, 2, 23, 60
    Rouses Britain, 2, 186, 191, 201, 203
    Warnings of invasion, 15-16, 25, 26, 35
    Views on probability of invasion, 35, 36, 103-4, 118, 129, 186, 187-88, 204
    Signals to President Roosevelt, 44, 58
    and internment, 46
    and Ireland, 58, 59, 60
    Refusal to contemplate peace, 60, 61, 62, 63, 64
    and the French Fleet, 87, 88, 91, 92, 93, 94, 95, 97, 98
    As leader, 70, 71-72, 153
    Speeches. 13 May, 2; 19 May, 35; 4 June, 7, 48; 4 July, 97-98; 20 August, 134; 17 September, 185-86, 201
Chiefs of Staff, Joint, 15, 16, 26, 38, 39, 45, 50, 72, 87, 94, 95, 153, 164, 170
Ciano, Count Galeazzo, 110, 114, 115, 161, 193
Cliff End, 139, 146, 148-49, 209
Cobh (Queenstown), 76
Cocks, Seymour, 104
Cologne, 18
Columbia Broadcasting Services (CBS), 114
Colville, John, 62, 99, 126, 187
Combined Intelligence Committee (CIC) (formerly Invasion Warning Sub-Committee), 140, 154, 155, 190
Commandos, 106
Committee for Imperial Defence, 21
Commons, House of, 7, 20, 72, 74, 97, 98, 104, 124, 185, 193, 201
Compiègne, 90
Concordia Network, 115
Co-ordination of Defence, Ministry of, 15
Copenhagen, 27
Cork, 76
Cornwall, 147, 166
Cotswold Bruderhof, 47
Cotswold Hills, 164
Coulsdon, 141
Coventry, 22(fn), 31, 40
Crewkerne, 147
Crieff, 32
Cripps, Sir Stafford, 122
Cromer, 14

Tollervey, Pte, 155
Tone, Wolfe, 8
Tottenham, 141
Toulon, 92, 96
Trafalgar, Cape, 7, 203
Transport, Ministry of, 135
Trenchard, MRAF Sir Hugh, 21, 22, 80, 119
Truro, Bishop of, 32
Tunbridge Wells, 105, 127
Turcoing, 198
Tyne, River, 13, 37, 141

Uckfield, 147
Ulster, 59, 64, 65, 66, 76
Ulster Defence Volunteer Force, 34
Union of Soviet Socialist Republics (USSR), 12, 17, 51, 60, 100, 120, 122, 123, 124, 125, 160, 190, 192, 193, 194, 201
United States of America (USA), 1, 51, 58, 60, 93, 94, 96, 102, 120, 123, 124, 161, 162, 192, 201

Vatican, The, 67
Venlo, 68
Ventnor, 129, 132
Versailles, Treaty of, 42
Vichy, 97
Victoria Cross (VC), 11, 107, 132
Victoria Station, 166, 178
Vietinghoff, Gen von, 198
'Voice of Peace', 115, 116
Vordingbord, 27

Waldberg, José Rudolf, 155, 156
Wales, 8, 76, 115, 136, 144, 169
Wall, Joseph, 8, 9
Waltham, 147
War Cabinet, 14, 15, 25, 26, 38, 39, 59, 87, 91, 95, 115, 129, 190, 204
War Office, 25, 30, 50, 58, 102, 118, 126, 140, 153, 187
War, Secretary of State for, 26, 184, 187
Warsaw, 116, 160
Wash, The, 11, 50, 54, 55, 76, 103, 104, 132, 185
Washington D.C., 60, 61, 94, 175, 176, 187
Washington, Sussex, 147
Waterloo Station, 175
Wedgwood, Col Josiah, 11, 12
Wehrmacht (German Army).
  In French campaign (1940), 36, 38, 70
    Condition in 1940, 72–74, 201
    Early disinterest for invasion, 13–14, 101
    Support for invasion, 24, 136, 194
    Plans for invasion, 111–13, 120, 145–48, 180–82, 209–11
    Disagreements with *Kriegsmarine*, 122, 123, 138, 148, 151, 161, 198
    Mentioned, 1, 43, 82, 196, 197
  Oberkommando des Heeres (OKH) (High Com-

mand of German Army), 5, 13, 15, 73, 121, 122, 136, 147, 149, 151, 153, 182, 183, 188, 190, 205
Army Groups. A, 146, 147, 180, 198, 205
  B, 205
  C, 146, 147, 205
Armies. 9th, 146, 147, 150, 188, 205, 210, 211
  16th, 146, 147, 148, 149, 188, 198, 205, 209, 210
Corps. VII, 146, 149
  XIII, 146, 152, 198, 200
  XXXVIII, 146, 210
Divisions. 7 Infantry, 146, 209
  8 Infantry, 146, 211
  17 Infantry, 146, 152, 198, 200, 209, 210
  26 Infantry, 146
  28 Infantry, 146, 150, 210
  34 Infantry, 146
  35 Infantry, 146, 209
  1 Mountain, 146, 209
  6 Mountain, 146, 210
  7 *Flieger*, 27, 28, 29, 49, 148, 149, 152, 210
  22 Air Portable, 28, 29, 43, 49, 149
Weizsäcker, Ernst von, 63
Welsh Nationalists, 155
West Ham, 46, 163
Westminster, 21, 178
Wever, Gen Walther, 79
Wexford, County, 145
Weybourne, 25
Weygand, Gen Maxime, 88
Weymouth, 146
Wheatley, Ronald, 4
Wicklow, County, 66
Wight, Isle of, 46, 111, 112, 129, 185
Wilhelmina, Queen of the Netherlands, 28
Windsor, Edward, Duke of, 116
Winterbottom, Gp-Capt F.W., 187
Winterhilfe, 161
Wodehouse, P.G., 19
Wolkoff, Anna, 44–45
Wolverhampton, 76
Women's Voluntary Services (WVS), 105
Woodarg, Major, 174
Woolf, Leonard, 52
Woolwich Arsenal, 163
Worcester, 9, 25
'Workers' Challenge' (Plan S), 115
Worthing, 147

Yarmouth, 13, 14, 37, 189
York, Archbishop of, 47
York, Frederick Augustus, Duke of, 8
Yorkshire, 33, 127
Ypres, 192

Zeebrugge, 11
Zeesen, 18
Ziegenburg, 198

224